Imagining Insiders

Literature, Culture and Identity

Series Editor: Bruce King

This series is concerned with the ways in which literature and cultures are influenced by the complexities and complications of identity. It looks at the ways in which identities are explored, mapped, defined and challenged in the arts where boundaries are often overlapping, contested and re-mapped. It considers how differences, conflicts and change are felt and expressed. It investigates how such categories as race, class, gender, sexuality, ethnicity, nation, exile, diaspora and multiculturalism have come about. It discusses how these categories co-exist and their relationship to the individual, particular situations, the artist and the arts.

Imagining Insiders

Africa and the Question of Belonging

MINEKE SCHIPPER

CASSELL
London and New York

Cassell
Wellington House, 125 Strand, London WC2R 0BB
370 Lexington Avenue, New York, NY 10017-6550

First published 1999

This book is based on *De boomstam en de krokodil: kwesties van ras, cultuur en wetenschap* (Amsterdam: Van Gennep, 1996).

British Library Cataloguing in Publication Data
A catalogue record for this book is available from the British Library.
ISBN 0 304 70478 4 Hardback
      0 304 70479 2 Paperback

Library of Congress Cataloging-in-Publication Data
Schipper, Mineke.
        [De boomstam en de krokodil. English]
        Imagining insiders : Africa and the question of belonging / Mineke Schipper.
            p.   cm. — (Literature, culture, and identity)
        Includes bibliographical references (p.   ) and index.
        ISBN 0-304-70478-4.—ISBN 0-304-70479-2 (pbk.)
        1. Race.   2. Difference (Psychology)   3. Africa—Civilization—Western influences.   4. Civilization, Western—African influences.
        5. Whites in literature.   6. Africans—Race identity.   7. Afro-Americans—Race identity.   8. Sexism.   I. Title.   II. Series.
        CB195 S2813   1999
        305.8—dc21   99–10213
                                                                                    CIP

Typeset by BookEns Ltd, Royston, Herts.
Printed and bound in Great Britain by Biddles Ltd, Guildford & King's Lynn

For Maryse Condé and Richard Philcox

Contents

Acknowledgements   ix

1   Insiders and outsiders   1
2   *Homo caudatus*: European imagination and its cultural outsiders   13
3   'The white man has no friends': The European Other in
    African oral and written literatures   30
4   African roots and American black culture   56
5   Negritude, Black Consciousness and beyond   77
6   Black is beautiful or the whiteness of feminism   103
7   Emerging from the shadows: Changing patterns in gender
    matters   122
8   Knowledge is like an ocean: Insiders, outsiders and the
    academy   150
9   Towards a culture of interdiscursivity   171

Interviews
    Léopold Sédar Senghor   183
    Wole Soyinka   186
    Buchi Emecheta   189
    Sembène Ousmane   192
    Maryse Condé   195

Bibliography   198
Index   217

Acknowledgements

It is impossible to mention here the names of all the friends, colleagues and students, especially those in Africa, who over the years have generously contributed with enjoyable discussions and indispensable comments and reflections to my intercultural education

The Arts Faculty of Leiden University with its Research School of Asian, African and Amerindian Studies has provided a stimulating place with ample space for interdisciplinary contacts, exchange of ideas and intercultural perspectives.

I am grateful to Edward Said for his enlightening comments during our public debate in Amsterdam in December 1994; to Ernst van Alphen, Bernard Arps, Theo D'haen, Peter Geschiere, Wilt Idema, Henk Maier, Jarich Oosten, Reimar Schefold, Rik Schipper and Wasif Shadid (Leiden); to Kwame Anthony Appiah (Cambridge Mass.), Mieke Bal (Amsterdam), Robert Young (Oxford), John Picton (London), Wanjiku Mukabi Kabira and Sultan Somjee (Nairobi), Jean-Pierre Guingané and Sanou Salaka (Ouagadougou), Joseph Semboja (Dar es Salaam), Anne Adams and Biodun Jeyifo (Ithaca), Eileen Julien and Kalidou Sy (Bloomington), Aliko Songolo (Madison), Clémentine Faïk-Nzuji and Chantal Zabus (Louvain-la-Neuve), Bernard Mouralis (Paris), Kenneth Harrow (East-Lansing), Abiola Irele and Julia Watson (Columbus), Steven Shankman (Oregon), Valentin Mudimbe and Elisabeth Mudimbe-Boyi (Stanford), Ariel Dorfman and Arif Dirlik (Durham), for their friendship and support.

I wish to express my sincere gratitude to Léopold Sédar Senghor, Sembène Ousmane, Wole Soyinka, Buchi Emecheta and Maryse Condé who whole-heartedly and patiently shared their ideas with me in extended interviews, of which selected passages have been included – interviews which had never been published in English.

I also want to express my thanks to Janet Joyce, director of Cassell

Academic and to Bruce King, editor, who cordially invited me to be the first
author in their new series *Literature, Culture and Identity*.

A Dutch version of this text was originally published in Amsterdam, by Van
Gennep (1996). Permission to reuse this material for an enlarged, reshaped,
updated and adapted English edition is gratefully acknowledged. Earlier
versions of Chapters 7 and 8 appeared in *Research in African Literatures* (vol. 27/
1, spring 1996 and vol. 28/4, winter 1997). I thank Indiana University Press for
permission to include these materials in modified form. All translations are
mine unless stated otherwise.

I am happy to acknowledge the sources of poetry quoted in this book and
to thank the following publishers for granting their permission:

Editions Gallimard, Paris, for a passage from Léon Damas, *Black Label*
(1956); Editions du Seuil, Paris, for a passage from Aimé Césaire, *Ferrements*
(1960); Ad Donker Publishers, Johannesburg, for a passage from Mafika Gwala,
Jol'iinkomo (1975); Alfred A. Knopf, New York, for an extract from Langston
Hughes, 'The Negro Speaks of Rivers'. (The author and publisher offer their
apologies if any material has been included without permission, and will
happily include acknowledgement in any future edition.)

Last but not least, I am deeply grateful to the Rockefeller Foundation.
Without its royal invitation to come and work on my project at the Villa
Serbelloni in Bellagio and without that paradisiacal stay at Lake Como, this
book might not yet have been born.

1

Insiders and outsiders

You have to understand your neighbour's language before you judge him.

Douala proverb, Cameroon

Race transforms people who learn to do what we do into the thieves of our culture and people who teach us to do what they do into the destroyers of our culture; it makes assimilation into a kind of betrayal and the refusal to assimilate into a form of heroism.

Walter Benn Michaels

In *Hopes and Impediments* (1988: 15), Chinua Achebe emphasizes how much Europeans cherish the information they receive from their own 'channels'. As far as the channels of Others are concerned, Europe seems to prefer those that have been 'disinfected', those that willingly become 'purveyors of old comforting myths'. Achebe pleads for equal partnership, but recognizes the impediments that block the way to the attainment of such a solution as long as the point of departure remains the assumption that only the representatives of a single group are qualified to interpret the world. Such an assumption prevents dialogue and perpetuates a situation in which the Other is a stereotype that is exploited to label people and to justify their exclusion from a mutually beneficial partnership.

From this perspective, the authentically African was 'naked' and the more primitive, the more real. Unfortunately for this stereotype, Achebe notes, such 'unspoilt' creatures are rapidly dying out, and European colonial views of Africans have to be readjusted by counter-images. Of course, Achebe is aware of the simplifications in which he is indulging. He admits that not all white people can be held responsible to the same degree for what happened in history, but his aim is clear. If a number of Europeans contributed to a better understanding of Africa in Europe this has not necessarily led to a real dialogue with Africans. According to Achebe, Europe is not ready for such a dialogue (1988: 19); prejudices about Africans continue to block the way. The struggle between images and counter-images is not an easy one, for dominant groups experience great difficulty in extending equality to others, and 'equality is the one thing which Europeans are conspicuously incapable of extending to others, especially Africans' (15). What to do with Achebe's remarks?

Throughout the centuries, human beings have created binaries, devising images of themselves as opposites of Others. They have embedded such images in stories, songs and other forms of artistic expression. Scholarship too has been influenced by people's imagination and existing narratives (e.g. Fox Keller 1985, 1992). However, the boundaries between own and foreign are mobile and constantly redefined and manipulated; new situations followed by new interpretations make people modify earlier assumptions. This is an ongoing process which continues, as a result, to affect the facts, in practice as well as in theory (Kuhn 1970).

In the twentieth century, a Western multinational Otherness industry has developed. Academics seriously looked into the fate, content, form, presence and absence of the West's Others. They defined whether, where and how these Others were supposed to exist; to be seen or to be ignored. The resulting inventories of stereotyped images classified Others' roles − either positive or negative − in advertisements, literatures, film, popular culture and the human sciences. Over the past twenty or thirty years, considerable scientific research has been devoted to this question from Western insiders' perspectives. A well-studied case is the *homo caudatus*, a geographically moving product of Western imagination: depending on the historical context, the man with the tail (as explained in Chapter 2) was situated now in one continent, now in another.

Western scholarship has classified its Others according to physical appearance, behaviour, language, customs. Thus packaged, they are presented: this is how they look, this is their reality. Such ideas are continually being adapted. In recent years, older views of the Other have frequently been analysed by studying documents in which Others were, over time, looked at, described, painted, photographed and filmed (e.g. Nederveen Pieterse 1990). Many studies have examined how our ancestors or academic predecessors (stereo)typed the various categories of people they conceived of as Other. (Said 1979; Miller 1985; Brantlinger 1988; Breman 1990; Young 1990, 1995).

Besides views of ourselves and of others, there are others' views of themselves and of us. However, there is little demand for alternative perspectives and curiosity about the views of others tends not to be particularly strong. Although Pliny once declared 'Ex Africa semper aliquid novi' [Always from Africa (comes) something new], little attention has been given to the sources of the news. Who reported what and why? European views are quite different from those of its victims. One needs to re-examine the available source material and to determine the degree to which diverse views are represented, the degree to which research in history, sociology, anthropology and literature has been skewed by differences in the amount of effort devoted to describing, studying and teaching particular peoples. Such quantitative differences obviously affect their chances of being seen, heard and (re-)presented. The same proviso holds true for research results on matters of gender. This is particularly the case for the perspectives of African women living in Africa which inside as well as outside the academy have been neglected or completely ignored, for decades after their male counterparts had been taking the floor, talking back and presenting their views.

As an object of research, however, the Other became more and more problematic when scholars became aware of the obscuring barriers of power between their own subjective gaze and the Other as an object of research in a Western (white, colonial) history and culture (e.g. Clifford 1988). Because so many mistakes had been made in the past and because Western researchers were said to be descended from slave traders as well as colonialist and sexist ancestors, a new generation of scholars (emphasizing at the same time their political correctness) began to assume a distance from this cultural and academic heritage, showing how wrong and disgusting their predecessors had been. The Other became so fashionable in Western academy that words such as 'difference' and 'Otherness' have come to function – in the words of Edward Said (1989: 213) – as a talisman, serving to guarantee political correctness.

In some manifestations of self-hatred one could hear a sobbing sound, cynically condemned by Pascal Bruckner in his *Le sanglot de l'homme blanc* (1983). According to Bruckner, Western culture's dominant position made the Euro-American (but who is that?) fatally nostalgic for an invented paradise of a southern hemisphere, on which his life and his certainty depended. This paradise was based on two ideas: 'there they have a new and unspoilt kind of socialism' or 'there they have a spirituality we lack' (153). This was accompanied by the uncritical acceptance of the Other. Bruckner's caricatural description refers to the excesses of cultural relativism, which was useful as a reaction to evolutionism but, taken to an extreme, became a dead end (Lemaire 1976; Schipper 1989).

Is there an alternative? To what extent are people fatally caught up in their inherited ideas, even if they wish to go against them? After all, the power relations of the past, in which the academic world is enmeshed, continue to exist. On a practical level, imagined stereotypes lead a life of their own. In Western public opinion, the term 'colonized' seems to be associated with 'Third World' and has come to mean something like underdevelopment and a third rate status.

Have the discussions of Otherness come to nothing then? At least one positive result is the numerous studies, collections, documentaries and exhibitions which have contributed to making many aware of the ongoing stereotyping of the Other in Western imagination. Ironically, all these efforts to make an inventory of the representations of savages, slaves and colonized peoples were once more in response to the views from one perspective only. Once again, the result was a product of Western thinking and the West. Consequently, the new analysis of representation generally tells more about those who described and analysed than about those represented.

For a long time most Otherness studies were significantly silent about the question of how Self and Other were described from other perspectives. It seemed as if marginalized groups were only allowed the position of Other not Self; of object not subject. Power relations define the division of roles. All the same, white Westerners have always been viewed and described from the outside. Often without knowing it, they have been the object of views and opinions all over the world. They have been closely observed and commented upon as 'natives' in their own countries by people from abroad who came as visitors or settlers to the West.

Gradually researchers have lost their cultural innocence. The Other has become a concept that can no longer be easily dismissed by scholars. It is true that in daily life one's own background is still taken for granted and deviant views are easily discarded as illogical, as non-compatible input (see pp. 24ff.), but numerous examples of other 'logics' can be found by those who search for them (Tambiah 1990). Concern for what happens outside traditionally cherished and sanctioned channels is a matter of awareness. It has not only resulted in greater knowledge, but has also changed assumptions:

> It has forced a reinterpretation of basic themes, calling into question the very assumptions of the disciplines themselves. It has thereby increased our awareness of the way in which knowledge is produced and organized. In important ways, it has exposed the foundations of the disciplines. (Bates *et al* 1993: xxi)

Even among those academics who are 'deaf' or 'hard of hearing' as Edward Said (1989: 223) observes, 'women, natives, or sexual eccentrics, erupt into vision ... to challenge and resist settled metropolitan histories, forms, modes of thought'. The question of cultural identity is continuously being formulated and reformulated and global history tells more than one narrative to those who listen.

Identity is related to the question of the difference between us and others: a difference in culture, social class, sex, religion, age, nationality, living area, etc.

From all these different combined identities, views are developed of Self and Other. As soon as people feel threatened as a group, they attach great importance to their identity.

Guy Michaud (1978: 112) elaborated a concept of collective identity, highlighting a cultural point of view as:

- experienced subjectively and confirmed by members of a group;
- derived from the consciousness of belonging to the group;
- determined by boundaries excluding the Other in general and marking out the differences with certain groups in particular;
- boundaries and differences based on a system of relatively intuitive images (of the Self as well as of the Other), determined by a set of negative (avoidable) aspects and a set of positive ones. The positive aspects (presented by the group as an ideal model) constitute a kind of defensive ethnocentrism, resulting in chauvinism, nationalism, patriotism etc.
- a relatively coherent ideology established on the basis of these characteristics and attitudes and found in the discourse of the group, as expressed in all kinds of texts.

These characteristics not only apply to 'foreign' cultures or so-called minorities, but to all collective identities. The subjective is a determining factor in human behaviour; there is always a difference between how people view themselves and their group and how they see others. The cultural interpretations of one's own identity and its surrounding world merge from childhood. They are experienced as natural, that is, if not disrupted (Erikson 1980; Goffman 1986). Ideally, we should be able to consider ourselves against the background of others, in the same way as we put others against our own background.

The second half of the twentieth century offers a dramatic contradiction. On the one hand there is the technological advancement which covers our planet as a levelling cosmopolitism and on the other a continuous protest against it by a variety of groups in the name of nationalism, race, culture or other forms of collective identity. People will always rebel against whom or what demands their unconditional adaptation, because otherwise they are 'nowhere'. This easily leads to *ethnocentrism*. This deep-rooted human feature which is so much easier to detect in others than in oneself can be defined as a group attitude in which a self-evident central position is given to one's own cultural group amid other groups and in which one's own group characteristics are valued positively and those of others negatively (Memmi 1968: 195; Preiswerk and Perrot 1975: 49; Lorde 1985: 115). There is a relationship between ethnocentrism and racism, even though physical aspects play a role in racism and not necessarily in ethnocentrism. Still, both resemble each other in that they obscure the image of those who belong to the out-groups as a result of the value judgement of the in-group.

Racism is the belief in the superiority of one's own race as against other races, with the intention of gaining privileges and the right of domination. For a long time the Western hierarchy of race typology was based on supposed scientific statements which turned out to be untenable. Unfortunately, their disproof has not resulted in the disappearance of racism. Racism occurs wherever biological characteristics are used to define a group and racialized characteristics receive negative connotations. In his book *Racism* (1989: 74) Miles rejects the term 'race' as analytically inadequate and uses instead the term 'racialization' to denote the conceptual process in which social relations between people – and finally differentiated social groups – are based on attributing significance to human biological characteristics (Anthias and Yuval-Davis 1992: 11).

Physical aspects play a role in racism as well as in *sexism* (but not necessarily in ethnocentrism), as both are based on similar arguments, derived from assumed natural difference in capacities and needs and the belief in the superiority of one category over the other in order to gain privileges and the right of domination. These so-called differences are used to justify inequality in economic, political and cultural relations (Anthias and Yuval-Davis 1992: 12).

Reactions to both racism and sexism are comparable: thinking in terms of equality; thinking in terms of difference and thinking in terms of diversity or hybridity. These three approaches do not necessarily exclude each other.

Emphasis on equality is a response to Western racism which had systematically racialized biological differences to justify slavery and colonization (Fanon 1961; JanMohamed 1983). The highlighting of equality was meant to show that Africans or people of African descent had no less contributed to culture than white people, be it in the field of art, literature, dance, music or science. The invisibility of black culture had to be blamed on those who had ignored or denied its value. Research inventoried and studied the riches of African cultures. The conclusion was that black people are essentially the same as white people and their culture just as interesting and rich. Those who denied this were racially blinded.

Thinking in terms of difference was a second option: colonialism, racism and enforced assimilation had previously led to a dominant discourse about race. It assumed an unbridgeable biological and cultural gap between black and white. Black people's reaction was to emphasize this difference by claiming a culture of their own, a history of their own, aesthetics of their own, all based on an essence of their own, free from and independent of the Other. In this category one finds Panafricanism, Black Renaissance, Negritude and Black Consciousness, with artists, writers and scholars in search of their roots, of African and

American black traditions, 'the ties that bind' (Magubane 1987). Western culture, the dominant canon and white standards and norms are rejected; and the collective heritage of black norms and values are celebrated. The word 'black', as a political statement, is written with a capital B. No more question of the ideal of equality.

For those who thought in terms of equality as well as for those who argued in terms of difference, the assumptions were inevitably affected by a history of slavery, colonization and racism. Both reactions related to previous Western perspectives on Self and Other; the definition of black as equal to or completely different from white is superimposed on Western ideas and texts. A third option has been to abandon binary oppositions such as black and white, slave and master, colonized and colonizer, Africa and Europe: in practice Blackness has not been an unproblematic common denominator either.

The same three options are also current in feminist contexts: striving for equality, emphasizing one's Otherness and rejecting the construction of a single collective womanhood or identity, have alternately been chosen as starting points for research. From a cosmopolitan perspective many writers seem to have gone global, thus solving dichotomy problems in a successful creolization formula for those postcolonial writers living in a Western metropolis.

> The hybridity of a migrant's art may well signify a freeing of voices, a technique for dismantling authority, a liberating polyphony of voices … it is a hybridity that remains primarily an aesthetic device, or a source of themes. Indeed, in certain lights it may seem that writers' connections with their Third World background have become chiefly metaphorical. (Boehmer 1995: 239)

Contemporary hybridity is not ahistorical, however, and cannot be understood without solid background knowledge from the cultures of origin. In the ongoing debate, cosmopolitan migrant writers are sometimes accused of being appropriated by the neocolonial cultural centre and having lost their commitment or loyalty to their region of origin (Boehmer 1995: 245). This is also a dilemma for many Third World academics living in the West (as discussed in Chapter 8). The concept of hybridity, much in vogue in the West today, seems to suggest something new, but cultural hybridity has existed as long as cultures have been in contact.

It is encouraging to see how much scholarly attention has been devoted to mechanisms of inclusion and exclusion, to marginalization processes and diversities. We get to know more about what in the past, for moral, social, political and economic reasons, was ignored, denied, or erased. The awareness of mobility in the relations between insiders and outsiders in the context of culture, colour, gender, in the arts and in the academy has led to a variety of debates on 'cultural insiderism' (Sollors 1986).

This book is intended as a contribution to the discussion which for me began in 1964 in Congo, later Zaïre, now Congo again. After having studied French as my main subject, with Latin and philosophy as subsidiaries, I was appointed to the Université Libre du Congo. I entered the country as an ignorant outsider. At my arts faculty it had been unusual to look beyond Europe's cultural hedge and none of my teachers had ever mentioned Africa: for them there was no other Francophone literature than the French texts from France. No problem, or so it seemed: my task was to teach French language and literature, which I did with enthusiasm, from Corneille to Racine, from Mme de la Fayette to Flaubert, from Baudelaire to Sartre.

My Congolese students loved French literature and were preparing to be teachers, but I started wondering how this related to their culture and background. The curriculum was based on the Belgian education system and French was of course the official language. In the arts faculty there were as yet no African colleagues because of the Belgian colonial policy: first primary school for everyone, then secondary school and then, in the long run, 'we' will give 'them' higher education. However, independence came much earlier than foreseen, and consequently there were no more than thirteen university-trained Congolese in 1960. But in the library there were quite a few books by African writers and I initiated myself to Francophone African poetry, novels and plays. Freshly self-taught, I shared this knowledge with my students and we had long discussions. Although they liked the French writers, this new literature fascinated them because it related directly to their own continent and cultural experience.

That first generation of Francophone writers referred regularly to colonial settings and European characters. This aroused my curiosity: how did African writers represent Europeans, their appearance, behaviour, peculiarities? Did they see white people as outsiders or as human beings? How did Africans imagine Westerners, the travellers and the traders, the settlers and housewives? I taught with some intervals between 1964 and 1972 at the Université Libre which, rebaptized by Mobutu, became the Université Nationale. Gradually the idea came to me that I should do my doctoral research on the representation of Europeans and the West in African novels. I often talked about it with students as well as with others. Everybody had opinions on the subject. A retired clerk, who had worked for the Belgians in the colonial days, helped me with the typing of the manuscript and was perplexed: 'Surely, this is the truth. All these images have been in my head for so long, and here they are all of a sudden, right in front of me, on paper.' An African edition of the book appeared in 1973 and was quickly sold out. 'Almost nothing has been written on what we think about

Europeans and the West, and yet there are so many stories concerning them here in Africa,' students commented time and again in those early years of independence. For me it was an excellent training in different perspectives.

Over the years I have given a number of lectures on the subject. The comments were often telling. Two examples may illustrate this: the first comes from a group of theology students in Kisangani (Congo), who had invited me to give a presentation on 'The Image of the Missionary in the African Novel'. This rather delicate subject – the writers' image of the mission and Christianity was not all that positive – made me introduce my talk somewhat moderately: of course, this was fiction which might be different from their own experiences with missions and missionaries and fictional images should perhaps not be taken too literally. When I had finished, one of the students stood up and said: 'I totally agree with all you said, however, your statement on the images being fictional is incorrect. It is our reality that we recognize in these novels.'

'And still you took up theology?'

'No one knows the ways of the Holy Ghost. Probably we started studying theology in spite of rather than thanks to the missionaries. Who knows?'

Quite a different discussion followed after a lecture at the Royal Tropical Institute, Amsterdam, on the topic 'Perspectives of Europeans and the West in African Novels'. The audience consisted of a group of brewers who were going to set up breweries of a well-known Dutch brand in African countries. The lecture was part of their cultural preparation for Africa, but the majority did not appreciate my presentation. Obviously, the idea that 'we' were objects instead of subjects was unbearable. Several members of the audience had already been to Africa to become acquainted with their future personnel and assured me irritably that my talk was complete nonsense: Africans did not think that way. The Dutch brewers had conveniently overlooked the fact that the Africans they had met were their subordinates. The reactions were revealingly strong: this literature was rubbish. The well-known adage that subordinates always know more about their masters than the other way around was new to them.

Significantly more has been written on colonial Othering than on the Othering that came to supplant it. Such an imbalance in data continues to play its part and needs to be taken into account.

This book examines various ways in which insiders and outsiders have been imagined and defined. Chapter 2 discusses the Western imagination and its Othering practice, as illustrated by the invention of *homo caudatus*. It also investigates the cultural psychology mechanism which makes people divide the world into insiders and outsiders and its consequences for intercultural approaches.

Chapters 3, 4 and 5 present 'us' and 'them' and the boundaries separating Selves and Others, as imagined by Africans and people of African descent.

Issues dealt with are mutual relations, similarities and differences, a common 'us' in African and African-American cultural representation, versus Europeans, the West, white people as 'them' and whiteness as otherness.

In Chapter 3 the African representation of white people and the West in African novels is dealt with, preceded by a brief analysis of the origin of white and black people as explained in myths from oral traditions. Chapters 4 and 5 present various African and black perspectives on Africanness and identity: such intellectual and cultural movements are discussed as Panafricanism and the Harlem Renaissance, Negritude and South African Black Consciousness. During the twentieth century, black cultural movements started to flourish in reaction to white indifference and racism, focused on the significance of the African heritage in music, literature and the visual arts. These movements raised the question to what extent black culture should be a permanent phenomenon, an essence, or an historical phase. Of relevance to this question is the extent to which black and white have been or should be considered different categories. As Paul Gilroy has argued (1993: 199), 'there are strong tensions inside black cultures on attitudes towards tradition and modernity'. He offers the concept of diaspora as a way to speak about the 'apparently magical processes of connectedness that arise as much from the transformation of Africa by diaspora cultures as from the affiliation of diaspora cultures to Africa and the traces of Africa that those diaspora cultures enclose' (*ibid*). Blackness is apparently just as little a guarantee for unity as whiteness.

The discussions of gender and culture are also thriving. Poised between Western feminism and their own cultural traditions, African women and African-American women critically pick their way between old and new cultural legacies. Different views of gender matters are discussed in Chapters 6 and 7. In spite of common interests, the African and African-American contexts reflect enormous differences in gender issues, aims and strategies, depending on class, culture, history and hegemonic power.

Some theoretical issues in the ongoing academic debate about insiders and outsiders will also be examined, with examples from various disciplines. Chapter 8 deals with insiders' issues in the academy, with examples ranging from the disciplines of history and anthropology to sociology and literary studies. *Interdiscursivity* will be suggested as a concept offering some modest but interesting space for dialogue on a more equal footing (Chapter 9).

Identities are not ossified fossils from a distant past. The narratives of slavery, loss, colonisation, exile and migration serve a mnemonic function, as Paul Gilroy (1993) argues, 'organising the consciousness of the "racial" group socially and striking the important balance between inside and outside activity – the different practices, cognitive, habitual, and performative, that are required to invent, maintain, and renew identity' (198). Identities are as mobile and variable as the imagined boundaries between insiders and outsiders in cultures and scholarship. As the offspring of a common history of domination and subjugation, the mutual exchange of experience and reflection regarding each other's cultural insiderisms is important.

A discussion about the invention of boundaries is full of ambivalences and pitfalls. I cannot undo the fact that I am a European woman, living in a small country and belonging to a privileged class of academics, a non-native to both Africa and the USA. However, I believe this need not be negative *per se* (e.g. Bakhtin 1986). One of my privileges has been a long experience of living and working in Africa, where I first spent those years in Congo, and later as a visiting scholar and lecturer, shorter periods in several other countries in West, East and Southern Africa. Africans taught me not only much about Africa, but also about Europe as the periphery for those who consider Africa their centre. This experience has been very helpful as a training in awareness about the self-evident ethnocentrism with which we have been brought up in the West.

My frequent visits to the USA have always been a pleasure and I have come to appreciate the stimulating research climate, enjoyable enthusiasm and sincere friendship of colleagues in a number of universities. As a visitor from outside the USA I have also learnt how difficult it has become openly to discuss tricky issues related to race and gender matters in the American academic world, a worrisome development in a country so proud of its freedom and democracy. Open debates on insiders and outsiders are sensitive but indispensable. If such debates are shunned out of fear of conflict or dismissal, what will happen to the fragile flowers of academic openness and tolerance? At several conferences, I have seen them wither away in suffocating bushes of fearful or dogmatic political correctness and (Self or Other) silencing censorship.

In this book I have taken the risk of discussing some controversies in which I was personally involved. After serious consideration I decided to discuss these experiences here: they are meant (and hopefully will be read) as a modest contribution to a respectful intercultural dialogue which can only develop thanks to debates on diverging views.

The title of this book, *Imagining Insiders*, refers to insiders (and outsiders) as subjects and objects of race and gender imagining. A completely detached perspective does not exist. We all have our traps and interests, as men and women, as people of European and African descent, as privileged academics in a global class society; but we can weigh those biases rationally and critically, and present the results of honest efforts to colleagues in our field of knowledge production. In the words of Elisabeth Mudimbe-Boyi (1998: 209), 'there is no critical monopoly nor reserved domain in any intellectual inquiry or field of research'.

Over the years I have interviewed a number of African writers, some of whom have become close friends. Those long and intense interviews have been very rewarding and I am glad to be able to share here some of the insights given to me. At the end of the book I have included some passages from interviews with five well-known writers – the passages related to the foregoing issues. Not only those conversations with writers, but also the contacts with African, Caribbean and American colleagues have made clear to me how indissolubly interconnected our cultures and experiences have become.

2

Homo caudatus

European imagination and its cultural outsiders

Everybody calls what he is not used to barbarism; really, it seems that we have no other sight of truth and reason than the example and idea of opinions and traditions of the country where we live.

Michel de Montaigne

The purpose is not really to indict the past, but to summon it to the attention of a suicidal, anachronistic present: you are a child of those centuries of lies, distortion and opportunism in high places, even among the holy of holies of intellectual objectivity.

Wole Soyinka

In 1987, when the Dutch author Harry Mulisch was not nominated for the prestigious AKO prize, he dismissed the list of nominees with the comment: 'Third world literature' (*Trouw*, 16 May 1987). When I later asked him what he meant by that, he answered: 'Third rate.'

'Do you mean to say that Third World literature is third-rate literature?'

'Yes,' Mulisch said, 'the lights don't work there either, do they?'

Third world equals third rate: quite a common line of reasoning, but does the culture that is economically and technologically the most advanced necessarily also produce the best literature? For Mulisch, of course, the best literature consists of the books he has written himself. The matter might be more complicated for anyone who bothers to wonder whether the lights were working when Homer wrote the *Iliad* or Cervantes *Don Quixote*.

The West has been left with an evolutionist legacy: following Darwin's example with living creatures, societies and cultures have been put on a scale ranging from most primitive to most advanced. On the basis of its economic power and technological development, Western society also sees itself at the top of the list culturally.

But why should literature flourish solely in conditions of comfort and luxury? What exactly are the criteria that would justify the conclusion that Western literature is more 'advanced' — and in what direction one might ask — and is consequently superior? Ruth Finnegan (1977: 266) rightly refuted this evolutionist view:

> The prejudice which connects poor material conditions with lack of artistic achievements dies hard. But it must be made clear to a dispassionate enquirer that in the light of the evidence now available from all over the world, any generalised attempt to postulate a direct correlation of economic with poetic development would be simple-minded.

Cultural differences have rarely been acknowledged as self-evident. On the contrary, people tend to reject differentness and the definition of what is human often extends no further than the borders of one's own group, country, race or sex — the borders of one's own language, continent and culture. The barbarians are always the others. Before it acquired its negative connotation of 'uncivilized', the Greek word *barbaros* originally meant 'speaking incomprehensibly, foreign and strange'. More or less the same thing happened with the word *silvaticus*, which originally meant 'forest' or 'living in the forest'. *Sauvage* or *savage* came to mean 'wild' and the word *paganus*, initially a 'villager' or 'rural person', now pejoratively became a 'pagan' (Sinclair 1977).

Thus the Greeks viewed the Romans as barbarians. Romans did the same with the peoples they subjugated. Aryans looked down on Jews and Jews on Palestinians. Europeans felt they were more civilized than Indians and Africans, but did not realize that to these peoples Western barbarianism had become proverbial. In China, the Wall was the dividing line between culture and barbarism. The philosopher Shao Yong (1011–1077) expressed this ethnocentric mentality quite clearly when he stated: 'I am happy because I am a human being and not an animal, a man and not a woman, a Chinese and not a barbarian, and because I live in Loyang, the most beautiful city in the world' (qtd in Sinclair 1977: 20). The tendency to judge others as inferior to one's own group is widespread, for the truthfulness of world views is often less important in gaining acceptance than is the extent to which they serve prevailing interests.

Homo caudatus

In the days when voyages were still a rare adventure, people at home were only too willing to believe any and every story told by travellers about what they had seen. There was much less interest in verifying their accounts than in the undeniable fact that they had been there and were relating what they had seen with their own eyes. If, in the course of their travels, they had not actually seen something but had it from hearsay, then having been in the vicinity was quite enough. Perhaps the main reason travellers met with such easy credibility was that their compatriots shared their views, their language and their culture: the people they were describing had to be different — an irrefutable point.

Views are accepted not only because, on the grounds of whatever information is already available, they seem to ring true, but also because they serve a prevailing interest. As is evident from the notions adhered to by Harry Mulisch, scientifically untenable ideas sometimes survive for surprising lengths of time.

There was, for example, the *homo caudatus*, human but with a tail, a creature that has appeared at numerous spots and on numerous occasions in Western history. The *homo caudatus* or 'tail-man' is a creature one would actually prefer to view as not belonging to the human race, difficult though it might be to deny the resemblance. The crux of the matter is whether he has a soul. If he does not then of course he cannot be baptized. This product of distant expeditions and European imperialism is also often associated with cannibalism and uninhibited lust, negative qualities generally attributed to barbarians. The *homo caudatus* represents the Other as an inferior species. In his study of its history, Penel (1982) referred to the Greek satyr and the medieval devil, often depicted with a tail, as the ancestors of the 'tail-man'. References found in the works of Pliny (first century), Saint Augustine and Saint Jerome (fourth century) and Saint Albert the Great (twelfth century) later served as 'evidence': by merely quoting them, one had the backing of serious authors, the Classics, the Fathers of the Church.

It is striking to note how the home of *homo caudatus* moved from the Mediterranean and North Africa to Latin America and Asia, the Malay Archipelago and the Philippines. From the many accounts I have selected two Dutch ones. The first is by Jakob de Bondt, who assumed the Latin name Bontius, as was the habit among scholars in those days. In 1642 he published in Amsterdam a study in Latin entitled *Natural History and Medicine in the Western Part of the Dutch East Indies*. The author was a doctor in this area, where *caudati* allegedly lived. He called them satyrs:

I have seen several satyrs of both sexes who walked in an upright position and I also saw a female satyr who hid and covered her face with both hands with just as much modesty, if I may say so, as our most virtuous girls, in the presence of the men she did not know. She wept, moaned and did everything so exactly like a human being that one might

say all she was lacking was speech. The inhabitants of the island Java say
that satyrs, the males as well as the females, are quite capable of speaking
but that they do not want to because they are afraid that they would
then be forced to work. But in my opinion, that is quite ridiculous. The
Dutch who live there ... say they are born of the lust of local women
who have monkeys and guinea pigs impregnate them. (in Penel 1982: 48)

In an account of his expedition, another traveller Struys (1681) was initially
rather sceptical. He had heard about tail-people but did not believe in them.
Then one day in Formosa, when a travelling companion stepped into the
jungle to relieve his bowels, he was for no apparent reason, murdered by a
native. The guilty party was apprehended and sentenced to be burned at the
stake. While the man was tied to the stake awaiting his execution, Struys made
this discovery:

I saw something I had previously been unable to believe; his tail was
more than a foot long, completely covered with hair, just like the tail of a
cow. When he saw that the spectators were surprised about what he had
and they did not, he said that the flaw, if that was what it was, was due to
the climate, since everyone in the southern region of that island had one,
just like he did. (in Penel 1982: 45).

The relation between these travellers and their informants was certainly not
one of equality, as evidenced in this statement about fellow *caudati*. However,
such trivialities did not bother the public: it knew what it wanted to hear and
the traveller willingly furnished descriptions translated into binaries with
which people at home were already familiar.

Until the eighteenth century no cultural theories were linked to the
phenomenon. Since then, however, the tail-man has come to play an increasing
role, not only from the natural history angle but also because of his popularity
in the literary imagination which has nourished his perpetuation.

For a long time there was no consensus among the anatomists who
commented on the tail-man. Some said that on rare occasions a human being is
born with one or two extra vertebrae. Others claimed that what one was
dealing with here were satyrs and referred back to Ancient authors. Pliny, for
example, situated pans and satyrs in Africa and the Orient. Hypothesis and
fantasy went hand in hand in Le Cat's *Anatomy of the Human Body* (1765).
According to him, if pregnant women were scared by a monkey during the
second or third month of pregnancy they gave birth to tail-babies. The fright
fixed itself in the minds of women, which was why their babies were born with
tails. (in Penel 1982: 51).

In *The Singularities of Nature* (1766), even Voltaire took *homo caudatus* seriously. An enlightened man, he did not fail to seek reasonable arguments to back his standpoint. His sources included:

- Jesuits who worked as missionaries among the heathens;
- travellers to distant regions;
- the scholar Maillet, who fervently held that the *caudatus* was a species;
- a small 'empirical' study he conducted among the black servants of his acquaintances.

Voltaire concluded that the *caudatus* did indeed exist, but in countries far warmer than his. If specimens were to be found closer to home, then of course they would be in rural regions; savages and peasants had a great deal of contact with animals and were, in a sense, animal-like themselves. His line of reasoning also went back to the Classics, where the satyr was described as the product of a relation between a human being and a monkey. Naturally 'our' girls did not do anything like that, he assured his readers, but 'in warm countries' that kind of thing could be expected (in Penel 1982: 54). One cannot help noting that in Voltaire's writings, as well as in those of other authors, it is only the women who have relations with monkeys.

A literary example was presented by Voltaire in *Candide* (1759): far away, in the distant land of the Oreillons (savages in South America), Candide and his servant Cacambo were resting in a meadow near a cool brook when they heard the high-pitched shrieks of women. Were they shrieks of pain or pleasure? They set off to find out:

> The shrieks were uttered by two completely naked girls who were walking nimbly down the meadow path, followed by two monkeys gently biting them in the buttocks. Candide was overcome by compassion ... He reached for his Spanish rifle, fired two shots and killed the monkeys.
>
> 'Thank God, my dear Cacambo, I have saved these poor creatures from a great danger.' (in Penel 1982: 52–53).

It soon appeared, however, that there had been a grievous misunderstanding; the two women were enraged. Candide could not understand why, but Cacambo explained that 'in some countries, monkeys win the affection of ladies' (53) and in his opinion it was not really all that hard to understand, since they were quarter-people. Then Candide recalled the words of his old teacher, Pangloss, who had told him about fauns, satyrs and egypans who were seen by important persons in Ancient times. The two women immediately complained to their fellow savages who, as might be expected, were naked as well. Armed with arrows, clubs and axes of stone, they tied up Candide and his servant. Some of them warmed the cauldron and others came with spits on which to roast them (in Penel 1982: 53–54). If the monkeys were quarter-people, then the savages were at most half-people, according to the perceived thinking of the time.

By the end of the eighteenth century it became increasingly clear that there was no way to defend the notion of the *homo caudatus* as a species. All the facts indicated that the elongated coccyx is a freak of nature, just as there are rare cases of human babies born with six toes. It is indeed an abnormality that occurs now and then all over the world. For example, in the *British Medical Journal* (January 1989: 55) a case was described (illustrated with photo) of a baby boy newly born in the North Manchester General Hospital 'with no abnormality obvious apart from his tail – 5 cm long. It was a true tail, an extension of the coccyx, moved intermittently, and was covered with fine downy hair. The tail was excised on the day of birth under local anaesthesia'.

The *homo caudatus* was just another product of the imagination, like all the other stereotypes associated with the noble as well as the evil savage (Sinclair 1977; Lemaire 1986). There are numerous examples of both kinds in Western literature (Hoffmann 1973; Joachim 1980; Milbury-Steen 1981).

At the beginning of the nineteenth century there was, nonetheless, a heated debate among scholars about 'Niam-Niams', a man-eating tribe of tail-people said to have been discovered in the dark heart of Africa. Anthropological research revealed, however, that they were a tribe clothed in animal skins, who wore belts with a long strip of leather hanging down the back. By the late nineteenth century, most studies and encyclopedias referred to the tail-man as a kind of fable.

Caudatus thinking

What remained was the myth that there were people who were inferior to European whites and that the natural hierarchy studied by biologists coincided with a moral and aesthetic progression. There was also more emphasis on the differences between civilized man, barbarian and savage. It would be virtually impossible, or so the myth went, for a savage to become civilized. The differences were elaborated upon in academic treatises and the racial theory of Comte de Gobineau was one of the most popular. He wrote a four-volume work *On the Inequality of Human Races* (1835–55) in which he provided evidence that he and the other members of his own kind constituted the highest category of the human race. Faced with the notions of freedom, equality, brotherhood and the abolition of slavery, the scientific evidence was supposed to legitimate permanent inequality on the grounds of racial traits.

As Benedict Anderson has observed, 'the dreams of racism have their origin ... above all in claims to divinity among rulers and to "blue" or "white" blood and "breeding" among aristocracies. No surprise then that the putative sire of modern racism should be, not some petty-bourgeois nationalist, but Joseph Arthur, Comte de Gobineau' (1983: 149). The superiority of the aristocracy was then extended to the colonies, 'generalizing a principle of innate, inherited superiority' — permitting large numbers of bourgeois colonials 'to play aristocrat off centre court' (150).

Racial theories and practices went hand in hand. If blacks were not real human beings, then there was nothing wrong with slavery and the Europeans could do unto savages as they had been created to do, that is rule over nature. The nineteenth-century theories were undeniably linked to the interests of the group that benefited from them. If an idea such as this one is refuted in the academic world, that does not, alas, automatically mean the end of racism. Many representatives of the academic world had been supporting this theory for so long that the solid roots of its popularity have not been eradicated until this very day.

In European *caudatus* thinking it was taken for granted that Africans were 'the heathens'. It seemed only logical that God had entrusted their pagan fate into the hands of Christians. The more extensive the slave trade became, the more often the story of the accursed children of Ham who had to serve their brothers became a frame of reference. For in Genesis it says 'Cursed be Canaan [the son of Ham], a servant of servants shall he be unto his brethren'. And the sons of Ham were black ... or were made black as punishment.

In the course of history any number of attempts were thus made to justify slavery and colonization. White people would sometimes wonder, for example, whether the blacks were really descendants of Adam and Eve, only to conclude that this was probably not the case. As late as 1900 C. Caroll published a book called *The Negro as a Beast or in the Image of God?* (cf. Burns 1949: 21). The title of one of the chapters was 'Biblical and Scientific Proof of the Fact that the Negro is not a Member of the Human Race'. If this comes as a surprise, in the 1960s a fundamentalist Dutch evangelical broadcasting company published a photograph of a Kapauke (a New Guinea Papua) whose facial features had clearly become less animal-like as a result of his conversion to Christianity. But who would ever dream of comparing a religious white man to a non-religious one and then conclude that the former's facial features were less animal-like than the latter's? The myth of the black savage, whether noble or aggressive or both, is deeply rooted in Western thinking, though usually now without a tail. Disguised in a wide range of subtle metamorphoses, this kind of *caudatus* thinking which presents people from foreign cultures as somehow deviating from the 'natural' order still crops up in all kinds of texts, from exotic, colonial and 'ordinary' novels to comic books, advertisements and literary criticism. Let me give just one contemporary example. In the novel *De herfst zal schitterend zijn* [Autumn will be splendid] by the Dutch author Jan Siebelink (1980) there is the following description of the black man whose virility threatens one of 'our' women:

> In the bar: music, the proximity of the ocean and the sweetish smell of negroes. Hella is dancing and singing … the negro smiles at her and his tongue and palate are pink and he asks her to come with him to his room. 'No,' she says. 'I am married, I am here with my daughter'. He laughs with his mouth wide open … Now the band is playing 'Black Blood' … Perspiration is dripping down Hella's forehead, running down her cheeks, going down her neck. The negro is perspiring too. His torso is swaying back and forth, he is gracefully moving his hands about and then she can tell from the look in his eyes … she is certain he has come. (Siebelink 1980: 14–15)

European perspectives on miscegenation have been part of the theories of race and racialized thinking in colonial Europe since the nineteenth century. Robert Young in *Colonial Desire* (1995), wrote an interesting analysis of this Western obsession with 'mixed' sexuality and hybridity. Africans too were preoccupied with the subject, as a number of African novels make clear (see Chapter 3).

Centres and peripheries

In the relations between cultures and in observation of these relations the fact that certain things are ideologically 'self-evident' plays a role. We are conditioned by our centre and, working outward from that basis, we establish our relation with the periphery. In connection with international trade, economists like André Gunder Frank and Raul Prebisch have described both these concepts and their relations. There are countries that belong to the centre of the world economy and there are others that constitute the periphery around this centre. In a centre–periphery system there are no independent regions. Regions can be analysed solely in relation to the larger whole of which they are part. The inequality of the regions that function within the system is one of the characteristic features of the centre–periphery relation. The regions where the forces of production are the most highly developed constitute the centre of the system, which implies that they determine the structure and the functions of the parts. The less developed regions are peripheral in this system: they are economically dependent, which inhibits their advance and promotes the development of the centre. This analysis has been criticized frequently by other economists as it puts the blame and responsibility for this state of affairs exclusively with the West (thus withholding, in advance, any initiative from the developing countries concerned). In the 1980s governments on the periphery who committed major mistakes and shirked responsibility for their own policies became increasingly subject to criticism. Nevertheless, economic allocation and specialization are still largely dictated by the centres generating the strongest purchasing power. These forces also affect information.

Does the same hold true for culture? In spite of the forces attempting to penetrate it from the periphery, Western culture would seem to be an inviolable centre of power. Whoever rules the information flow also rules the culture. Whoever belongs to the centre defines itself and the periphery on that basis. Contributions from the periphery are overlooked, ignored or belittled. Criticism of the West for its Eurocentrism is regularly expressed from outside Europe's borders. At an international conference on 'Eurocentrism and the Disciplines' held in 1982 at the Free University, Amsterdam, Asian and African scholars revealed Eurocentrism's role in fields ranging from theology, psychology and medicine to economics, law and literary theory (Schröder 1982). The question is whether the difference between inside and outside Europe can be maintained.

Europe has sometimes simply projected the boundaries between the North and the South into the Mediterranean area. In *L'Eurocentrism, critique d'une idéologie* (1988a), the Egyptian researcher Samir Amin expresses his objection to such a North–South cultural divide which the West, by virtue of its economic position, has imposed on the Mediterranean countries. Western Europe, he claims, has forgotten that for centuries, the Atlantic world was on the periphery of the Hellenistic culture which was also influenced by contributions from outside Greece, from Egypt and the eastern territories of the former Persian empire conquered by Alexander the Great. What is more, Europe inherited much of this legacy from Muslim scholars (Sinclair 1977). Only since the Renaissance has the centre of this culture shifted westward, while Mediterranean culture has gradually come to occupy a peripheral position. Samir Amin (1988b: 13) objects to the fact that this new European culture is based upon a myth of Western geographical continuity as opposed to the world south of the Mediterranean, which thus became the new border between the centre and the periphery. He feels that the core of Eurocentrism lies within this mythical construction: in order to justify its existence the now prevailing cultural Eurocentrism has invented 'a mythical West' which it claims 'was always there, unique and extraordinary from the very start'.

The myth of Greek ancestors has also played an instrumental role: Greece is the mother of rational philosophy and 'the East' never got any further than metaphysics. The function of the Arabs is thus reduced to the mere transference of the Greek legacy to the Renaissance. Within this view, Amin feels, Islam never emerges above the Hellenic legacy and this same view conceives of the North–South borderline as permanent and self-evident, as if inherent to the region's geography and its history (Amin 1988a: 16). The myth 'logically' results in the notion that 'Third World is third rate'.

In addition to Samir Amin, Edward Said (1979, 1989, 1993) and others have taken exception to the views concerning man and culture held for centuries by esteemed scholars in the centre that, in the words of Wole Soyinka in his Nobel lecture in Stockholm in 1986, have been pronounced 'the holy of holies of intellectual objectivity'.

Of course, people try to accommodate what is strange and translate it into familiar codes on the basis of their own reality. All cultures apply their own corrections to reality. As Said (1979: 67) put it:

> It is perfectly natural for the human mind to resist the assault on it of untreated strangeness; therefore cultures have always been inclined to impose complete transformations on other cultures, receiving these other cultures not as they are but as, for the benefit of the receiver, they ought to be.

According to the Argentinian Jorge Luis Borges (1981), authors choose their own predecessors. The same holds true in academia: researchers choose from the views and commentaries that are at hand. A new text — whether literary or scientific — is written on the basis of the selection, rearrangement, reorganization, adaptation and revision of what has been written earlier. But with what intention are such changes made and what gives the revision its authority?

Socio-cultural identity

If reality is a construction, as sociologists of knowledge such as Peter Berger and Thomas Luckmann (1973) contend, literature is a secondary construction based upon it. The concept of identity is clearly embedded in both of these constructions. What processes determine our collective identity and how we become conscious of them is an old question. In the field of psychology, much research has been conducted into exactly how identity mechanisms work. The results would also be useful in the field of literary theory since psychological processes link language and thinking with each other as well as with knowledge and emotions, individual motivations and a personal world view. In her study of psychological processes, Marisa Zavalloni defines collective identity as:

> a cultural product that embodies all that has been recorded as history, institution, fiction, work of art and knowledge. The sociocultural environment, of which collective identities are indeed an essential part, may be seen as the sedimented product of centuries of interactive cycles, molded through psychological processes that can be considered as fixed parameters which reproduce and sometimes subvert its order. (1983: 206)

From this perspective, personal identity develops during a series of interactions with the sociocultural environment. Zavalloni formulated a method of *representational contextualization* (free association, introspection, interpretation and comments on one's place and role in the sociocultural environment) to gather data about a person's identity in terms of country, sex, religious background, vocation, social group, political commitment, peer group and family situation. Such data can be inventoried. Coded in language as *manifest thinking*, first-order data enable us to evaluate the sociocultural environment. But it is only one aspect of what is activated in the brain when a person comments on the various categories mentioned, for manifest thinking invariably co-exists with *second-order data*: the internalized images, collective memories, and traditions that are handed down from one generation to the next and that (as *background thinking* on the periphery of consciousness) constantly accompany our utterances, which are coded in language. The concomitance of words and background thinking constitutes one and the same psychological phenomenon which Zavalloni calls the *internal operant environment*:

> The associations between a descriptive category of one's identity group and one's image and memories have been found to be stable over time and seem to operate in the brain as units of representational thinking, a mixture of words and thoughts. (Zavalloni 1983: 208)

People are not necessarily conscious of the ways in which manifest thinking and background thinking function, but they can be made conscious of them. The pronoun shifters 'I' and 'We' play an important role in this process, for they link the members of the group emotionally in their social intercourse. In interaction with each other, the identity associated with the 'I' is repeatedly reinforced by reference to the 'We'. In fact, the complex interrelationship between background thinking and manifest thinking functions like a computer program that is continuously searching for compatible inputs which are selected on the basis of recognized sameness and differentness, positive qualities and negative ones, self and non-self. Such binary oppositions are fundamental to the construction of reality, for they imply that people or things that make a negative impression are inextricably linked to people or things that are experienced as positive, important, and legitimate. The possibility of imagining one's self in another person's place is generally restricted to the category of people who belong to one's own group. For this reason, the reality of the out-group cannot be experienced internally. As Zavalloni explains, 'Thinking about the being of these groups will give rise to an emptiness, a blank feeling' (208). Indeed, everything that does not have a fixed positive meaning in the internal operant environment tends to be registered as uninteresting, unimportant or untrue. Culture plays a crucial role in shaping the internal operant environment, for the products of culture-creators, artists, philosophers and researchers serve to reinforce individual motivations and arguments. According to Zavalloni, for example, structural similarities in the internal operant environments of culture-producers and culture-consumers correspond to the way human nature is depicted in art, literature, film, science, ideology and other realms of cultural production in their society.

In considering the extent to which power and interest determine what belongs to the centre and what belongs to the periphery, we can elucidate the relationship between a culture and its various subcultures through Clifford Geertz's (1973: 89) definition of culture as:

> an historically transmitted pattern of meanings embodied in symbols, a system of inherited conceptions expressed in symbolic forms by means of which men communicate, perpetuate, and develop their knowledge about and attitudes toward life.

Although groups invariably construe reality in ways that differ from those of other groups in that society, a separate subculture exists only when it exhibits a fixed pattern of specific differences from the larger cultural system of which it is a part and with which it shares features. The terms culture and subculture are therefore relative, for just as one might speak about European or African cultures, within which the cultures of Great Britain or Zimbabwe would be subcultures, one could refer to the culture of Great Britain with its black, gay and Anglican subcultures, or the culture of Zimbabwe with its Shona, Ndebele and 'Rhodie' subcultures. Thus, cultures and subcultures are constructed, imagined, in spite of the practice in which people do not restrict themselves exclusively to what belongs inside their imagined (sub-)cultural borderline.

Zavalloni's (1983) discussion of internal operant environment, manifest thinking, and background thinking as collective mechanisms helps us to understand the nature of cultural and subcultural identity. If one is programmed to conceive of culture as Western culture, other cultures will be regarded as peripheral, negative, inferior, uninteresting and/or unimportant. In this case, one's background thinking articulates the belief that there is no real culture outside the Western centre, because 'the lights don't work there': 'they' have not produced a Rembrandt, Bach or Beethoven. The literature of these Others is not considered part of the mainstream. Such background thinking is perceived as an accurate depiction of reality. The same holds for perspectives from other cultures.

Identity mechanisms tend to be reinforced by the way in which we deal with information that is in harmony with our internal operant environment and with information that is not compatible. However, even information which is accurate and acceptable might not be accepted because the people who encounter it lack the receptivity to assimilate it. If information contradicts elements of their background thinking they have no motivation to alter such elements. One's own culture and the information received constantly reinforce each other through the same identity mechanism; indeed this reinforcement accords an aura of objectivity and 'reality' to both of them.

Many examples could be given from the field of literary studies to illustrate the resistance of scholars to the input of the Other. When the Nigerian scholar Emmanuel Nwezeh (1985) criticized Albert Gérard's view of comparative literature as too European and therefore inapplicable to Africa, he also explained why he felt that some of Gérard's comments were 'paternalistic' and 'neo-colonial'. When Gérard was invited to comment on the matter, he expressed surprise at Nwezeh's polemical tone and declared himself to be 'an academic who has devoted twenty years to the study of African literature and does not intend to enter into a discussion about it' (Nwezeh 1985: 41). In other words, he rejected new input from outside, because he regarded it as non-compatible with his own professional standing in the field. Such a policy of exclusion – of women and children this time – is also obvious in a comment by Claude Lévi-Strauss in his study of the Bororo: 'The *entire* village left the next day in thirty canoes. We remained behind with the women and children in the *abandoned* houses' (qtd in Michard and Ribery 1982: 7, emphasis added).

I have met a few proponents of the unwritten law that one must be black to study literature written by black authors and the response to African criticisms of methods and techniques used by some white researchers has been the charge that these criticisms were introducing a normative point of view. However, normative points of view existed long before the criticism of the dominant discourse was made; in fact they were so profoundly embedded in people's background thinking that they were no longer aware of their own biases – and not only in the field of African literature. Examples abound: D.W. Fokkema (1985) has criticized the field of women's studies for its 'anti-empirical subjectivist tendency', on the grounds that those conducting the research were themselves the subject of this research. According to him, this situation introduced a normative standpoint into the academic discussion and excluded the possibility of independent verification of research results. He added that 'the unwritten law that women are the only ones who are qualified to engage in women's studies is similarly based upon an undesirable intermingling of subjective interest and research procedure' (Fokkema 1985: 253). Yet he fails to consider how his own subjective interests prevent him from assimilating the input of the Other and how these interests enter into his own definition of empirical research.

Women speaking to women are no exception to this rule: they may also fail to respect the perspective of the Other. After a lecture by Anglo-Indian critic Gayatri Spivak, the Nigerian scholar Folabo Soyinka-Ajayi remarked that she 'did not find deconstruction that relevant to the analysis of her work'. In response, Spivak condescendingly declared, 'There can be no learning when the field is not prepared ... When one says Africa, quite often ... we forget that Africa is a place with universities and so on' (quoted in Jeyifo 1989: 5). Ajayi, who would have welcomed a 'critical' dialogue on the subject, felt that she had been treated instead to an 'insulting diatribe'. For our purposes, the most revealing aspect here is the restrictive use of the pronoun shifter 'we'. The term obviously did not include Ajayi, who could hardly be expected to forget that there were universities in Africa.

Cultural distance and cultural hierarchies

Such confrontations demonstrate the necessity of continually re-examining the premises upon which the academic community operates and the way in which statements are verified. To what extent have members of this community been programmed by their status, their gender, their culture? How have differences in (sub)culture, class and gender been integrated into a hierarchical system of assumptions that govern the descriptive and analytical work of scholars in the field? How does power influence the result of research in literary and cultural studies?

One might pessimistically conclude that uncontaminated research is impossible and that scholars should refrain from examining, describing and interpreting the products of societies to which they do not belong.

In reaction to the danger of domination, Otherness-studies have launched the idea that one can only speak about a group as a specialist if belonging to the group itself by culture, race, sex, social class, etc. According to this argument, outsiders can never say anything reliable about 'us' because they do not speak from within. I do not agree. If this is true, a dialogue between people who always differ will, by that very fact, be aborted from the start.

Of course there are experiences that someone from outside does not share with insiders, but this also holds true the other way round. Insiders' and outsiders' views can be both enriching and restricting. Due to a certain detachment, someone who looks in from outside observes things that are not obvious to the insiders, since they are too self-evident, too close to their situation and experience. On the other hand, outsiders lack this intimate knowledge and experience. This applies to all groups. If an anthropologist from Asia or Africa does research on the customs of European natives, the perspective will yield interesting observations. Views of Africans on colonial Western novels and films, as well as novels and stories about the colonial occupation, white characters and their habits, are revealing for similar reasons. What strikes Africans that Westerners 'naturally' overlook because of their background? Those who strictly adhere to their own insiderism, will never receive an answer to such questions.

While a cultural insider has the advantage of certain knowledge, the boundaries of knowledge and experience between insiders and outsiders are constantly shifting. One can become an insider in different ways: 'doing the enlightening and enabling research; showing capability for empathy; under-standing, if not taking the perspectives of one's research subjects; testing the knowledge gained with those who live the culture; living the culture; and learning the relevant languages' (Mukherjee 1990; Ogundipe-Leslie 1993: 109).

Eurocentrism and other types of ethnocentrism give people blinkers, but blinkers can be disposed of, whereas the idea that the Other as defined and constructed by 'us' cannot study us nor we the Other labels and imprisons all people in the prejudices of their own group.

People can question their acquired certainties and assumptions and from this critical stance closely observe, ask questions, formulate carefully and submit their results to representatives of groups to which they do and do not belong, who act and react from varied perspectives and with different questions. This is how a critical dialogue develops.

In the past it was often assumed that the situation could be resolved by respecting a certain distance between researchers and the objects of their research, thereby assuring the objectivity of observations. However, even intersubjectivity is no guarantee, because the subjects consulted for purposes of scientific control tend to come from the same culture, social background, nation or continent as the researcher. Only a greater awareness of our own cultural context can enable us to detect the ways in which we tend to repudiate certain inputs as non-compatible. The confrontation between discourse and counter-discourses is particularly important in the arts, literature and the various disciplines in the humanities.

In *Playing in the Dark* (1992), Toni Morisson analysed narrative devices, strategies and language in the fiction of white American writers representing black characters. She pleads for investigations 'of the ways in which a non-white Africanist presence and personae have been constructed ... in the United States, and of the literary uses this fabricated presence has served'. The critical perspective should be averted 'from the racial object to the racial subject; from the described and imagined to the describers and imaginers; from the serving to the served' (90). Of course, this has been done more extensively over the last decade. The study of Western literature and literary criticism on these matters reveals indeed that the opinions of both writers and critics in this part of the world are often based less on aesthetics than on 'Westhetics'.

Perspectives are unavoidable, but they are also reversible and changeable. Writing offers the possibility of unsettling what is written by writing back. This has been done to an increasing degree by those who had been discarded on the basis of established scientific or cultural criteria.

During the time of slavery, writing and freedom were directly associated with each other. Where mankind came to be defined on the basis of people's ability to read and write, reading and writing naturally impressed those who were excluded from both. When learning to write is forbidden by the Others' laws, it becomes urgent to prove to 'them' that 'we' are human beings who are also able to write books. Henry Louis Gates Jr (1987) has argued how creative writing thus became, for American slaves, 'a political statement. It started with *Poems on Various Subjects, Religious and Moral, by Phillis Wheatly, Negro Servant to Mr. Wheatly of Boston* (1773) which was not read as literature but as a political document; she thus wrote herself into humanity thanks to her poetry. Although she followed the conventions of Western neo-classical literature, mentioning Milton, Pope, Gray, Addison and Watts as her examples, a literary tradition began with her of black writers who wanted to prove their humanity in spite of a long Western tradition of slave traders and scholars who were deemed to have proved the opposite. The fact that politics and culture are interwoven is apparent not only from such a poetics but also from the previous Western train of thought on to which it is grafted (Gates 1987: 73).

White domination and prejudice have also provoked reactions in Africa. In orally transmitted myths, for example, it is explained how the difference between black and white came about. Such stories of origin developed after the arrival of the Europeans. African writers have written back, in their own novels and poetry, to the Western stories of the 'discoverers' and the colonial novels. Their novels set African visions of Africa against European visions of Africa while, in the poetry of Africans and of people of African origin in the diaspora, belief in a common Pan-African identity was professed. That belief has been expressed in cultural movements such as indigenism, the Harlem Renaissance, Negritude, Black Arts and Black Consciousness. These movements often look back to an idealized past, or anticipate a utopian future, in order to make the present bearable. Sometimes they produce a reversed discourse in which the Westerner is the 'Other'.

In his classic *Portrait du Colonisé précédé du Portrait du colonisateur* (1966), Albert Memmi describes the two well-known replies of the colonized to the dominant argument of the colonizer:

1. The assimilation with the colonial culture, which always fails because the colonized is by definition doomed to remain an outsider. Such a failure can have dramatic consequences: in 1915 the Haïtian poet Edmond Laforest, as Michael Dash (1981: 24) tells us, tied the Larousse encyclopedia round his neck, jumped from a bridge and committed suicide by drowning. For later Negritude poets he became a symbol of what happens to one who fatally associates himself with the colonial culture.
2. The break with colonial culture, the second answer, leads to protest, self-glorification and dogmatic emphasis of differences. Such a reaction is to no less bound up with the very thing that it reacts against than is attempted assimilation.

Both replies are found not only in the literature but also in the scientific work of those whom the colonialist's exclusivist perspective labelled outsiders. In both cases the original discriminatory claims remain as a subtext, determining the history of the new culture. There is no way out, purity does not exist.

Outside Africa information on African representations of Europeans and the West in oral and written texts, in myths, stories, paintings, films and theatre continues to be scanty. That is why the next chapter addresses Africa's imagined outsiders as they came into being in oral and written literature.

3

'The white man has no friends'

The European Other in African oral and written literatures

A people is always misunderstood if only its rulers are quoted.

Bernard Dadié

The much felt presence of the foreign conquerors marked the beginning of irreversible changes on the continent. Reactions to this lengthy occupation can be found in the visual arts, music, theatre and above all literature, although they have remained largely unknown outside the circles where they originated.

In precolonial oral literature, Westerners hardly played a role. Later they became characters in stories and songs. In many cultures the most important oral genre in which white foreigners figure, besides ordinary human beings, is the myth of origin or creation, explaining in multiple forms and versions why there are black and white people.

Two main themes determine the relationship between black and white people in African oral and written texts. They correspond with Albert Memmi's categories of response referred to earlier. On the one hand there is admiration for the power of the whites and Western culture leading to imitation and assimilation, albeit with reservations and mixed feelings about the consequences of the European presence in Africa. On the other, there are sharp protests against the many injustices of domination, and much critical comment on the white outsider.

In both cases strong interconnectedness and intercultural influences are undeniably visible in the works of colonized authors. The same holds for colonial literature by Western authors. Indeed, right from the first contacts, European and African literatures entered each other's cultural spaces. As Elleke Boehmer (1995: 102) observed: 'There is an intriguing coincidence in the fact that metropolitan writers began to acknowledge in their work the presence of Others around the same time as colonized writers were appropriating European genres and symbolic conventions to express their own identity.'

Of course, the interactions and interconnectedness do not dispense with the differences in power between invaders and invaded. Still, the colonial centre had certainly not foreseen that the cultural boundaries between Europe and Africa would be blurred forever. In Africa, the European Others had long been represented in oral stories and songs before African writers depicted them in their poetry, novels and theatre.

Black and white in oral literature

All over the world, people have sought explanations for the mysteries of the environment around them. To the people of Africa, the rule of the white man was one of those mysteries. In Congo I first heard a tale in which the difference in power is accounted for (but there are many variants in Central as well as West Africa). The Congolese version goes as follows: God the Father had two sons, Manicongo and Zonga. He loved Manicongo just as much as he loved Zonga. One day he decided to put them to a test. He summoned them and told them to go forth the next morning at daybreak and bathe in a little nearby lake.

Zonga, the youngest son, was obedient and sensible. He stayed up all night and the next morning he arrived at the lake even before the first rooster's cock crow. He dived into the lake and to his surprise he saw that his whole body had turned white.

By then Manicongo, the eldest son, was also awake. He had not stayed up all night. After having a good meal and plenty to drink, he had danced and made merry until the small hours of the morning and then fell into a deep sleep. No wonder he overslept. He jumped up and ran to the lake, but just as he was about to dive in the water receded. Only the palms of his hands and the soles of his feet managed to touch the water for a split second and they turned white. For the rest, Manicongo was still as black as he had always been.

God the Father praised his youngest son and rewarded him for his sensible conduct. Zonga could select whatever he wanted from all his father's riches and he quickly chose the paper, the pens, the telescope, the rifle and the gunpowder. There wasn't much left for poor Manicongo but a couple of copper bracelets, a few sabres, a hoe with which to work the land and some bows and arrows. From that moment on, the two brothers could no longer live together in Africa and God decided to separate them. Zonga crossed the ocean and became the father of the whites and Manicongo stayed in Africa and became the father of the Africans. Ever since then, the whites have become richer and richer and the blacks have remained just as poor as they were.

The story explains not only how the difference in skin colour came about, but also the reasons for separation of the two brothers. Having richly rewarded his youngest son, God decides that he has to leave Africa. The unequal gifts, it is argued, make their living on the same continent impossible. In fact the story reveals and justifies a race, class and space hierarchy. It clearly reflects some of the racist stereotypes which colonizers used to blazon abroad, such as the prejudice that Africans would prefer to drink and dance instead of being responsible people. Significantly, it is thanks to the youngest son's good behaviour that his skin turns white. Having heard this story told on different occasions by different people, mostly students from different areas, I wondered whether it was a real African story, but they said it was.

Such myths were passed on orally from one generation to the next in order to explain historical developments that proved both unfair and inescapable. The visions represented in them stem from the time when the colonial situation was already an empirical fact, as was the ideology of the colonizer. These myths of creation are clearly marked by white colonial discourse, as spread by the colonial culture through the missions, education and the administration.

Some variants of the story end with the conclusion that Zonga, or his descendants 'would return to bring wealth and happiness to Mother Earth'. This is why the arrival of the first white people in Africa was welcomed with the usual hospitality: they were considered the children of Zonga who had returned to honour their pledge. However, they did not; they were bad and greedy: 'They gathered treasures only to transport them to the other side of the ocean. Twenty million black Africans were deported in this way', as Saïdou Kane (1995: 12) puts it. He adds that the Africans, of course, wondered why the descendants of Zonga had not kept their promise.

Veronika Görög-Karady (1976) has written an interesting study about African creation myths concerning black and white people. She categorized them according to three themes: the theme of destination, the theme of trial and the theme of the committed error. In some stories the differences between white and black are viewed as a freak of nature. Just as there is a richly varied world of plants and animals and just as there are sheep and cows in different colours, so there is also diversity in colours among people. In some examples, the existence of differently coloured people is presented as an enrichment of the species. This emphasis is not present in other cases, where the diversity of colours among people is purely coincidental and depends on the kind of material available in a particular place: those made out of white sand get white skin and those made out of black clay get black skin. Thus, inequality is not always brought into the picture. In the practice of telling, however, 'innocent' outward features usually prove to be associated with inequality and difference in status. After all, these stories are aetiological and their function, at the time, was to explain how things had come to be the way they were.

The story of the two brothers in the lake combines two themes: both a trial and a committed error are present. If Manikongo had not had a party and had gone to sleep, like his brother, he would have been able to reach the water in time. But of course the story is there to explain contemporary reality.

The origin of difference, with its far-reaching consequences is sometimes attributed to sheer arbitrariness or fate – people being unable to change it. It can also be a matter of preference of one of the ancestors for children of one particular kind. There is a Dogon story about a woman who gave birth to a white child and a black child. The mother is convinced that the white child will bring bad luck and throws him into the river. Nommo, God himself, then takes the child, raises him and provides him – and consequently his offspring – with knowledge of all things. Ever since, white people have been superior and have been in power (Ambara Dolo, in Görög-Karady 1976: 284).

Many stories conclude that, as a consequence of the difference and resulting inequality, the brothers can no longer live together. While at first there may even be a preference for the black child, as in the Dogon myth, this eventually turns out to conform to the dialectics of progress: in the end he is in the least favourable position. It also happens that the creator or parents love the white child more (because he would look more like them) than the black child. Eventually, the whites and their offspring are better off.

Often in the myths the African is the first to exist; the European is born later as the second son. In many cases he is originally an African whose skin turns white later due to events in the story. This is in keeping with the universally known story of the two sons, the younger one being cleverer and friendlier than his disobedient, spoiled or lazy older brother. Just as in the story of Manicongo and Zonga, the younger brother ends up in the better position.

However, in narratives where the white man is created first, he still has the final advantage. There are also stories in which the black man appears first, but with a different kind of argument: 'the man from above', who decided to populate the earth, created people from clay, but was dissatisfied with the product from his oven. That is the reason why he made a fresh attempt and the result was the mulatto. Ultimately, he managed to create a white man: 'after that, he broke his oven and took a rest' (Jeannest Kabynde 1883, in Görög-Karady 1976: 280).

Sometimes two different creators are introduced in a story but then, once again, the white man is better off. Inequality can also originate from unequal treatment of the children by the first parents, or because the father favours one child and the mother the other. In all cases, inequality accompanies posterity as an inescapable fate.

Finally, a Bashi view of creation from Congo: the creator, Nyamuzinda, first makes a chicken which he thereafter constantly carries in his right hand. With the chicken he starts on a journey, but nowhere in the emptiness does he find a living being. He creates earth with its mountains and then he orders the chicken — it is the third day — to lay eggs from which human beings can be born. She lays forty and the next day forty human beings appear. One of them, Mushema, becomes the forefather of all the earthlings. Together with his wife Mwabunyoko (created after him) he has many children who have to disperse across the globe, but Mushema is poor. He is not able to give them an inheritance and Nyamuzinda comes to his aid:

What happened? Nobody knows. One thing, however, is for sure: at the break of day, all children held a gift of God in their hand. One had a cow, another had an ox, a third had a goat, and so on. Chihanya, the forefather of the Bashi, woke up with a pot of milk in his hand. That is the reason why the Bashi like milk and cows so much.

However, the people thought that Nyamuzinda had endowed them unequally. This envy sparked quarrel among the children of Mushema.

The forefather of the Europeans, whose name has been lost, could hardly recognize himself when he woke up. Not only had he received a special gift from Nyamuzinda (stationery and firearms) but also his skin had turned from black, like his brothers', to white, like the one the Europeans have at present. When his brothers saw this, they asked him: 'Where do you come from? You are not a human child like we are. Our mother Mwabunyoko did not give birth to you and who can understand the things you hold in your hand?'

It was decided to slaughter a young chicken and to read the meaning of all this in her intestines. It then became clear that Nyamuzinda himself had changed him thus and that he had revealed only to this creature the secret of the gifts he had given him. Just like Kelemera, he too was expelled from his native region. He left for a distant country, named Bulayi [Europe], but it is not known which way he took. Did he die first, then arise from the grave to be taken to his country invisibly? Was he carried by the clouds or did he follow the path of the rain? Mystery. One thing is for sure, he took his gifts of God with him. And that is the reason why his offspring, the Europeans, are still in possession of the stationery and the firearms. (Van Hoef, in Schipper 1980: 32)

In this Bashi story, all children have been created by one creator. They originate from the eggs of one chicken. The difference arises only much later as a result of unequally distributed gifts. This causes trouble. The most favoured son has to leave; he has miraculously been turned white. And so the forefather of the Europeans no longer fits in.

Whether the most disadvantaged one has or has not been taken into protection by God does not seem to make any difference to the outcome. Time and again the human being with the white skin takes the most advantage of the positive or negative situation in which he (it is hardly ever a 'she') finds himself

The inequality of black and white represents but one of numerous misfortunes which find their way into narrative. All fundamental and inescapable bearings on everyday life – such as the existence of illness and death, the trials of pregnancy and birth, sorcery, or the fact that we have to work for our daily bread – find their explanation in origin myths.

Many stories about difference in skin colour are unmistakably linked to the historical fact of colonization: Europeans came to colonize and Africans were colonized. The explanation for the inequality in material wealth and technical skill between black and white people was couched in a mythical story in which the European is the Other. He is or becomes the foreigner, the outsider; he is from far away or sent far away at the dawn of time because he is too different to fit in with real people and ordinary life. He is represented as the stranger belonging to an unknown world, living under water or in a country overseas; or he is imagined as a spirit or a ghost from the kingdom of the dead. Numerous oral stories on the subject make clear that the idea of the white man as the Other, as the one who does not belong, is firmly rooted in the collective imagination. The domination of this imagined Other, though, is framed in the context of colonial reality.

In order to explain the power and apparent good luck of the Europeans, African stories tell how and why the white people came to have the first choice when resources were distributed; how and why they received the paper and books, the stationery, the guns, the machines and the money. All sorts of qualities are attributed to them, from supernatural to material. In many stories the light skin is clearly qualified as a sign of beauty and, in a number of cases, the positive aesthetic qualities of the white Other are associated with positive ethical ones. In this respect, such stories display an obvious lack of self-esteem: the storytellers must have been struggling with their attempts to answer the why of the harsh colonial situation. The positive image of the white man in these stories may have to do with its explanatory function: the ethical qualities are advanced as a justification for the profitable gift of the technical skills that the ancestors of the white men received.

As negative 'white' qualities, the delicate health and the malign, jealous, egotistic character of the whites are mentioned, as well as their aggression and systematic exploitation of Africans. Such observations, however, are hardly present in the creation and origin myths, but in different kinds of stories that began circulating at the beginning of colonization, for example, prophecies, chronicles, anecdotes (Görög-Karady 1976: Chapter 5).

All in all, the Africans present a remarkably gloomy and negative image of themselves in these oral creation stories, a picture of victimization and material poverty. They seem to associate dependence with inferiority. This was exactly the message brought by the colonial Europeans systematically confirming the supremacy of Western culture, to which one could gain access by means of their religion and their schools. The language of the stranger came to play an important role. As Calvet has shown in *Linguistique et colonialisme* (1974), the emphasis on the importance of the European language was implied at the same time that the cultural value and importance of the African languages was being denied by the colonial government. This has had far-reaching consequences, about which fierce debates are still held.

Fanon used the concept 'discourse of the Other' in *Peau noire, masques blancs* (1952). This he termed the master's discourse of law and order, which assumes its form in the relation between the colonized and the colonizer. Whoever tries to identify with the discourse of the Other becomes assimilated, a 'white mask', and follows the (foreign) rule instead of taking an independent position revealing this Other.

The colonial message of their own superiority was brought and diffused in various forms by Europeans in their colonies, one of these being the mythical colour representations. Black and white were used as general metaphors for sin, hell and Satan on the one hand and purity, holiness and angels on the other, in order to justify the colonial relationships from the white side. This discourse has obviously given birth to a large number of stories seeking to explain the origin of white domination in Africa.

However, two observations are necessary here. The first is that, besides the narratives discussed above, there are numerous origin myths which completely ignore the question of the origin of black and white people. Others mention the matter only in passing, making clear that this is not an important issue in the narrative as a whole as, for example, in the Nigerian Jukun creation story concerning the origin of witchcraft (Meek 1931: 193-196). The numerous townspeople who had been swallowed by the king's mother, fall out of her stomach after she has been killed by her son: 'those which she had swallowed first, when restored to life, had white skins like white men; those she had swallowed later, had red skins like Fulani; while those she had swallowed last reappeared with the black skins of Negroes' (195).

Second, there is an enormous variety of ways in which the realities inhabited by colonizers and colonized have become inextricably interconnected. Texts are singled out for analysis as the favourite medium in academic research. As Paul Gilroy (1993: 36) has argued, the play of racial signification has usually been conceived in terms of the model provided by textuality, while the powerful functioning of music as a fundamental artistic means of signifying has been underestimated. People's intercultural mixtures are not only reflected verbally, but also in the performing and material arts.

In written as well as oral literature and in the arts, African explanations of the European outsiders' presence are intended as a means to handle the reality. Such coping is expressed in cultural works, defined by Obeyesekere as 'the process whereby symbolic forms existing on the cultural level get created and recreated through the minds of people' (1990: xix). Until now, this fascinating interrelatedness of African performing, verbal and material arts has hardly been studied. Such a combined verbal/material approach will throw new light on the functioning of the arts in African cultures and societies, including the representation of black and white. In this chapter, though, I shall restrict myself to literature.

In the version transcribed by Saïdou Kane (1995), the Manicongo and Zonga story continues after decolonization: 'The bad whites had left only to exploit Africa via the neo-Africans that they themselves had educated. The bad children of Zonga had brought up some of the children of Manicongo to be bad blacks.' Those who were against plundering were stifled. The new whites who arrived after independence did not much listen to the peasants' stories either. So, what are the good children proposing?

> Most of them, also educated by white schools, are convinced that the white development model needs to be applied [but] the school needs to reconquer the past which was robbed of its subsistance ... This school will have to be open to the future. There the African child will not have to learn how to imitate the West in all its facets, but rather, like the Japanese, to take the shortest route – and yet remain African. So that a world emerges in which the children of Manicongo and Zonga will be able to honour the pledge of their ancestors. (Kane 1995: 12)

Whites and the West in the African novel

The theme of the white man's power was also the subject of the continent's written literature. Here, however, conditions were hardly ever presented with resignation; rather the unequal colonial relations became a topic of debate: 'from the white men, we have to learn the art of conquering without being right', as one of the characters put it in *L'aventure ambiguë* (1961: 53), by the Senegalese author Cheik Hamidou Kane.

The medium of the novel proved very suitable to the needs of African writers who wanted to address colonial reality as they had experienced it. In their work, the novelists uprooted the myth that riches and power make the white man superior.

Europeans do not appear to have considered the question of what Africans might think of them. As already argued by Melville Herskovits in *The Human Factor in Changing Africa* (1962), African literature lends a helping hand in answering such questions of representation from inside the colonized communities. He rightly referred to the importance of African written literature, not only to Africans but also to the Western world. Many novelists presented a picture of the society in which they were raised. Until the 1960s, in French-speaking and English-speaking Africa alike, theirs was a colonial society. African literature reflects what oppression meant for those who were its victims, or what it means to give up one's language and culture for those of an intruding power. The novels written in European languages turned the European colonial perspective upside down and replaced it with African views of the colonial myths of race and colour.

Until the mid-1960s, whites and the West continued to have a significant role in African literature. Various authors admitted that they initially wrote more for a European than for an African reading audience: if one was to change the colonial situation in any way, one had to address the colonizer in his own language. However, the authors did not think along the lines of fundamentalist manichean structures (JanMohamed 1983): not every white character was necessarily presented as evil, nor were all African brothers and sisters the epitome of virtue.

Yet the fact remains that, like Europe, Africa has also developed its myths about 'others'. Just as Europeans tend to see the African first as black and then as human, in Africa the striking fact that Europeans are white is there before any other feature seems to be noticed. In either direction, these primary reactions are identical.

Obviously the Other does not look like us and is thus 'peculiar'. The picture that Europeans have of Africans bears some striking similarities to the one Africans have of Europeans. Briefly summarized, from the European point of view, African Others look different from a normal human being: they smell, they resemble animals (apes, gorillas), they are sexually dangerous (the 'virile' black man who is a menace to 'our' women), they steal, are lazy and uncivilized – such are the prejudices expressed in the prevalent Western myth.

The curious thing is that African literature bears witness to similar myths about white people. In this case though, the Europeans are the ones who look like animals, apes (who have straight rather than kinky hair) or pigs (they are just as pink) and they have a funny smell. They are rapists (in Africa the colonial men took at will the local African women or children). Their rude behaviour is uncivilized, they steal (emptying Africa of its riches); they are lazy (Africans do all the work for them and are paid very little). And, what kind of civilization does the West have as a continent that counts two destructive world wars among its achievements?

The image of the white man, just like its counterpart, consists of numerous observations that are indicative of mistrust and misunderstandings, dividing black from white. The most striking thing about the white characters in a number of African novels, in addition to their superiority complex, is that they exhibit pathological greed: they are eternally hungry for more money, more property and more power. The God of the whites lives in their wallets, one of the authors observes, which is why 'In God we trust' is written on their money. If you look at the white man, you understand what being civilized means to him:

> You have to have money, lots of money, to be civilized. The money, *that* is the civilization. As long as we are poor, we are meaningless in the eyes of the whites. Some people continue to think that courage or faith are important, but all those things come to you naturally if you have got money. If you have got money, everybody prays for you and everybody respects you. (Beti 1954: 96, 130)

The Western hurry, love of money, individualism, all these traits would seem to be proverbial to the African: 'The whites just keep rushing on, they want to stay ahead of us. We take our time ... some day they will stop. After all, you can't keep running on for centuries on end. They will realize that two or three or four weeks' vacation is not enough for the kind of life they lead.' And what can one see happening in the city? Africans are starting to take on the pernicious rhythm of hurry. They too are in a hurry: 'no time left for lengthy handshaking, for enquiring about someone's health or for asking how the family and friends are' (Dadié 1959: 215, 134, 21). African solidarity is in danger of being replaced by a European *chacun pour soi*, in Benjamin Matip's opinion (1956: 21). In African novels, comments such as 'a white man has no friends' or 'we are not like the whites, we don't just let people starve to death' are as numerous as significant examples of the novelists' counter-discourse. In the words of the beggar in *Le regard du roi* by the Guinean novelist Camara Laye (1954: 97): 'A white man does not know what humility or modesty is, that is why white men never have compassion for anyone. If people only knew better!'

Such comments illustrate the way earlier myths on Self and Other were inverted by the first generations of African novelists. Colonial relations made mutual understanding impossible. Most colonizers were totally unaware of what was being thought about them, while Africans were only too familiar with the stereotyped ideas which Europeans had about them. Of course, masters are never hesitant to speak freely in the presence of their servants; they can well afford to do so. In colonial times, the Africans were wise to save their opinions for after working hours. Among themselves they discussed in great detail all the peculiarities of the white man, emphasizing that white did not necessarily mean right.

In the following pages, I shall first describe two types of foreigners who played an important role in the picture of white people imagined by African writers: schoolteachers and missionaries. I shall then look at the imagined European woman in the African novel. Her presence in colonial society certainly contributed towards the stereotyped image of Western women in Africa, which was gradually reinforced by films, television and advertisements. But the image itself was born live, in the reality of colonialism, and was used by the first novelists to their advantage as a form of 'writing back to the Imperial Centre'.

The white school

Colonial schooling for African children was purely Western and rather limited. Children in the British colonies were taught the history of the Dukes of Kent, while children in the French colonies learned about *nos ancêtres les Gaulois*. In the words of Albert Tevoedjre (1958: 70): 'Our philosophy was that of Descartes or Bergson, our drama was that of Racine, our sense of humour was that of Lamartine or Musset.' The Marseillaise resounded at regular intervals, as did other heart-warming songs of *la patrie*. In the English colonies it was no different. Schoolchildren were taught to sing the following song whenever a missionary arrived in a village colonized by the French:

La France est belle
Ses destins sont bénis.

Vivons pour elle,
Vivons, vivons unis.

Passez les monts, passez les mers,
Visitez cent climats divers,
Joyeux au bout de l'univers,
Vous chanterez fidèles:

La France est belle ... (Beti 1956: 245)

At first some schools had trouble getting children to enrol, since people preferred to wait and see what the school would be like. In some parts of Congo, poor orphans were the first to be sent to the schools. In other places village elders sent their slaves to school first. More often, however, 'the best sons' were the first to attend the white school. Interest in education soon became so widespread that there was not enough room for the large numbers of children who wanted to register. Schools were usually viewed as a positive contribution on the part of the colonizer (as was healthcare).

In *L'aventure ambiguë* (1961), Cheikh Hamidou Kane presents his main character, Samba Diallo, as one of the first boys from the region of the Diallobé to go to the white school, called 'the new school' to differentiate it from the Koran school which had long been in existence in West Africa. In his novel, Kane expresses the tragic side of the culture shock experienced by his people. After the arrival of the Europeans, it is suggested, people were forced to adopt Western culture and to despise their own.

Before taking a decision about the new school, the Diallobé discuss the problem among themselves: should we send our children to the white school or not? The chief hesitates, he cannot make up his mind. After thinking it over for a long time — in a talk with the Master of the Koran school — he slowly formulates his thoughts, doing his best to weigh the advantages against the disadvantages:

> If I tell them to go to the new school, they will all go. They will learn all the ways to tie wood that we did not learn. But while learning they will also forget. What they will learn, is that worth just as much as what they will forget? I would like to ask you, is it possible to learn one thing without forgetting the other thing, and what you learn, does that compensate for what you forget? ... If I tell the Diallobé not to go to the new school, they won't go. Their homes will collapse, their children will die or be made into slaves. Misery will be their fate and their hearts will be filled with resentment. (Kane 1961: 49).

These last words are spoken by the chief's sister, a lady held in high esteem, called the Grande Royale. Before deciding to have the children attend school, she first analyses what has led to the present situation, a chapter of history in which the Diallobé had been forced to play a role by 'them':

> We have to learn from them the art of conquering without being right. Moreover, the battle is not over yet. The foreign school is the new form of warfare that they have come to wage with us and we must send our elite there before we make it compulsory for all. It is good that the elite

will be once more in the vanguard. If there are risks involved, then it is the elite that is best prepared to cope, because most closely linked to its own self. If there is something good to be gotten from it, then it must also be the elite who benefit from it first. (Kane 1961: 53).

Of course the schools helped to increase the influence of the West and the older generation, still illiterate and brought up solely according to their own local traditions, must have felt deeply distressed. Generational conflicts and contradictory views of society are presented in many novels as an increasingly common phenomenon. In Cameroonian Mongo Beti's (1954) novella *Ville cruelle*, for example, a youngster observes: 'I did not go to school that long but it was useful, at any rate I learned not to be fooled any more by old people' (Beti 1954: 94). The opposite perspective is represented in an old man's complaint in *Les dernières paroles de Koimé* (1961: 9), a novel by Raphael Koffi from Ivory Coast: 'The white men burn the brains of our children with their insane books and weird stories. The children who go to the school of the white men, the children who learn what the white people know become very different, under their black skin their soul is almost white.'

Times are seen as changing so drastically, that older people wonder where the world is going. Youngsters will no longer be the same if they continue imitating the white man. The older generation's main worry is whether the youngsters will still take care of older relatives, as has been the tradition.

Mongo Beti's early novels are aimed at revealing the corruption and injustice of colonial society, but also the problematic power mechanisms dominating traditional practices which he does not idealize. In *Mission terminée* (1957), for example, the main character, Jean-Marie Medza, has been at the white man's school. The relatives he is visiting in a remote village consider him a learned man, although he has just failed the oral part of his baccalauréat examination. At a gathering one evening, this great scholar has to answer all kinds of questions. After everyone has agreed that time spent at school will make the younger generation earn a lot of money, just like the white people, an old lady formulates the concern and uncertainty of her generation:

'Son,' the woman with the irritated look hailed, when people were quiet again, 'if you are going to earn just as much money as them, does that mean you are going to live the way the whites do?'

'What do you mean?'

'You'll live in houses with a fence around them, in the evening you smoke cigarettes while you read the newspaper, you don't drink the water from our well any more, you would rather drink red wine than our palm wine, you drive cars, there is a tablecloth on your table, you have servants, you only speak their language. And maybe you will start to dislike the sound of the tam tam in the night, just like they do. That is all right. But me, I ask you this question: and what about us, what are you going to do with us? Can we come into your homes, just as we go to the homes of our other children, whenever we like? Can we talk there and laugh there without anyone telling us to be quiet? And with bare feet, if we want? And eat from the same dish as you, even if we don't use a fork? Son, is all that still going to be possible?'

'Yes, of course,' I said just to stop her from going on, 'of course you can treat us the same as you treat your other children.'

'Do you believe that, son?' she said highly skeptically. (Beti 1957: 118).

Of course the old lady is quite right to be sceptical is the message we get. She is imagining the world of the educated Africans as the opposite of the 'traditional way of living'. Not only will there be all that money, but also the white way of life, significantly characterized by the separation mark of the fence around the house, excluding unwelcome poor relatives such as herself. Next to the material well-being of those who went to school, there will be 'their' French language and a rejection of 'our' music. From the perspective of those who did not go to school, new boundaries will be created by the white school, materially as well as culturally.

Though African authors have written a great deal about the school as an institution or about school experience (often based on their own), very little has been written about European schoolteachers. The few comments that novelists have made about them are positive. Colonial schoolteachers are presented as more honest, more idealistic and clearly less prejudiced than other white people. In Oyono's *Une vie de boy* (1956), for example, the headmaster keeps his distance from the rest of the colonial community at the district commissioner's party. The Commandant has invited all the white people of Dangan to a reception in honour of his wife, who has just arrived from Paris. Much of the conversation pertains to prevailing stereotypes such as the smell of the Africans, their drinking, laziness and unreliability. Oyono presents the attitude of the schoolteacher as an exception to the general colonial rule of putting other people down to make yourself appear better.

Monsieur Salvain holds the opinion that all races are equal and that by nature whites are no more intelligent than Africans. At his school he offers evidence to back this idea. His standpoint is familiar to the local Africans as well as to the whites, who tend to regard him with distrust. At the reception Salvain does not say anything for a long time, but when the doctor's wife complains that there are no moral standards in the country he cannot help but comment that there are none in Paris either. The reactions require no further explanation. These observations are presented from the perspective of Toundi, the main character and servant of the Commandant, who writes of his experiences in a diary:

> The remark ran through the bodies of the Europeans in the room like an electric current. They shuddered, one by one. The doctor's ears grew blood-red. Only Madame remained unmoved, and the American ladies who had been so busy whispering among themselves that they had heard nothing. The man who disinfects Dangan with DDT was breathing heavily. He turned sharply to the schoolmaster:
>
> 'What ... what do you ... what do you mean by that?' he stammered.
>
> The schoolmaster made a little grimace of contempt and shrugged his shoulders. The other man rose and walked over to him. The schoolmaster watched without concern. Was the disinfector going to fly at his throat? The moment was tense.
>
> 'You nasty little rabble rouser,' he snapped.
>
> 'Please, please, Monsieur Fernand,' said the Commandant, coming between them. Monsieur Fernand went back to his seat and was about to sit down. As his behind touched the bottom of the armchair, he seemed to collapse as if he had been bitten by a scorpion. Once or twice his arms thrashed the air. He opened his mouth, shut it, then ran his tongue over his lips.
>
> 'You're a traitor, Monsieur Salvain,' he said, 'a traitor. Ever since you came to this country you have behaved in a way unworthy of a Frenchman. You're stirring the natives up against us. You keep telling them that they are as good as we are — as if they hadn't got a high enough opinion of themselves already ...'
>
> Monsieur Fernand sat down. Gullet nodded his head at the end of his neck in approval. Other heads followed this lead. Madame's head remained still.
>
> 'Poor France,' said Gullet, blowing his nose.
>
> The schoolmaster shrugged. (Oyono 1956: 78; transl. John Reed)

In this novel, Oyono uses the realistic device of the narrator and main character's view from below: the narrating and focalizing subject is Toundi who carefully observes the details of the whites' behaviour, their prejudices, their chauvinism, their obsessions and neuroses. Thus white private life becomes the object of the colonized's gaze. Toundi, however, is an ambiguous character: he is intrigued by the world of the whites and the dream of assimilation. Unfortunately, as Richard Bjornson (1991) has observed, the French colonial system offers Africans 'a set of equally untenable alternatives: if they accept its promises at face value, they will be exploited and eventually confronted by its denial of their humanity; if they adopt the self-serving attitudes behind the colonialist rhetoric, they will lose touch with what is most valuable in themselves' (87). What option is left then? Despite French nationalism at school, despite the colonial ideas about the superiority of the Western languages and culture, despite the individualistic methods of bringing up children (matters critically referred to in a number of other novels), education continues to be highly valued while criticized for its narrowness and the limited number of schools. In the novels, narrators and characters explore the crossroads where colonial schools and African cultural values meet, preparing multiple ways of talking and writing back.

Some colonials, such as George Hardy in *Nos grands problèmes coloniaux* (1929: 78), felt it was not advisable to expand local schooling too quickly: 'Education in the colonies cannot be modest enough. The danger is not that we do not teach the people enough. The danger is that we might teach them too much.' The complaint of the Africans, however, was that the school curriculum was so clearly focused upon the whites' own interests, that it remained confined to small groups and at an elementary level. Hardly any efforts were made to adjust the school system to the lives of the Africans. Still, schools were thought important. It was where you could learn to read and write, just like the Europeans. Pens and books had been part of God's mythical legacy to the ancestor of the whites and therefore certainly a means of access to colonial riches and power. The main criticisms were that you could not learn enough there and that the number of schools were far too small: after three hundred years of colonization, only one in ten children went to school in Senegal (Tevoedjre 1958: 60).

The missionaries and their God

Many of the first generation novelists present missionaries as characters in their novels. These authors were often brought up at missionary posts where they attended schools run by priests. There is ample evidence of their first-hand experiences with missionaries whose mistakes and lack of understanding of African cultures have often been described.

The missionary would sometimes be confused with the image which Africans had in mind of 'the God of the whites'. In *Le pauvre Christ de Bomba* (1956: 9) Mongo Beti describes the French priest, Drumont. When visiting the villages Drumont distributes little pictures of Christ surrounded by children.

The village children are surprised to see how much Christ looks like Father Drumont: the same beard, the same robe, the same cord around his waist. The village catechist confirms this impression that indeed Jesus and the priest are one and the same (28).

In *Le roi miraculé* (Beti 1958: 250) there is the same kind of visual association. A polygamous chieftain is obsessed by the idea that for everything he has done he will have to answer, some day, to God:

> a mysterious being who might very well be more powerful than Akomo (the forefather) and – who knows? – might look just like the missionary Le Guen, with the same thin lips and the same stern blue eyes, a man who constantly lectures him about the sin of polygamy.

Missionaries must often have failed to realize the extent of this problem; one that was enlarged by their unleashing torrents of clichés about white purity and black sin, white saints and black devils. In Europe it was common practice to use terms of this kind, which was why they spoke to the Africans of a soul that was black with sin and would turn white after its conversion to Christianity. These moral colours were unwittingly applied to the visible bodies as well.

In a missionary bookshop in Kinshasa in the 1960s – after independence that is – I found an illustrated children's Bible (printed in France) in which the story of Cain and Abel was enriched with pictures of a black evil Cain killing his pink and innocent brother Abel. Why did Europeans use these colour symbols? Perhaps the notion of their own superiority led white people to associate white with innocence and black with evil: we are fine and the others are not was the way in which it came across. In *Un nègre à Paris* (1959: 96), Bernard Dadié quasi-innocently formulates his impressions of the churches in Paris: wherever you go you see a wrathful God with a whip in his left hand and a box of candy in his right. A God who looks exactly like the white man in Africa with his medals in one hand and his prison in the other one. As far as the angels are concerned, 'the good ones are white, the bad ones are black like us. They are called devils'.

In the churches there are statues of saints, but not a single black one. As Dadié's character observes: the blacks had apparently not yet been admitted to paradise and, should they arrive there unexpectedly, Saint Peter would take one look at them and send them off to Beelzebub. And yet he has not lost hope that some day, if they do their best, the blacks will have a saint of their own. That, however, will lead to other problems, because then one will have to invent another colour for the devil, no simple matter of course! (64).

In Mongo Beti's (1956) novel *Le pauvre Christ de Bomba*, Denis, a servant at the mission station, is a fervent follower of Father Drumont and has always admired his authoritarian manner. In his diary, Denis makes clear that he is not happy with the change taking place in his master's behaviour:

> I don't know why he's taken this fancy for listening to all this foolishness. Until recently, he would just have sent this fellow packing, whereas today he seemed really to be discussing seriously with him, listening to all his illiterate nonsense. I'm sure it's a mistake to explain things carefully to them. Quite enough to tell them that they'll roast in Hell, that's all. Oh, what hopeless people. (Beti 1956: 103; transl. Gerald Moore)

Like Oyono's (1956) hero in *Une vie de boy*, Denis keeps a diary and his assertive main perspective makes clear that he is more Catholic than the Pope and certainly more orthodox than the Father who in the past used to have a different conception of his missionary work.

For a good part of his life as a missionary Father Drumont viewed the Africans as children in need of a strict upbringing. He wanted them to submit to a specific pattern of behaviour, a pattern that is totally incomprehensible and irrelevant to them. For example, because it is the first Friday of the month, he forbids the people of a 'heathen' village to dance. The catechist he sends there to announce this prohibition fails to get the people to stop their celebration. Then Drumont himself sets off to do so. Enraged, he pounces upon the xylophones and dashes them to pieces, the drums fall to the ground with a great thump, much to the fury of the village chief, who rushes over to the priest roaring with rage and intent upon murder. The villagers hold back their chief and caution him to leave the priest alone because he is a white man and if any harm comes to him, then the other white men, his brothers, will come: 'Let him go his way and don't offend him. You can never be sure with them' (101). After everyone calms down, the priest tries to defend his case, but fails to convince anyone as to why the dancers should stop. In the discussion that ensues, the priest has little choice but to keep quiet:

> 'But how should we live without our dancing? You whites have your cars, your aeroplanes, your trains ... But we have nothing but our dancing. And now you want to take that from us. What could we do instead?'
> 'You could pray to God, and worship Him.'
> They were silent for a moment, looking at us musingly. The moonlight poured down the sloping roof like heavy oil. Soon, our questioner spoke again: 'Father, it seems to me that if Jesus Christ had really thought of us, he would have come himself to discuss the matter with us. Then perhaps he would have consented to let us dance. That's how it looks to me: what do you think?'

'Exactly so. Jesus Christ ordered me to tell you ...'
'Told you? But you are a white man, Father!' (Oyono 1956: 101; transl.
Gerald Moore)

The priest's arguments are not convincing and he is aware of his own
weakness. As the story develops, he becomes more attentive to the people and
their thinking. Instead of talking he now listens to them attentively and starts
distancing himself from earlier ideas. Conversing with the people, Father
Drumont begins to understand to what extent the people associate
Christianity with colonization, something he had not been able to see during
his years spent in Africa.

Christianity did not simply replace the old religious customs. The reason for
converting was that it might be rewarding: the whites were stronger and
perhaps their god would give more strength to the Africans. The secret of the
white man's power might be in his religion. One evening when Father
Drumont wonders why the Africans first converted to Christianity and have
now abandoned the faith, his cook Zacharia explains the reality of the
situation:

'The first of us who ran to religion, to your religion, came to it as a sort
of ... revelation. Yes, that's it, a revelation; a school where they could
learn your secret, the secret of your power, of your aeroplanes and
railways ... in a word, the secret of your mystery. Instead of that, you
began talking to them of God, of the soul, of eternal life, and so forth. Do
you really suppose they didn't know those things already, long before
you came? So of course, they decided that you were hiding something.
Later, they saw that if they had money they could get plenty of things
for themselves – gramophones and cars, and perhaps even aeroplanes
one day. Well then! They are turning from religion and running
elsewhere, after money, no less. That's the truth of it, Father. As for the
rest, it's all make-believe.' (Oyono 1956: 56; transl. Gerald Moore)

In fact, the whites do not seem inspired by their own religion and they do
not provide good examples of Christian conduct: they neither love their
neighbours nor attend church regularly. The Europeans apparently no longer
pray to their Father to give them their 'daily bread'. Either they prefer to earn
that bread themselves without any help from the Father or their bellies are so
full that they stay in bed rather than go to church. That is the way Climbié sees
it in Dadié's novel (1959: 128).

Many conflicts between missionaries and their flocks result from differences
in their conception of 'morality'. Missionaries had learned that polygamy is

'heathen' as it offends against both secular and Christian norms. In their own society unmarried mothers were to be pitied, and only people who were legally married could sleep together, or so the missionaries said. They transported the sexual taboos formerly prevalent in Europe to their new congregations in Africa where quite different views were traditional. The Africans do not understand the idea of celibacy and jokingly worry about the priest's purity. He in turn worries about the 'impure' ideas of his converts.

The problem of illegitimate children bothers the missionaries more than the parents, although the latter are threatened with excommunication. Special days are reserved for the baptism of these children. In *Un nègre à Paris* (1959) Dadié wonders whether God makes a distinction between 'legitimate' and 'illegitimate' (181). In *Le pauvre Christ de Bomba* (Beti1956) polygamous and unmarried mothers pay a special price for the baptism of their children. Father Drumont writes *ex fornicatione ortus* on their baptism certificates. No one knows or dares to ask what it means.

Beti's (1958) novel *Le roi miraculé* concerns a polygamous chief who has to send away all but one of his twenty-three wives when he converts to Christianity, something quite impossible according to tribal tradition: bride-prices have linked these women for life to the chief's clan. The wise men of the village propose a compromise, thus enabling the women to remain in the village without being married to the chief. The missionary refuses to accept this solution, because the women might 'seduce' the chief to revert back to his 'sinful' ways. One of the Africans who consults with the white man fails to see what would be so terrible about that:

> 'What difference would that make, Father,' Azombo shouted. 'A couple of times now and then, what harm could that do? Don't Christians ever sleep with a woman who is not "their wife in the eyes of God"?' Le Guen was sure he had already preached in the wilderness too long and took leave of the Ebibot clan. (Beti 1958: 187)

This passage points up the hypocrisy of colonial double standards. The whites do as they like, or they say one thing and do another: the church has no power over them. The missionaries now want the Africans to fulfil the Catholic church's ideals of chastity. To save the status quo some people try to convince the missionaries of their right to polygamy by choosing biblical names of polygamists such as Salomon, David or Jacob, but the missionaries refuse to relent.

Once Father Drumont learns to listen, he blames himself for having had so little understanding of the Africans during all those years as a missionary: 'If only I had taken the trouble to look around,' he laments toward the end, when his own errors become clear to him.

The unifying theme in *Le pauvre Christ de Bomba* (Beti 1956) is the white missionary's changing connections with colonialism. At the end of the book, Father Drumont feels so discouraged that he leaves Africa for good. His pessimistic conclusion is that it is impossible for the white missionary to bring the Gospel to Africa unless he openly declares war on the oppressive regime, which would never be tolerated. That is why the novel begins with a significant warning:

> I don't wish to deceive the reader. There has never been a Reverend Father Superior Drumont in African experience, probably there never will be one – not if I know my Africa. That would be too much luck for us.

On the same note the author ironically adds that the African characters, though, 'have been taken straight from life. And there is no incident here which is not strictly and demonstrably authentic'.

Herskovits (1962: 135–136) observed that in real life the missionaries had great difficulty in obtaining information on African criticism of Christianity: politeness and self-interest prevented them. The novels, on the contrary, are quite outspoken on such matters.

The white woman

In *Le deuxième sexe* (1949) Simone de Beauvoir – and with her many other feminists who stood up for the rights of the (Western) woman – notes similarities between the plight of women and that of blacks. Both, it was argued, are in the process of liberating themselves from the paternalist hold of the white man. The white man tries to keep them 'in their place' – the place traditionally ascribed to them. The white man may generously praise the virtues of the 'good negro' who, unaware of his true situation, is childlike, merry and acquiescent, just as he praises the 'goodness' of the woman who is 'a real woman', vain, immature, irresponsible, the woman who recognizes the man as her superior and is gladly subservient to him.

But who has ever heard an African man express his heartfelt solidarity with the tragic fate of the poor oppressed white woman? This Beauvoirian comparison is clearly a product of the West – in any case it is not a view shared by African novelists. There are no traces of such a common fate in any African novel; on the contrary. In the minds of colonized Africans a white woman is imagined as the most privileged of human beings, not to be pitied but rather to be envied. In view of the colonial situation this is quite understandable. In the colonies a white woman was highly appreciated: in proportion to the number of men there were relatively few European women, which is why they were treated as a precious species.

From an African novelist's perspective on colonial society the European woman lives in a beautiful mansion surrounded by a lovely garden, leads a life of luxury, does not have to lift a finger (which indeed she mostly does not do) except to command her numerous and often dedicated servants.

In the colonies a woman who would have been an average person in Europe, a woman who would have had to clean her own house and take care of her own children, has endless opportunities to exert power over her servants. And there is nothing to stop her from abusing this power.

Some novels describe how the white woman in Europe cherishes dreams of wide-open spaces, gardens of Eden in sunny Africa where a new life beckons far from the fog and shabbiness of home. Soon after arrival in the land of her dreams, however, she is quick to change her tune. In the heat of day the paradise of her dreams is more like an inferno and she longs for everything she has left behind in the distant mother country. This accounts for all her sighs, lamentations and cries of woe. Despite her privileged position, she is often depicted as a thoroughly discontented and ill-tempered being.

The white colonial woman as a character in African novels rarely has a status of her own; she has no occupation and is totally dependent on her husband and his position. Although exceptionally allusions are made to a woman who is schoolteacher, barmaid or prostitute, in general the white woman is only known as Mrs wife of Mr so and so. The problem that seems to occupy much of her time is her appearance: her complexion, her figure, her clothes, her jewellery. In the very restricted circles of colonial society there is fierce competition among the women, each eager to be the most beautiful. If they do not succeed nothing seems to console them. Another favourite pastime is exchanging critical comments on Africa and the Africans. These are obsessive, inexhaustible topics of conversation, providing unending opportunities for some people to feel superior by putting down others.

There is no end to the complaints expressed about the accursed country: the wretched climate with its beastly heat and sudden cloudbursts, where the tennis courts can easily be flooded, where there is not a single good hairdresser and where there is no way to stop perspiring. And then those black people all over the place! There is nothing to be done with them, they are hopelessly lazy, they lie, they steal. They drink too much, smell horrible and they are dirty. 'First thing every morning, it's the smell of alcohol and unwashed body, wafting in from the veranda that tells me my boy has arrived.' such are the ladies' conversations in *Une vie de boy*. (Oyono 1956: 50, 71)

Toundi's Madame at first has an aversion to such negative conversations; having just arrived, she is not yet contaminated by the local prejudices. The story is an example of how a European woman changes for the worse in a colonial situation. At first, she is happy with her husband and enthusiastic about life in Africa. Unfortunately, the Commandant is often away on business and Madame is bored: there is nothing but boredom in the town of Dangan. Thus she starts an affair with the prison director, a tough he-man whom the Africans called White Elephant because he is 'a man among men'. Madame soon realizes that her servants know what is going on and this makes her nervous and unreasonable. Despite her initial kindness, she now becomes extremely nasty. Like most other white women, she now calls her servants lazy good-for-nothings and regrets not having immediately believed what the others told her: 'The prison director knew what he was talking about when he said what you needed was the big stick,' she went on. 'Well, that's what you're going to get, that's what you're going to get. We shall see who wins in the end!' Among themselves, the servants complain about being 'dependent on the whims of such a bitch!' (111).

The Commandant gets wind of his wife's affair and makes a horrible scene after which they make up. But Madame remains embarrassed in front of her servants, especially Toundi the 'houseboy' with whom she is in frequent contact. Just to get rid of him she has him arrested for a robbery he did not commit. He is imprisoned, tortured and dies of the injuries.

Toundi's Madame is one of the colonial women whose lack of occupation and lack of imagination make them vain and unstable, answering to Simone de Beauvoir's description of the 'truly feminine woman', the empty-headed, frivolous, childish, irresponsible woman, whose situation she compared to the subservient black man. From the perspective of the colonial situation this comparison is not valid: the unfavourable representation of white women in the African novel is made worse by their racism and prejudices. The image of the victim does not fit them into this context at all.

In these novels the white women are unhappily married. As a character in African novels, the white woman is either the seductive femme fatale or the disappointed, lonely wife. The men have mistresses — white as well as black — but some wives are also unfaithful, as in the case of the Commandant's wife in *Une vie de boy*. It is plausible that old Dallas-like films shown in Africa contributed toward this view of the white marriage and there was some justification for it in reality.

Relationships or love affairs between white women and black men in Africa met with huge difficulties. The colonial situation did not allow for it. The women usually remained so distant and aloof that there was no question of coming any closer. The reverse situation of white men having affairs with black women was naturally accepted or tolerated, because it did not go against race and gender hierarchy. In the metropolis in the home country more opportunities did present themselves for relationships between white women and black men, though even there public opinion was not in favour of inter-racial relationships.

As far as the novels are concerned, most of the love affairs between a white woman and a black man take place in Europe. The most striking point, however, is that these relationships meet with a tragic end, usually a death. It is as if the authors are trying to make it clear that in a society where the white man is the boss he will not let anything or anyone get out from under his thumb. Never a happy ending holds true not only for the mixed relationships in Africa itself, but also for those in Europe.

Like so many of his generation, Oumar Faye, the main character in Sembène Ousmane's novel *O pays, mon beau peuple* (1958), has been a soldier in France. After World War II he met a French girl there, Isabelle, whom he marries. In the beginning her parents object, but gradually they accept Faye as their son-in-law. Then the couple moves to Africa, where they are confronted with the overt hostility of the local white community: Faye has learnt a great deal in Europe; he has self-confidence and he cannot stand to see whites exploiting and mistreating blacks. When he actively opposes this abuse, the tension grows. Isabelle has no colonial experience and cannot understand why the other whites are so hostile to her and her husband. Faye feels that the notion of black freedom is so abhorrent to the whites that if and when a black man openly exhibits his freedom they will in one way or another get back at him. A black man having a white wife is an intolerable infraction of colonial rules.

One evening when Isabelle is home alone two white men visit her and try to convince her to leave her husband. One of them even offers to 'take her over'. Enraged, she refuses. The men then attempt to rape her, believing that any white woman married to a black man is a whore. She chases them off by threatening them with a rifle (140–141).

This attempted rape fits into the colonial scheme of things: the one in power controls the women, the white women as well as the black, and the white woman who marries a black man is an inferior being, a worthless prostitute who does not deserve respect. By raping her, both she and the black husband are humiliated.

Faye's relatives are also unhappy with his marriage; it is not in their tradition to choose a wife against your parents' wishes or without their consent. In the end, the family accepts Isabelle to a certain extent, but life continues to be difficult:

> You and I [Oumar Faye says to his wife] had upbringings as different as the colours of our skin. One ambiguity can destroy our unity. Always bear in mind that we live between two worlds, between day and night. It

is not conceivable to any white man or any black man that we can live
together happily as man and wife. (Ousmane 1958: 88)

Ultimately Faye is murdered by an African bribed with money of the whites.
Ousmane points out the prejudice against mixed marriage and concludes that
there is no place for love between a white woman and a black man in colonial
Africa, just as there is no place for blacks to act as truly free men.

In other novels as well tragedy puts an untimely end to whatever love there
is between a white woman and a black man. It is striking that most of the
marriages between whites also end in failure, but in the novels this is not due
to accident, death or other disaster but to adultery on the part of one or both
partners.

Significantly, young African women begin to compare their own situation
with that of the privileged Western women. This is put into words by Sophie,
the mistress of a European engineer in Oyono's *Une vie de boy* (1956). She has no
identity problems and does not feel she is their inferior in any way. One day,
when she has to sit at the back of the truck instead of in front with her white
boyfriend, she mumbles to herself: 'Those good manners of these whites, if they
only use them for each other ... Shit! My ass is just as delicate as their wives''
(60). And she asks rhetorically: 'What have they got that I haven't got?' Sophie is
quite sure of herself: she takes initiatives on her own, and survives as a winner.

Many girls, though, start to worry about African men becoming interested
in white women and sometimes preferring them, especially when studying in
Europe. African women had fewer opportunities to go to Europe at the time.
They wonder whether European women have some mysterious charm. They
hear stories about Europe and watch the ways in which colonial white women
behave. Then there are the pictures, magazines and advertisements: the white
woman's appearance seems to represent an example to follow.

The white woman is usually depicted in African novels as bourgeois and
narrow-minded. Though often beautiful, slim and well-dressed, she is also a
vain, unstable, unfaithful, lazy and silly creature. In novels her appearance is
nonetheless idealized by African male characters and imitated by the females.
Following the white woman's example African girls wear tight dresses or
slacks that clearly accentuate their curves. They straighten their hair, put on
lipstick and nail polish and do their best to master the language of the whites.

These developments worry the older generation for in their eyes white
women are the epitome of evil and shamelessness. If this becomes the ideal of
'our' girls, all the local moral traditions are in danger of being abandoned.

Literature reacts to traditions by continuing or by going against them;
mostly, however, one can see a combination of both. This is true for myths of
origin as well as for novels. The stories of creation, as a genre, preserve the old

form and choose the white stranger as a new character, in order to explain white colonial rule. Whites and the West have been a main theme, especially of the Francophone African novels of the 1950s and 1960s discussed here. There is sharp disapproval of colonialism, though some positive aspects of the West are not overlooked. Of course the picture that the novels create of the whites is subjective, but it can be assumed to coincide with ideas still prevalent in African society about the whites and the Western world.

There is a great deal that Europeans can learn from these novels, not only about Africa and Africans, but also about their own history. The colonial situation illustrates how easily people tend to abuse their position of power; in present-day Africa this has once again proved to be more a question of human weakness than of skin colour. In contemporary African literature, white people no longer play a role of any significance. Times have changed as has literature.

4

African roots and American black culture

What they held in common was their utterly painful relation to the white world. What they had in common was the necessity to remake the world in their own image, to impose this image on the world, and no longer be controlled by the vision of the world, and of themselves, held by other people.

James Baldwin

When asked what is important for getting ahead in life, poor blacks are almost as likely to choose being of the right sex and more likely to choose religious conviction and political connections than to choose being of the right race. Well-off blacks, however, think race matters more than any of those characteristics.

Jenny Hochschild

The problem of the twentieth century, as the black American W. E. B. Du Bois said as early as 1903, is the problem of the 'color line'. As the migration age passed, those words gained more worldwide significance than he had ever anticipated. However, debates are being reframed and, as in Du Bois's days, the various perspectives on the history and role of blackness continue to depend on the imagining subjects, their positioning, their social, political and personal interests.

The main themes in this chapter and the next will be concerned with the boundaries between insiders and outsiders in black cultural movements and the extent to which the 'color line' served as a source of inspiration for writers as a criterion for 'real' literature. In other words, who in the field of culture did or did not belong to 'us' and why or why not? Or, to quote this time a reverse variation of Sophie's words from Oyono's (1956) *Une vie de boy*: 'What have we got that they haven't got?'

Another topic will be the role of intellectuals and artists as leaders of the black community: do they have a special responsibility which enables them to be spokes(wo)men for 'ordinary people'?

Some interesting new approaches try to link the history of modernism with the history of blackness instead of continuing to separate the two. In *The Black Atlantic* (1993) Paul Gilroy, for example, criticized and transcended the invented gaps between modernity, nationalism and ethnicity, while in the context of the USA the limitations of traditional racialized views of modernism are criticized for ignoring American cultural nationalism as a shared national identity by both black and white writers (e.g. Hutchinson 1995). Perspectives on insiders and outsiders have been broadened by a plea in favour of radical democracy across the 'color line', as Cornel West does in *The Future of the Race* (1996), in a re-assessment of Du Bois's idea of the Talented Tenth.

One of the early solutions imagined to the problem of the 'color line' in the diaspora was Panafricanism: it posited the idea of an undivided Africa as the promised land for black people from all over the world. This dream especially appealed to black Americans and Caribbeans, or Africans and Caribbeans living in Europe. Some groups in African countries have also felt attracted to Panafricanism.

What do black movements on either side of the ocean have in common? According to Wilfried Feuser (1976: 293), similar tendencies can be found over different periods and areas in the field of literature: 'with an early flowering of poetry, fiction, and drama in the New Negro movement, a steady traffic of ideas across the Atlantic via Haiti and the French West Indies, and the eventual take-over by the negritude movement'. Here, the nineteenth-century expression 'New Negro' referred to a new class of well-educated blacks from the post-Civil War period; their literature flourished in the years after World War I:

> The black race produced one after the other such remarkable personalities as Claude McKay, Jean Toomer, Countee Cullen, Langston Hughes, and Sterling Brown, without counting a number of lesser poets ... The dimensions of the phenomenon were equaled only by its suddenness at least that's the impression gained by its contemporaries. (Wagner 1973: 149)

The *New Negro Movement* or *Black Renaissance* is often referred to as the *Harlem Renaissance* after the cultural centre of the movement in Harlem, New York. The New Negro Movement may be considered as the overall socio-political framework in which the Harlem Renaissance functioned as the centre of artistic and intellectual activities, defending and boosting black cultural identity. Over the years – Du Bois had his own struggle to capitalize the 'N' – the word Negro was gradually considered to be degrading and was abandoned. It was replaced by Afro-American and then by African-American, a term which has become the most politically correct for many Americans of African descent.

While some people emphasize the importance of the naming of their choice, others believe that these names have lost their political menace, as Henry Louis Gates (1992: 139) notes with respect to the following rather complacent comment taken from the *New York Times* (22 December 1988):

> Blacks may now feel comfortable enough in their standing as citizens to adopt the family surname: American. And their first name, African, conveys a pride in cultural heritage that all Americans cherish. The late James Baldwin once lamented, 'Nobody knows my name.' Now everyone does.

No sooner has a term been accepted by the establishment than other people start to rebel against it. This is the case with the young black writer Trey Ellis: 'When somebody tries to tell me what to call myself in all uses just because they come to some decision at a cocktail party to which I was not even invited, my mama raised me to tell them to kiss my ass' (*Village Voice*, 13 June 1989). According to Ellis African-Americans is not always the best term to be used (Gates 1992: 139).

The use of yet another variant has recently been proposed: American Black, advocated by Nikki Giovanni (1994) and others. Katya Gibel Azoulay (1996: 138) supported the idea as follows: 'Those who wish to transcend, bracket, or hyphenate their identities should live and be well, but for now, I'll support the use of "american" as an adjective and "Black" as a noun.' In everyday language in the USA the word Black obviously remains the most widely used.

Panafricanism: from Oronooko to Malcolm X

In Panafricanism, the common denominator used to be that Africans and people of African origin belong together. Thus a growing sense of racial solidarity and a new self-awareness could unite Africans of the diaspora with those in Africa. This did not necessarily include a physical return to Africa. What mattered, from the beginning was the sense of belonging to a common origin and the connectedness of people as the 'African world'. The key phrase 'Africa for the Africans' and the pursuit of a cultural and political Panafrican unity are part of this context. Panafricanism glorifies the African past and is proud of African traditional values.

By now, so much has been written on Panafricanism, that there is no need for a detailed outline of its history here (e.g. Geiss 1968; Langley 1973; Esedebe 1982; Magubane 1987). Panafricanism *avant la lettre* started as early as the seventeenth century. According to some it began in 1688, birth year of the Glorious Revolution in England, resulting in the liberal parliamentary system, later embraced by African nationalists and Panafricanists. In the same year, a remarkable novel was published, *Oroonoko* by the English writer Aphra Behn, which was set in the Caribbean and for the first time featured a black person Oroonoko (portrayed sympathetically) as the main character. Also in 1688 the first protest against the system of slavery was publicized in America, coming from the Quakers of Philadelphia (Geiss 1968: 32).

In the wake of the transatlantic slave trade, Panafricanism travelled back and forth between Western Europe, Africa (especially West Africa), the Caribbean and the USA. The Panafricanist George Padmore (1956: 879), born in Trinidad, called it a delayed boomerang from the times of slavery. In the same 'golden triangle' (in fact a quadrangle) marked by slavery, a dynamic exchange of ideas resulted in intercontinental Panafrican politics and a common cultural heritage. All geographical points of departure and arrival of the human trade were involved in the development of Panafricanism.

Important Panafricanists from the Caribbean include: Edward Wilmot Blyden, Henry Sylvester Williams, Marcus Garvey, George Padmore and Claude McKay. The father and grandfather of W. E. B. Du Bois were both of Haitian origin. Du Bois, one of the first black Americans to gain a PhD, was the founder of the National Association for the Advancement of Colored People (NAACP) and for over twenty years the principal director of *The Crisis*, the organization's magazine. Du Bois was one of the most dynamic and visionary leaders of Panafricanism. Through the organization of international congresses he brought black leaders from many countries into contact with each other.

Francophone Caribbeans have also played a key role in the rise of cultural nationalism in Africa. Writers and intellectuals such as René Maran, Aimé Césaire, Frantz Fanon (all three from Martinique, French Antilles), Jean Price-Mars (Haiti) and Léon Gontran Damas (French Guiana) have contributed to the Négritude Movement (discussed in Chapter 5).

After World War I Du Bois received support in Europe for his Panafrican Congress movement, from Antillian intellectuals and politicians in France; other European contacts dated from the beginning of the century. In 1919 he organized a Panafrican Congress in Paris. The ideas of black French intellectuals worked catalytically on the African pursuit of independence and on the American Civil Rights Movement. On the Francophone side the greatest influence has undoubtedly been exerted by the works of Fanon (e.g.

1952, 1961), whose strength and vision continue to inspire today's debates on matters of race, nationalism, humanism and the future of Africa (Sekye-Otu 1996).

In the USA Panafricanism became a real political movement around 1900, but it remained remarkably Anglophone, with black English and African representatives from the British Empire and their brothers (as far as I know, sisters did not play much of a role) from across the Ocean. American Panafricanism was firmly rooted in abolitionism and, after the Civil War, in an emancipatory movement which led to the Harlem Renaissance and later became the driving force behind the ideas of Black Arts, Black Aesthetics and Black Power.

In the long run, the political effect was rather small, due not only to a lack of material means, but also to a lack of political will. In 1957 Nkrumah declared that the independence of his country would not mean a thing unless it was part of the overall liberation of Africa. At the All-African People's Conference in Ghana in December 1958 he made clear that as the President of Ghana he was delighted that so many people of African origin had come to Accra. It meant that they felt strongly involved with the liberation movement in Africa:

> We must not forget that they are part of us. These sons and daughters of Africa were taken from our shores, and despite all the centuries that have separated us, they did not forget their ancestral links. ... Many of them made no small contribution to the cause of African freedom. Names that spring immediately to mind are those of Marcus Garvey and W. E. B. Dubois. Long before many of us were even conscious of our own degradation, these men fought for African national and racial equality. Long may the links between Africa and the people of African descent continue to hold us together in fraternity. (Esedebe 1982: 200)

Over the years many famous African and African-American political leaders have continued to express solidarity with each other and have protested against the sufferings caused by whites to their brothers and sisters on either side of the ocean, ranging from lynchings in the USA to a bloodbath in South African Sharpeville. It was of great psychological importance to the black American community when the new African states became independent around 1960. There is almost general agreement about the link between the strong development of the American Civil Rights movement in the 1950s and 1960s and the decolonization of Africa (James Baldwin 1962: 117).

In 1963 the Organization of African Unity (OAU) was founded. In spite of black solidarity, representatives of African origin from the USA, Caribbean and

Brazil were not admitted as members. However Panafrican identification between Black Power and Africa were important and often called upon by leaders in political and cultural demonstrations. In July 1963, for example, Malcolm X addressed the OAU summit:

> We in America, are your long-lost brothers and sisters, and I am only to remind you that our problems are your problems. As the African-Americans 'awaken' today, we find ourselves in a strange land that has rejected us, and, like the prodigal son, we are turning to our elder brothers for help. We pray our pleas will not fall upon deaf ears ... Your problems will never be fully resolved until and unless ours are solved. You will never be recognized as free human beings until and unless we are also recognized and treated as human beings. (1966: 73)

In practice, however, the ties were more a matter of conviction than a factor for structural political change. Malcolm X was granted no more than the status of observer at the summit in Cairo. In that capacity he was permitted to submit a memorandum to the delegates in which he urged them to support the cause of American Blacks. The next day the 'Harlem riots' started in the USA (July 1963). The OAU has never been able to turn into actions its words of solidarity addressed to black America. Still, Malcolm X was right: the problems and solutions on both sides of the Atlantic are linked.

Culture in discussion

In Kwame Anthony Appiah's *In My Father's House* (1992a), he studies the idea of 'the negro' and an 'African race' in the discourse of some 'archetypes' of Panafricanism (as he calls them) – Alexander Crummell and W. E. B. Du Bois. He shows that their ideas were founded on a dubious racial hierarchy derived from nineteenth-century European and American thinking. The same racially determined ideas are also the basis of Senghor's negritude (discussed in Chapter 5).

For American black leaders, writers and intellectuals it was out of the question to stay neutral with regard to matters of Self and Other. It was impossible to take a consistent position which would not conflict with oneself, with members of the group, or others. This was equally so for those writers who tried to find their own way through the impenetrable thickets of a dominant culture teeming with obtrusive white examples and white critics. In such circumstances, how could one organize a strong cultural opposition? Around 1910 it was a novelty for black poets to receive white critical attention. A remarkable flourishing of black literature, music, dance and cabaret took place in the 1920s with Harlem as its centre. One of the reasons for this flourishing was the large-scale migration to the north of labourers, intellectuals, artists and protest leaders. The Harlem period linked earlier oral traditions with African-American modernism (Baker 1987).

During the 1920s many whites started to go to Harlem to 'forget the war and engage their new Freudian awareness by escaping into black cabaret life', (*Negro Digest* 1969, quoted by Redmond 1976: 142). It has been suggested that such white interest was founded on stereotyped views. The blacks were in vogue, as Langston Hughes put it. He was one of the blacks who found a white patron; for some time he was supported by a monthly grant from a rich old American woman. It freed him from endless material problems so that he could commit himself to writing in complete freedom. Eventually, he felt forced to break with her because she wanted to programme his work. In keeping with the stereotype image she had of black people in Africa, she regarded him as a primitive with primitive rhythms and a primitive soul. As he explained in *The Big Sea*: 'but I was not Africa, I was Chicago and Kansas City' (1940: 325). The relationship ended in the usual cul de sac of white stereotyping of blacks. The financial support of blacks by rich whites came to an end after the Wall Street Crash; it was followed by the international economic crisis of 1929, the beginning of the end of the Harlem Renaissance. At the same time, the interest of the whites in black culture strongly declined. By then, however, this 'literary spring' (Wagner 1973: 149) had given birth to a black discursive modernism, as a blending 'of class and mass', in a 'poetic mastery of form' and 'deformation of mastery' (Baker 1987: 93), as a result of the painful struggle for black self-determination.

During the Harlem Renaissance literary criticism was just as politically and racially tainted as the poetry itself. The most important themes were racial pride, the misery of the lives of black people and romantic visions of Africa. Writers and artists were in a difficult position. They were attacked from all sides: by the whites because they were supposedly not 'universal' enough, and by their own people because they were supposedly 'not black enough' (Redmond 1976: 140).

But what did 'black enough' mean? The idea of what is black, too black, black enough or not black enough appears to be unstable. A striking illustration of the uncertainty about what could be considered beautiful and what could not is the problematic appreciation of black popular culture. Was it authentically African and therefore beautiful, or was it some backward remains from the time of slavery which had better be repressed and forgotten? Even Alain Locke had to be convinced initially of the artistic value of spirituals, as Zora Neale Hurston observed (Van Notten 1994: 43). It appeared to be a dilemma, for instance, among the black students of Howard University Choir:

> Perceiving themselves as Americans rather than African-Americans, the students initially refused to perform black songs, generally regarded as degrading and primitive. Their objection was based not only on the spirituals' roots in slavery, non-standard grammar, and dialect lyrics, but also on the fact that they were never performed at white universities. (Van Notten 1994: 43)

The favourable reactions of white critics contributed greatly to the gradual reappraisal of spirituals in black cultural establishment circles.

Just as in Africa Nigerian critics fluctuated in their response to Tutuola or in the Caribbean where writers rigidly imitated Symbolist poetry, so American studies adopted unquestioningly the artistic norms of dominant white culture. This attitude had to do with self-hatred, a result of internalized dominant white views. As for the USA, Henderson (1969: 88) draws a connection between the white vision and the way in which the blacks came to consider their own cultural heritage:

> The devil is black, sin is black, death is black, Cain is black, Grendel is black, Othello is black, ergo Othello is the devil. The black man is the devil. The devil is the black man ... And honesty compels me to point out that *our* songs, *our* games, *our* myths embody a good deal of anti-black feeling and attitude ... It is, frankly the *nigger* component of the Black Experience.

An intensive discussion on aesthetic norms and values developed during the Harlem Renaissance, especially in Marcus Garvey's popular magazine *Negro World*. The debate also involved the place of propaganda in the arts. In 1914 Garvey had founded the Universal Negro Improvement Association (UNIA). In the mid-1920s this organization had grown into the largest Panafrican mass movement of all time, with divisions in more than forty countries, a power that had to be reckoned with. Marcus Garvey never showed the slightest doubt as to the direction which black literature should take:

> We must encourage our own black authors who have character, who feel loyal to their race, who feel proud to be black, and in every way let them feel that we appreciate their efforts to advance our race through healthy and decent literature. (qtd in Martin 1983: 8)

Garvey's dynamism and the impression that his work made on the masses raised a lot of discussion and resistance. In 1922 the leader of the UNIA was in trouble and in 1925 he was imprisoned for fraud. From that time onward his importance in the New Negro Movement dwindled and Du Bois's NAACP was relieved when his rival's star had set. Garvey had mockingly called The National Association for the Advancement of Colored People the National Association for the Advancement of CERTAIN People. The 'Talented Tenth', Du Bois's name for a class of black leaders, consisted mainly of people with a lighter skin who lived in the better houses of Harlem.

At times the 'color line' took some strange twists and turns. Some angry young Blacks, such as Wallace Thurman, were strongly opposed to what they considered old-fashioned moralistic and at times propagandistic (as a concession to Garvey?) views of art. They themselves proposed a more avant-gardist point of view of unlimited artistic freedom without any political or moral compulsion. Of course personal motives were also involved. Dark-skinned Thurman felt marginalized by African-American, middle-class representatives who seemed to place priority on lighter skintones and who 'grieved over the New Negroes as a lost generation reduced to a spectacle for white America' (Van Notten 1994: 13). Notwithstanding such controversies on aesthetic standards and perhaps even due to the dynamism they provoked, the Harlem Renaissance is still praised for being an extraordinary artistic movement (e.g. Gates and McKay 1997: 929).

The fact that in practice blacks often refused to accept their 'own' writers and artists unless they had been given the stamp of approval from 'the dominant race' underlay an important cultural debate in the 1920s. It concentrated on three central topics.

First, Garvey and his followers emphasized that the race itself should decide on the value of its own artists, without caring about the prevailing outsiders' norms. They should not leave the whites to decide who were 'our' poets, political leaders and moral advisors. Someone like Claude McKay, for instance, often said to be the best poet of the Harlem Renaissance, had become famous mainly because of his publications in white literary magazines and thanks to a series of white tutors, godfathers and sponsors. How convincing could such a writer be in his own circles?

A second point of aesthetic discussion, not uncommon in European cultural history either, was whether the arts were supposed to deal realistically with misery and care, destitution and destruction or confine themselves to the positive, refined and 'noble' aspects of life. In the American context, the main question in the black discussion was what the Other, the outsider, the white person, might think about 'us'. Like Faustus, the blacks had two souls. They looked at themselves with the examining and normative view of the Other, with a 'double consciousness', in Du Bois's own terms. This was precisely the inner compulsion against which Thurman and his sympathizers rebelled. Although the Harlem Renaissance did not manage to break down this double consciousness, its cultural harvest has been rich and diverse, in spite of, or more likely thanks to, its contradictory opinions on the arts.

According to Garvey, some writers prostituted their intellect: he accused them of revealing the worst sides of the people under supervision of the whites. He hinted at, among others, Claude McKay, whose *Home to Harlem* was, in his opinion, 'a damnable libel against the Negro' (Martin 1976: 26). Garvey's followers did not rule out the institution of a literary censor to safeguard the race against adverse literature.

Du Bois's 'Talented Tenth' also came to be divided on the question of how black characters ought to be portrayed. A questionnaire on the subject was distributed among prominent black and white Americans; the questions and later a selection of the answers were published in *The Crisis*. The questions show how vulnerable and dependent were the positions that many blacks adopted. Here is the list as published in *The Crisis*:

1. When the artist, black or white, portrays a Negro character is he under any obligations or limitations as to the sort of character he will portray?
2. Can any author be criticized for painting the worst or the best characters of a group?
3. Can publishers be criticized for refusing to handle novels on the ground that these characters are no different from white folk and therefore not interesting?
4. What are Negroes to do when they are continually painted at their worst and judged by the public as they are painted?
5. Does the situation of the educated Negro in America with its pathos, humiliation and tragedy call for artistic treatment at least as sincere and sympathetic as 'Porgy' received?
6. Is not the continual portrayal of the sordid, foolish and criminal among Negroes convincing the world that this and this alone is really and essentially Negroid, and preventing white artists from knowing any other types and preventing black artists from daring paint them?
7. Is there not a real danger that young coloured writers will be tempted to follow the popular trend in portraying Negro character in the underworld rather than seeking to paint the truth about themselves and their own social class? (*The Crisis* February 1926: 113)

The seven questions of *The Crisis* were not only the subject of a heated debate in the Harlem Renaissance, but continued to be a sensitive matter in the next decades. In 1978 Chinua Achebe wrote his essay on Conrad's racism (drawing upon what he calls 'some rather trivial encounters' in the USA). More recently in *Playing in the Dark* (1992), Toni Morrison again discussed comparable issues in her critical analysis of the representation of African-American characters in American fiction.

According to Langston Hughes, the whole discussion was irrelevant since a writer will write what he wants, irrespective of what others think about it. Another commentator, H. L. Mencken, argued that it was nonsense for white people to look at blacks exactly the way blacks looked at themselves (Van Notten 1994: 48). Of course he was right, but it was easy talk for someone standing on the other side of the 'color line'. As usual, ideas appeared to be closely connected with cultural power relations.

A third important issue of black aesthetics was the place of propaganda in the arts and whether or not cultural integration was desirable. Garvey's UNIA supporters were reasonably clear in theory: integration was undesirable and propaganda for the good cause was indispensable. In practice the opinions were less clear, especially among artists:

> Sometimes they vacillated between one position and the other. Often they tried to eat their cake and have it too, arguing in theory against propaganda while being unable in practice to escape the all encompassing reality of North American racial prejudice. (Martin 1983: 17)

In his essay 'The Negro Artist and the Racial Mountain', which was published in a white magazine, Langston Hughes raises the problem in his own manner by way of an anecdote:

> One of the most promising of the young Negro poets said to me once, 'I want to be a poet – not a Negro poet,' meaning, I believe, 'I want to write like a white poet' – meaning subconsciously, 'I would like to be a white poet;' meaning behind that, 'I would like to be white.' And I was sorry the young man said that, for no great poet has ever been afraid of being himself. And I doubted then that, with his desire to run away spiritually from his race, this boy would ever be a great poet. But this is the mountain standing in the way of any true Negro art in America – this urge within the race toward whiteness, the desire to pour racial individuality into the mold of American standardization, and to be as little Negro and as much American as possible. (qtd in Martin 1983)

The choice is, indeed, between two racially different viewpoints; one presents itself as exclusively black, the other as universal (meaning according to the adherents of the first point of view the dominant norm of the white elite).

It is significant that black artists felt compelled or were compelled to declare themselves for or against cultural separatism, whereas white artists and writers could consider the dilemma non-existent. One question was whether a black writer could still back the non-integration point of view if he enjoyed white support. Or, to what extent did an anti-propaganda point of view by definition coincide with a pro-integration perspective? Martin (1983: 20) argues that the latter two inevitably go together, 'for why use one's artistic gifts on behalf of racial struggle when one's larger purpose was to escape altogether into a colorless world?'

Among Garvey's supporters, black nationalism and racial pride were popular. It was the movement with the largest black support among the labour masses and therefore a factor to be seriously reckoned with by other black leaders. This probably explains the ambiguous attitude of other leading Renaissancists. Du Bois, Garvey's great rival, was just as inconsistent on this issue as in his argument about the binding force among blacks all over the world. (Appiah 1992a; Gates and West 1996)

Writers continued to change their views according to public and context. This ambivalence should not be surprising: it is the feeling of being both insider and outsider at the same time, depending on the moment and the context. Richard Wright explained 'white-mindedness' thus:

Because the blacks were so *close* to the very civilization which sought to keep them out, because they could not *help* but react in some way to its incentives and prizes, and because the very tissue of their consciousness received its tone and timbre from the strivings of that dominant civilization, oppression spawned among them a myriad variety of reactions, reaching from outright rebellion to a sweet, otherworldly submissiveness. (Wright 1953, qtd in Henderson 1969: 99))

According to Henderson, whitening skin creams and wigs with sleek hair were still being sold in the 1960s.

Ralph Ellison described the ambivalent position of the American blacks as the carrying of an uncomfortable burden which can also be a source of delight. The author of *Invisible Man* (1952) decided not to take a defensive attitude; he refused to identify with an image that the whites had created, but also refused to conform with an image created by blacks.

This viewpoint became much more common in the 1990s and probably easier to hold, considering the fact that mainstream American culture has annexed many more prestigious black writers as 'its' authors and that Toni Morrison has been awarded the Nobel Prize.

Claude McKay's poem 'If We Must Die' once stood as the ultimate proof of the argument that the best poetry is inspired by racial conflicts and confrontations. This celebrated militant sonnet was one of the most popular poems of the whole period, written in 1919 after a series of racial riots which took hundreds of lives. Incidentally, it appeared for the first time in a white liberal magazine, *The Liberator* (July 1919):

> If we must die, let it not be like hogs
> Hunted and penned in an unglorious spot,
> While round us bark the mad and hungry dogs,
> Making their mock at our accursed lot.
> If we must die, O let us nobly die
> So that our precious blood may not be shed
> In vain; then even the monsters that we defy
> Shall be constrained to honor us though dead! (in Randall 1988: 63)

This poem became so well-known that Sir Winston Churchill even quoted it in his address to the joint meeting of the American Senate and Congress in an attempt to persuade the Americans to join the British side in World War II (Feuser 1976: 294). In that context 'us' defending ourselves against 'them' acquired rather different connotations.

McKay has often been considered the poet of anger and protest. Yet even he was not consistent: 'Though he lashed out at whites, his closest friends were white; while he wrote defiant, angry and militant verse, he denied that it was inspired by the Blacks' predicament' (Redmond 1976: 171).

The same hesitant attitude characterized Countee Cullen, who would at one time emphasize the importance of black tradition and at another argue that blacks should be able to write poetry without featuring spirituals or blues. Henry Louis Gates Jr and Nelly McKay describe him as an 'African American determined to succeed in the white-dominated field of literature [who] shied away from being labelled a racial writer; yet he won his greatest poetic renown for his most race-conscious lyrics' (1997: 1303).

The literary forms which McKay and Cullen used were mainly based on conventional rhyme patterns from the Anglo-Saxon tradition. Both died in the 1940s leaving behind a body of poetry which is innovating in its selection of themes, but certainly not in its formal aspects. They are named (by Senghor and Damas among others) next to Langston Hughes and Jean Toomer as a source of inspiration for the negritude poets in Paris in the late 1930s.

Langston Hughes was probably the most innovating of the three, because his philosophy of life and perspective were determined by 'Negro life' and the 'jazz spirit': 'no one would deny today that Hughes had become the outstanding poet of Harlem' (Wagner 1973: 410).

This 'Poet Laureate of the Negro Race' has exerted a tremendous influence on black American poetry. Derived from jazz, his style of writing, his themes and techniques were to determine a tradition of colloquial poetry in blues form. From a literary point of view, Hughes was far ahead of his time. Long before the beat generation was born, he read poems to the music of a jazz combo, for example, with his famous poem: 'The Negro Speaks of Rivers'. Not surprisingly this was dedicated to W. E. B. Du Bois; it returns to a distant past, a Pan-Africa history, linking 'rivers older than the flow of human blood':

I built my hut near the Congo and it lulled me to sleep.
I looked upon the Nile and raised the pyramids above it.
I heard the singing of the Mississippi when Abe Lincoln
     went down to New Orleans, and I've seen its muddy
     bosom turn all golden in the sunset.

I've known rivers:
Ancient dusky rivers.

My soul has grown deep like rivers. (in Randall 1988: 78)

He wrote this poem when, still young, he placed his identity and roots in far-away Africa. Some years later he came to Africa and felt he had made a mistake: the Africans did not consider him their brother, and one of them even called him a white man. Africa, he would remark in *The Big Sea* (1940: 103) — and not without self-mockery — was the only place where this had ever happened to him.

Black Arts

The Harlem Renaissance, with its tremendous interest in its own art, literature and history, was a solid base for the Black Arts Movement to return to in the 1960s. The strongest link between the two cultural periods and movements was Langston Hughes, the prominent Harlem Renaissance writer who remained active throughout the 1960s. His themes were: racism, protest, unity of race, racial pride, the black woman, jazz, blues, religious music, violence against blacks and the possibility or impossibility of integration. The same themes return with the Black Arts Movement. Hughes had always rejected cultural segregation, but at the same time refused to assimilate culturally. Together with Sterling Brown he has been called the 'black grandfather' of the new poetry of the 1060s. Saunders Redding (1939: 115) associated Hughes's poetry with 'the dark perturbation of the soul – there is no other word – of the Negro'; soul being the 'American counter-part of negritude', but with a difference: 'not only do the unlettered use it, but the Ph.D. as well'. Unlike negritude, soul is not a theory but an experience, 'a highly condensed potent folk myth which black Americans are exploring and living every day'. Where the word negritude would not be used by Senghor's countrymen to speak about themselves, the American term soul was used by illiterates as well as educated people. Henderson (1969), triumphantly writing on the subject, defines soul as 'all of the unconscious energy of the Black Experience' (124).

The black experience increasingly inspired black writers to an anti-integration attitude: 'If we can't have our rightful place in this country, then we're gonna tear it up' (Henderson 1969: 126). The idea of a black revolution gained growing support.

White norms and literary techniques were repudiated by black writers. They continued on the road cleared by Hughes and others and found their inspiration in folk poetry, jazz music, the everyday life of the ghetto, all sorts of black images and examples. The new writer refused to be restricted or taken in by the old white canon: he was 'more chauvinistically Negro than any Negro poet before him. The sixties brought a Negro poet who tended to be both a separatist and a militant' (Jackson and Rubin 1974: 85).

The term militant becomes superfluous from then on, if associated with black: the latter implies the first. Black writers make people conscious of their own value: 'Black is beautiful'. They confirm their blackness against the hegemony of whiteness, and in the USA it implies being militant, dangerous, subversive, revolutionary. Henderson argues that writers realize these implications more than the Harlem Renaissance artists ever did.

Ever growing numbers of blacks refused to accept that only the whites should decide which roles the blacks were allowed in culture. The place and significance of black culture, music, art and literature had been legitimized for too long by white critics instead of their black colleagues. This harsh reality was described by Larry Neal in his essay 'The Black Musician in White America', which also contains a plea for a rethinking of white cultural aesthetics by, and out of, the Black Arts Movement (Baker 1988: 151). The rhetorical question was: How can a white person, who is no part of 'our' identity explain the significance of blues, whereas we ourselves are the physical manifestations of blues? (Grant 1968: 260). It is clearly a plea for an emic approach, which Afrocentrists still advocate today, 'derived from *within* ... an internal understanding without the fault of Eurocentric social sciences' (Asante 1987: 172).

The Black Arts Movement figured as the artistic pendant of Black Power. Martin Luther King was killed in 1968. In the 1960s 'We shall overcome', at first sung by black and white together, was gradually replaced by Black Power slogans and 'Afro outfits':

Young black Americans, wearing Afro hairdos and African jewelry, attended cultural festivals, back-to-Africa rallies, black-power conferences and poetry readings, and read community news published in revolutionary broadsides and tabloids. (Redmond 1976: 300)

After the gospels, the spirituals and the blues, the rappers of the 1970s became inspired by the old sermon techniques of the black churches, which they combined with 'boasting language' and music-mixing techniques: verbal virtuosity is accompanied with themes of black pride (Shusterman 1991: 621). This authentic source of inspiration for poets has resulted in *poésie parlante* with the rhythm and diction of everyday language and the vocabulary of the street experience. The poetry has a phonetic spelling or syntax of its own. These characteristics foster a sense of interrelationship: only the insiders can really understand what it is about. Black writers themselves decide what is suited for the ears of 'whitey' and what is not. The whites, for one thing, do not participate in the Black Experience and hence cannot evaluate it, great experts as they may be in their own culture. White critics have become irrelevant or as Larry Neal put it: 'We cannot abdicate our culture to those who exist outside of us.' Specialists of the black tradition say: 'White man, you don't know because you haven't listened to enough black sermons, and if you started listening when you were twenty-five, it was too late. You don't have the Soul-Sounds in your mind' (Henderson 1969: 79). In those years it was forbidden to say anything bad about the New Black Poetry. Houston Baker concludes in retrospect:

Black critical complicity emerged as a Black Aesthetic which sometimes proclaimed: 'If it is too loud, you're too old!' Which is to say, anyone (especially *white* ones) who had reservations, questions, or criticisms was deemed too pedantic, bourgeois, or unrevolutionary to comprehend the excellence of *all* black works. (Baker 1988: 175)

This answer to the previous systematic segregation by whites is a 'reverse discourse'. The Other is standing outside the cultural experience of Self, which remains the exclusive domain of people within the group. It is clearly specified who belongs, as shown in this fragment by Le Graham from Detroit:

Black poems are beautiful
egyptian princesses. afro-americans. john
o.killens

                                    ossie davies. leroi jones.
                                    malcolm x shabazz. robert
                                    williams. lumumba. A
poem for wooly-haired brothers. natural-haired sisters.
Bimbos. boots & woogies. Or nappy-headed youngsters

                                    Cause they want what i
                                    want: blood from revolu-
                                                        tions. A
                                    fast boat to Africa. ghana
                                    the cameroons uganda &
                                    nigeria. (Henderson 1969: 77)

In their most furious poems the poets jeer with utter contempt at the white
system and the establishment and do not refrain from obscenities and appeals
for violence and murder. For instance, Amiri Baraka, still called Leroi Jones at
the time, wrote the poem 'Black Dada Nihilismus':

Rape the white girls
Rape their fathers
Cut the mothers' throats. (in *De Volkskrant*, 28 May 1993)

Baraka started as an avant-garde poet in Greenwich Village, but in the 1960s
he left the white world, decided to become 'superblack' and took Malcolm X as
his radical example. Afterwards he gave up his exclusive Panafricanist point of
view; he preferred Marxism over the strict cultural nationalism in which he
grew increasingly disappointed. He is no longer read very much which, he
says, is proof of the validity of his political message (interview).

New Black Poetry (unlike the Harlem group) rejects *all* American values and
'mainstream' literature in particular. A large part of this poetry can therefore be
considered non-poetry or anti-poetry. In this respect it does not obviously
differ from other avant-garde literature, such as Dada, surrealism or, later, the
Beat Generation. However, one clear difference from all the other avant-gardes
is that the black cultural motives and references remained the characteristics of
the identity of African-American literature.

In *Afro-American Poetics, Revisions of Harlem and the Black Aesthetic* (1988)
Houston Baker analyses the history of his own changing views on the
Harlem 1920s and the Black Arts 1960s. Picking his way carefully to the

conclusion, he first goes back to the facts of the beginning, the birth of Afro-America, the product of a 'holocaustal Atlantic slave trade' run by white European males and involving between 50,000,000 and 100,000,000 African lives. Panafricanism, Harlem Renaissance and Black Power represented healing rituals because of a traumatized collective memory, a search for cultural space, an identity of one's own. In this 'autocritography' as Baker defines his enterprise, he takes, additionally and most significantly, a further critical step. He brings up his own position for discussion while reviewing his earlier ideas. He could simply have looked back to the 1960s in a nostalgic way, or he might have described those years in terms of triumphant heroism. It was indeed the power of the Black Arts to be able to strengthen vulnerable black identities. Yet Baker does not stop there, but also scrutinizes the negative sides of that power:

> Principal confusions of Black Arts workers and critics – myself included – involved a failure to distinguish between bullying militarism and revolutionary organization, between cults and intrest groups, between religious chicaneries and nationalistic politics, and finally, between verbal throwaways designed for political rallies and carefully articulated Afro American expressive texts. Bullet words and paramilitary posturing were read as signs of black 'power,' and a rhetoric of hard facts was mistaken for a realization of genuine expressive power. (Baker 1988: 175)

Many of the radical claims of the movement were short lived. Houston Baker's conclusion is that African-American street therapy, for one thing, managed to open doors for blacks in the business world, in the academic world and in professions which until then had always been inaccessible to them.

In this sense, it had not been vain – although it profited predominantly the black middle class. An optimistic note is that the 'moving spirit' of the African-American arts and culture can never be pinned down. In the 1980s it resulted in a spectacular eruption of black female talent which deserves 'our' full attention, according to Baker. Who is the 'us' here, one might feel tempted to ask.

From soul to negritude

The first Festival Mondial des Arts Nègres, held in Dakar in 1966, claimed the unity of all black culture in front of the rest of the world. It was an important event with leading representatives of African art and culture present. The chairman of the literary jury, Langston Hughes, presented the prizes to the writers, a special prize being awarded posthumously to W. E. B. Du Bois for *Souls of Black Folk* (1903) in recognition of its great influence on black intellectuals. The prize for the best report went to Nelson Mandela – who was already in jail – for *No Easy Walk to Freedom*. The real literary prizes went to Ngugi for *Weep Not, Child*; to Soyinka for his play *The Road*; and to the African-American poet Hayden for his collection of poems *Ballad of Remembrance*. At this first world festival the female writers went unnoticed and the fact that they were not nominated for any prizes was not commented upon.

At the colloquium on the function and the significance of African art and literature at the Dakar festival, Langston Hughes gave a lecture entitled 'Black Writers in a Troubled World' in which he compared 'soul' with 'negritude'. Their function was the same he argued: 'Soul is contemporary Harlem's Negritude, revealing to the Negro people and the world the beauty within themselves' (1966: 508). The examples he gave were his own 'The Negro Speaks of Rivers', which refers to Africa, and Senghor's 'Aux soldats négro-américains'. Both poems, he argues, show the cultural solidarity that black writers should keep in mind:

> As to Negro writing and writers, one of our aims, it seems to me, should be to gather the strengths of our people in Africa and the Americas into a tapestry of words as strong as the bronzes of Benin, the memories of Songhai and Mele, the war cry of Chaka, the beat of the blues, and the Uhuru of African freedom, and give it to the world with pride and love. (Hughes 1966: 509)

Off the Dakar coast is an island which was named Goeree or 'good roads' by Dutch slave traders. This 'good roads' or Gorée, as it is still called nowadays, offers a continuing living remembrance of the times of the slave trade: the slave cellars, in which people were chained, are still there. For Africans from the diaspora a visit to Gorée means reconnection with the traumatic history of their ancestors. The American writers and artists who came to Dakar in 1966 were back on the same coast which their forefathers left long ago. The contacts from the time of the slave trade onwards between Africa, Europe, the Caribbean and the USA that had been exclusively motivated by economic reasons had at last resulted in a positive and humane event: a Pan-African cultural *rendez-vous du donner et du recevoir*.

After a prolonged stay in Paris, the Guyanese Léon Gontran Damas, one of the fathers of negritude, gave a lecture during the 1970s at Howard University in Washington. He told young black Americans how much they owed to their avant-garde; to the poets of the Harlem Renaissance; to the NAACP; to Du Bois and Garvey; to Martin Luther King and Malcolm X. All of them had tried to achieve the same goal, which Damas defined as follows:

> the rehabilitation of the Race and of the word NEGRO which was thrown in our faces like an insult — whence the origin and the meaning of the concept of NEGRITUDE, literary expression of Panafricanism. (in Warner 1988: 22)

In this chapter I have not talked about the construction of whiteness in America because there are already several book-length publications on the subject, some quite recent (Frankenberg 1993; Roediger 1994, 1998; Sartwell 1998). The editors of the edition of *Transition* on 'The White Issue' (3/1997) expressed some reservations regarding the subject of this special theme because 'white studies' by, for and about white people might displace examination of groups that have only begun to be considered legitimate subjects of academic inquiry in the last thirty years. One can agree with this opinion as far as it is a matter of getting the balance of data right.

I started this chapter by referring to Du Bois's statement on the 'color line' in 1903 and his belief in the 'Talented Tenth' who would uplift the race. Over the years, the leadership has continued to be divided on the boundaries between insiders and outsiders, an issue resulting in dynamic disputes:

> With the coming of the civil rights era, and the partial fulfillment of Du Bois's agenda, the contending school of accomodationism was replaced by that of black separatism, of the Back-to-Africa movement, and later, Elijah Muhammad, of the Nation of Islam. (Gates 1997: 34)

Perhaps partly as a result of so much turbulence it has been a century of spectacular black American cultural achievements. From an end-of-the-century perspective, it is tempting to wonder about the future. Reviewing the admirable monument of 2,665 pages, *The Norton Anthology of African American Literature*, edited by Gates and McKay (1997), Caryl Phillips might well be right in his prophecy that 'in the twenty-first century, African-American literary endeavours are likely to take centre-stage' (*The Observer*, 6 April 1997).

In *The Future of the Race* (Gates and West 1996) the authors addressed the insiders–outsiders question in the perspective of the twenty-first century. by once more referring to Du Bois's (1903) concept of the 'Talented Tenth', which he had defined as 'the leadership of the Negro race in America by a trained few', a model based on his belief in an educated class. Both discuss his view of black leadership, the problematic concept of 'the black community' — as if there were no intraracial disparities of class, sexual consciousness, or political convictions — and the 'remarkable gap between the leaders and the led in Black America' (33). Gates emphasizes the growing divergence between poor and prosperous blacks. Blacks in the ghetto seem less and less interested in the 'easy manichaeism of the 1960s [which] serves us poorly in the 1990s' (37). The danger of black cultural nationalism is that it continues to mask 'how very vast black class differences really are' (38). Both Gates and West admit that the crisis of race is not finished, that there are groups of black people who continue to feel discrimination. Gates underlines the responsibility of black academics: what can we do? A good question that not only black academics should ask themselves. West transcends the 'color line', particularly worried about the future of democracy. He believes that 'in this age of globalization ... a focus on the lingering effects of racism seems outdated and antiquated' (107). For him a multiracial alliance of radical democratic forces seems the only way for humanity to survive (110). We return to this important point in Chapter 9.

The 'color line' has been central in cultural debates elsewhere. Two other variants of black culture will be discussed in the next chapter: the negritude movement born outside Africa as the spiritual child of Africans and Caribbeans and the South African Black Consciousness Movement, originating from apartheid and inspired by American Black Power.

5

Negritude, Black Consciousness and beyond

What is a negro?
And, first of all, what colour is he?

Jean Genet

Some will charge that we are racist but these people are using exactly the values we reject. We do not have the power to subjugate anyone. We are merely responding to provocation in the most realistic possible way. Racism does not imply exclusion of one race by another – it always presupposes that the exclusion is for the purpose of subjugation ... While it may be relevant now to talk about black in relation to white, we must not make this our preoccupation, for it can be a negative exercise. As we proceed further towards the achievement of our goals let us talk more about ourselves and our struggle and less about whites. We have set out on a quest for true humanity, and ... in time we shall be in a position to bestow upon South Africa the greatest gift possible – a more human face.

Steve Biko

Today we can no longer stick to the role of innocent victims. It is quite easy to be a victim. It is much more difficult to admit that the people who bring misery over us can also be black. We must acknowledge that we are responsible adults.

Maryse Condé

Neither in Europe, the USA nor Africa is it possible to group all African culture or literature under one heading, as though historical, political and cultural differences did not exist. Yet not only outsiders, but also many theoreticians and defenders of Negritude have tried to do this. Such generalizations have evoked protests on the part of writers and critics not only within the Anglophone camp but also among the Francophones whose cultural child was Negritude. This reference to *Europhonie* is important because, as far as I know, writers in African languages hardly ever preoccupied themselves with the subject.

Right from its beginning, advocates of Negritude and Black Consciousness have become opponents of the respective movements – hardly vice-versa. Both these important cultural movements have to be understood in their historical context. They have inspired a whole literature with the same themes and dilemmas as those found in the Harlem Renaissance, literary Garveyism and the Black Arts Movement, in line with the Panafrican view of cultural unity.

In this chapter Negritude and Black Consciousness will be looked at, mainly from an African perspective. Similar movements, such as Indigenism in the Caribbean or other more recent black developments in the diaspora (Coulthard, Dash, Glissant, Gilroy, Segal), will not be dealt with, though an exception will be made for a much neglected Surinamese movement.

Of course Negritude has an important Caribbean connection through poets such as Césaire, Damas and others. However, the main issue here is not so much literary history as the comparative question of the borderlines between cultural insiders and outsiders and how they shift according to the changing political climate.

The history of slavery, colonial occupation and cultural repression inspired common themes among numerous writers. In Africa the Negritude message was broached by West African writers before being utilized in Central Africa. The Congolese, for example, were unaware of the concept of Negritude for decades. The Belgian colonial policy of cultural isolation had indeed been effective. Negritude only began to flourish in Congo after independence in 1960. Internationally it was then already 'too late' (Ntamunoza 1976: 75) because after independence African literature started making new choices within the framework of a different political climate. In many places, Negritude dried up during the 1960s and the voices of most ambassadors of the movement gradually silenced. Senghor, however, made Negritude his life project. In South Africa the Black Consciousness movement came to life only at the end of the 1960s.

According to Aimé Césaire (1939: 44) it was in Haiti that Negritude first appeared. In his interview with the Haitian René Depestre he explains how and when he discovered the larger black world from the USA to Africa. He mentions in particular in the Caribbean the special history of Haiti which had already become independent in 1804.

Comparing Negritude and Indigenism in the Caribbean, G.R. Coulthard (1968: 46) concludes that 'the gradual build-up to Negritude and the final elaboration of the concept of Negritude took place largely in the West Indies'. For Senghor and most Francophones, however, Paris is the location of Negritude's inception. In their research, neither the Francophones nor

Anglophones have systematically examined comparable cultural activities in the Netherlands Antilles and Surinam.

Our Own Things

The Surinamese movement Wie Eegie Sanie (Our Own Things) started in 1950 when it was founded by Surinamese students in Amsterdam. It was not easy for a multicultural society like Surinam to establish what exactly were 'our own things'. They would surely be different for someone descending from Javanese immigrants, compared to someone with African ancestors.

In *Creole Drum* (1975) Voorhoeve and Lichtveld consider the movement as a striving for the ideal of a Surinamese culture and identity in a reaction to the imposition of Dutch language and culture. In this respect it resembled the reaction of Antillian students in Paris some twenty years earlier, whose manifesto *Légitime Défense* (1932) was a precursor of the Negritude movement:

> But compared with *Légitime Défense*, *Wie Eegie Sanie* represented a much more balanced reaction. Its spokesmen always stressed their essential openness to influences from other cultures. They even accepted Dutch culture as part of their cultural heritage, but they wanted to shape their own national culture, in which all Surinamese could participate. (Voorhoeve and Lichtveld 1975: 183)

This group was ahead of its time in the 1950s. It was not until 1989 that a booklet was published in the French Antilles with the intriguing title *Eloge de la Créolité*, in which the authors, including Patrick Chamoiseau, preached *créolité*. Obviously the different languages hamper communication, not only between the Netherlands Antilles and Surinam and the rest of the Caribbean, but also in Africa, especially between Francophones and Anglophones.

The history of Negritude has been dealt with, among others, by Lilyan Kesteloot (1963), Janheinz Jahn (1968), Marcien Towa (1971), René Depestre (1980), James Arnold (1981) and Michel Hausser (1988, 1991). The majority of publications on the subject are in French. Yet, without any knowledge of the European history of expansion, the counter-movement of Negritude cannot be understood.

From the colonial perspective, only Western culture was acceptable and the white example served as the ideal. 'Civilized' became synonymous with 'Western' and civilization could be learnt at schools founded by Europeans. The aim of French cultural politics was to create a loyal elite of fake French. The elite would ward off the danger of nationalism among the natives and perpetuate the colonial situation. The eternal norms of Western, in particular French, civilization were taught in the colonies. In the field of literature the result was sometimes cultural imitation, the production of a weak resemblance of what was no longer current nor original in Europe and irrelevant to any public. The French cultural politics of assimilation had such a pernicious effect that some writers even aimed at writing in such a 'French' French that Europeans would read their works without noticing that they were written by black authors: they chose European pseudonyms (Kesteloot 1963: 29).

In an interview with René Depestre (1971: 71), Aimé Césaire admits that he disliked his first poems so much that they were never published:

> I had not yet found a form of my own. I was still under the influence of French poets. To tell the truth, if the *Return to my Native Land* took the form of a prose poem, it was really [because] I wished to break with the French literary tradition and I did not free myself until the moment I decided to turn my back on its poetry. One might say that I became a poet by renouncing poetry. Poetry was for me the only means through which to break the regular French forms which were choking me ... To put it another way, the French language was an instrument which I wished to endow with a new expressiveness. I wished to write a Caribbean French, a black French, which although French would bear a black seal.

During the 1930s a change occurred among other poets too: the stronger the oppression, the fiercer their reaction.

According to Wilfried Feuser (1987: 259) the word 'negritude' was used for the first time in the nineteenth century, in an essay by Charles Lamb 'On Chimney-Sweeps', long before Aimé Césaire reinvented it. Negritude as a cultural movement also drew inspiration from Claude Mackay, Countee Cullen, Langston Hughes and other black American poets. Some of them met African and Antillian poets from the French colonies in Paris, which was an important intercultural meeting place for black writers and intellectuals. Magazines started to appear such as *La Revue du Monde Noir* (1931) and *L'Etudiant Noir* (1935). The editorial in the first *Revue du Monde Noir* emphasizes that one of the tasks of the magazine is 'to study and popularize, by means of the press, books, lectures, courses, all which concerns NEGRO CIVILIZATION and the natural riches of Africa, thrice sacred to the black race'. In *L'Etudiant Noir* an article appeared by Aimé Césaire entitled 'Négrerie: Jeunesse Noire et Assimilation' in which he opposes assimilation with the white race; he argues for authenticity and freedom (Ako 1984: 343).

Césaire recalled that assimilation was unavoidable in the 1930s; one could choose either the political left or right in France. For him left wing was the obvious choice, but he could not comply with the Communists either as they denied the special situation of black people:

> I argued that political issues ought not to hide our situation as blacks. We are blackmen, with a very special historical background. I suppose that in this I reflect the influence Senghor had on me. At that time, I knew nothing about Africa. I soon got to know Senghor who told me a lot of things about Africa. I was greatly impressed by all this. (interview with Depestre 1967: 74)

The term 'negritude' did not yet exist let alone a literary movement by that name. It would take another thirty years before the movement was given its name by Lilyan Kesteloot (1963) in the first literary study of the poetry of Césaire, Senghor and Damas. She spoke of the 'Mouvement de la Négritude' in quotation marks because it was unusual to call this poetry and its poets by that name. She was probably also the first to call Césaire, Senghor and Damas the three fathers of the movement. The mutual contacts in Paris stimulated the construction of a collective identity as a result of the experience that being black in the West meant being excluded, however accultured and French one's education was. Ideas of equality gradually developed into thinking in terms of difference, focusing on the questions: who are we as black people and in what respect are we essentially different from Europeans? This is the context which gave birth to the anecdote that, one day, walking with his Senegalese friend Senghor along the banks of the Seine in Paris or at the Place de la Sorbonne, Martiniquan Aimé Césaire said: 'We must bear out our negritude.' Nobody can prove that this is the way it happened. It has been supposed that Césaire had used the term, in *L'Etudiant Noir* in 1935, but this magazine only mentions the term *négrerie*. The growth of 'colour consciousness' (Appiah and Gutmann 1996) and its accompanying poetry were retroactively declared the 'negritude movement' in the 1960s, more than twenty years after Césaire had used the term in *Cahier d'un Retour au Pays Natal* in 1939 (Ako 1984). The flourishing of the movement is generally situated between the 1930s and the 1950s, Césaire, Senghor and Damas being its pioneers. Feuser (1987: 260) ironically refers to the three of them as 'the Trinity':

> If the Martiniquan poet thus assumes the role of father in the Negritude Trinity — 'In the beginning was the word' — Senghor must be the Son, while Damas is the self-proclaimed Holy Spirit: his first poems were, rather significantly, published in the journal *Esprit* in 1935.

Damas is the least well-known of the three as according to Femi Ojo-Ade (1989: 237), he did not play a political role. Césaire became *député-maire*, Senghor the first president of his country. Senghor, moreover, became the driving force behind the theory of the movement.

Looking back in 1971, Césaire reconstructs bits and pieces of the first stages of the development of Panafrican consciousness. He had heard of Marcus Garvey as a child. He had also read poems by Langston Hughes and Claude Mackay, which had been published in a collection of African-American poetry, translated into French in 1929. From a global point of view he underwent three kinds of cultural influence in his adolescent years: French, African and Afro-American from the Harlem Renaissance (interview with Depestre 1971: 75).

Numerous definitions have been given to Negritude. Césaire, defined it: 'Negritude is becoming aware of being black, admitting and accepting one's blackness, and taking responsibility for the history and culture that goes with it.' Senghor defined Negritude as 'the collective cultural values of the black world' (Kesteloot 1963: 111). Such definitions bring out the essential racial aspect. Other terms, such as *africanité*, *africanitude*, *négristique*, *négrisme*, *néo-africanisme* and *mélanisme* were based on the same idea: black people belong to the same race and therefore to the same culture. Africans and people of African origin appeal to their being black, they are proud of their being different from white people. As a reaction they start looking for 'their own things', values, history and cultural identity.

The body of Negritude ideas alternatively referred to a wide area of culture and politics, or to a strictly literary phenomenon. It is striking that the theoretical foundation (and undermining) occurred pre-eminently in Francophone circles. Most Anglophone Africans often rejected Negritude from the start. Soyinka expressed this in his famous statement that 'a tiger does not proclaim his tigritude, he pounces'. Later he explained what exactly he had meant:

> A tiger does not stand in the forest and say: 'I am a tiger.' When you pass where a tiger has walked before, you see the skeleton of the duiker, you know that some tigritude has been emanated there ... the distinction I was trying to make at this conference (in Kampala, Uganda, 1962) was a purely literary one: I was saying that what one expected from poetry was an intrinsic quality, not a mere name-dropping. (in Jahn 1968: 265)

In my own interview with Senghor, which has been partly included at the end of this book, the father of Negritude severely criticized his fellow writer for this statement:

You see, we are being attacked by both Anglophones and Francophones. Against my English speaking brothers who criticize us – among whom is my friend Wole Soyinka, who argues that the tiger doesn't speak about its tigritude – I argue that they fuel a French–English conflict, and I am not interested. To Wole Soyinka I reply: You're right! The tiger does not speak about its tigritude because it is an animal, but a human being does speak about its humanity.

With or without the umbrella of Negritude, 'black' themes cropped up in all places where black and white met on an unequal footing, on both sides of the Atlantic. Still, there were also differences. In Africa the British colonial policy of indirect rule gave rise to less vehement reactions in a number of cases, while the forceful French policy of assimilation provoked strong reactions. Both Negritude and the Black Consciousness movement used to emphasize differences between Self and Other, singing the praise of black identity as against white Otherness. Both black movements clearly demonstrate that people who are trapped in the straitjacket of colonialism and oppression need to confirm their cultural identity and create strategic myths of collective black solidarity which nourish both history and literature. Such myths may be similar and recognizable, in spite of distances and differences in language, culture, class, country, origin and gender. The search for a common denominator, a collective Africanness as against whiteness, is expressed in four general poetic themes.

In an earlier essay (Schipper 1989) I dealt extensively with these main literary themes which emphasize the unity of race, origin and history: suffering, revolt, triumph and the belief in an interracial dialogue. Here I will briefly summarize them before entering a more detailed discussion of Negritude and Black Consciousness, their mutual links and their connections with black movements on the other side of the Atlantic discussed previously.

Themes

Sartre analysed the phenomenon of black suffering in his famous essay *Orphée Noir* where he referred to the Passion (with a capital P) of the race (1949: 270): 'The conscious black represents himself in his own conceit as the man who has accepted all the burdens of mankind and who suffers for all, even for the whites.'

This 'Passion of the race' has inspired many poets. The past is evoked, history is analysed, evil is diagnosed: the suffering of blacks is the inevitable outcome of the savagery of whites. This theme has been expressed in many ways. The slaves sang their songs of suffering and longing for the hereafter in old spirituals such as 'Nobody Knows the Trouble I've Seen', before writers expressed the sufferings of their brothers and sisters in poetry, from the Caribbean to South Africa. In Aimé Césaire's *Et les chiens se taisaient* (1961), the author seems obsessed by the vision of the crimes committed by the white man. The atrocities are expressed in metaphors: the sea, the sun, the sky, the wind, the clouds, the whole natural world constitutes a horrendous picture of black sufferings, from which the groans of the victims rise:

> The cloud's head is the head of the old black man whom I have seen cudgeled at a market place, the low sky is a charcoal-box, the wind rolls burdens and sobs of sweating skin, the wind contaminates itself with whips and casks, and hanged men people the mapled sky and there are mastiffs with bloodstained hair, and ears ... ears ... barges made of cut ears gliding on the setting sun ... A rumour of iron collar chains ascends from the sea ... a gurgling of drowned people from the green paunch of the sea ... a cracking of fire, a cracking of whips, shouts of the assassinated ... the sea is burning.

The pain referred to is both physical and psychological. Not only are there allusions to the slave trade, the traumatic passage over the ocean with the toll of its deaths and the exploitation of those who arrived in the Americas but there is also the colonial alienation caused by people's lost languages and destroyed cultures; the forced assimilation to a foreign language, culture and education. This was well expressed by the Caribbean poet Léon Laleau (1931) in his poem *Trahison* [Treason]:

> The hopelessness I feel, deeper than all,
> Of taming with the words of France, this heart
> Which came to me from distant Senegal. (in Jahn 1968: 229)

All this has been engraved in people's traumatic cultural memories and vizualized in Caribbean and African-American black poetry, as well as in African writings referring to colonial domination. The passage I quoted from Césaire's text has been chosen from among hundreds of poems in French, English, Portuguese, Spanish, Afrikaans and Dutch.

To the poet who sings of suffering, revolt is never far off; he (to my knowledge there were no female poets in the Negritude movement and relatively few in the Black Consciousness movement) protests the injustice done to his people. The words of the poet are his weapons in the struggle for freedom; weapons often forged from words in a European language. One of Césaire's books of poetry is even called *Les armes miraculeuses* (1946). Just as in many poems of the Harlem Renaissance writers and the Black Arts movement, Caribbean and African Negritude poetry is a revolt against the outsider's cultural and political domination, in order 'to regain the bitter smell of freedom' (Césaire 1939: 87). Or, in David Diop's words: 'You, my brother, face full of fear and fright/Get up and shout: NO!' (1973: 48). The protest is expressed in many genres such as very popular resistance songs inspired by liberation struggles in Angola, Namibia, Kenya, Zimbabwe, Mozambique and South Africa.

In Negritude poetry 'white civilization' is under attack on all fronts. In his poetic work, Césaire successively condemns reason, culture, technology, ideologies and Christianity (Schipper 1972). In many protest poems the taste of victory is already present. The small step from revolt to triumph and self-glorification is evident; it is accompanied by poems idealizing the Black Self and a pre-colonial African Eden. There are many odes in many languages to this lost paradise.

This idyllic paradise has been sung by, among many others, Senghor (1964: 15) in poems such as 'Joal' (1941), inspired by a painful European solitude in Paris. His reference to 'an orphaned jazz, sobbing, sobbing, sobbing' creates an obvious link with Harlem jazz culture. A difference between diaspora and African poets of Negritude is that the former had no living tradition but wanted and needed to invent one in order to re-establish contact with their African past.

In Dutch there is, for example, the poet Frank Martinus Arion from Curaçao who dreams of his African roots in *Stemmen uit Afrika* [Voices from Africa, 1957]. In the introduction to the new 1978 edition he notes that from the 1960s onwards Dutch Antillian people became interested in the subject. His aim in this poetry was 'to combat white prejudices about Africa and black people in order to correct views of Africa and the Antilles'.

A romantic vision presenting Africa as a symbol of purity, sharply contrasting with a corrupted and destructive Europe, is referred to by Sartre (1949) as 'anti-racist racism'. As against white criteria of aesthetic appearances, there is the triumph of 'black is beautiful'. Thus, Léon Damas rejoices in 'Black Label' (1956: 52):

Whites will never be black
Because beauty is black
And black is wisdom,
Because endurance is black
And black is courage.

On the other hand, the three fathers of Negritude also proclaim that they wish to make the world more humane. The dialogue cannot begin, though, before old prejudices have been cleared away and both parties are on an equal footing enjoying the same rights. Or, as Césaire observed in the foreword to *Nouvelle somme de la poésie du monde noir* (1966: 3): 'As victims of colonial traumas and in search of a new balance, blacks have not yet achieved liberation. All dreams, all desire, all rancour accumulated, has to come out ... and as it opens out and finds its form of expression ... then it is called poetry.'

In the three themes mentioned — suffering, revolt and triumph — there is no space for dialogue; they represent three phases in terms of difference. The poet proclaims his position as an insider's view which excludes the Other, the outsider who was never interested in dialogue.

In Europe, Senghor has often been regarded as the reconciliator par excellence between blacks and whites. In *Liberté I* (1964: 401) he underlined that 'the black poem is not a monologue but a dialogue'. His poetry is more peaceful than that of other Negritude writers. Senghor explains this by referring to his 'harmony with African nature'. Thus he was able to write his poem 'Prayer for Peace' as far back as 1945 in which he asked God for peace and forgiveness: the Lord God should forgive white Europe in spite of its crucifixion of Africa (1964: 92).

This general and gracious pardon is intended as a gesture towards dialogue. Many sceptical comments have been made about Senghor. He certainly did not find favour with the younger generation who questioned his political practice, blaming him for being more keenly interested in good relations with France than in improving things back home.

There are also writers and poets who draw a political distinction between whites in power, who could consequently be held responsible for the injustices committed against people of colour, and peasants and workers in the Western world who were also victims. In his poem 'Pour Saluer le Tiers Monde', Césaire (1960: 85) envisages Africa as the first to reach out a hand to the 'wretched' of the other continents:

It is a swollen hand
A-wounded-open-hand
extended to,
brown, yellow, white,
to all the hands, to all the wounded hands
of the world.

The Haitian writer Jacques Roumain refuses to forgive the guilty. In 'Nouveau sermon nègre', he compares the suffering of the black man to the suffering of Christ. But whereas Jesus asks his Father to forgive his enemies 'who know not what they do', Roumain (1972: 306) cries out: 'We will not forgive them, for they know what they do.' However, his solidarity is not restricted to black brothers either, as is evident from the last lines of his poem 'Bois d'ébène' [Ebony]:

> Just like the contradiction of features
> Resolves in the face's harmony
> We proclaim the unity of suffering
> And of revolt
> Of all the peoples on the surface of our earth
> And we brew the mortar of fraternal times
> In the dust of the idols. (234)

From this perspective of class consciousness, Negritude loses its raison d'être: a different kind of solidarity is created that no longer requires the accentuation of the colour of a man's skin or his belonging to a particular 'race'. 'The Negro has been created by the white man', Fanon once said. Negritude has been a reaction to this state of affairs, though in a sense it has also prolonged it as long as the writers defined themselves 'according to the colour of the other group', as Sembène Ousmane put it in the foreword to his *The Money Order* (1966).

From Negritude to Post-Negritude

Mainly thanks to Senghor, the movement became well known. Senghor became an important and respected figure in such international circles of literature and the arts as UNESCO and Présence Africaine; he also was the first African to be elected as a member of the Académie française. Senghor has been an admirable and dynamic ambassador for the promotion of African culture. Many studies have been devoted to his poetry and ideas. He always considered his brainchild 'négritude' a permanent phenomenon, as he personally confirmed during an interview I had with him in Amsterdam. On that occasion, he once more underlined his belief in the unity of values of black civilization, even though the circumstances and themes were subject to change. According to him, the polemic against Europe was over now, but that did not in the least affect the continuation of Negritude:

> What we want is a dialogue. I advise, or rather we advise, a Euro-Arabo-African consultation, not only on an economic, but also on a cultural level. We are very attached to African civilization; at the same time we want to be open for civilizations from other parts of the world, Europe in particular.

In the *Civilisation de l'Universel*, Europe and Africa both have their well-defined contributions to make:

> With its spirit of method and organization, Europe will bring us, mainly, its scientific and technical discoveries. Africa, I mean black Africa, will bring its communitary and artistic values, particularly its philosophy of life, based upon the complementarity, and, in the arts, its sense of analogical image, of rhythm and of melody.

But why should such qualities be divided along the lines of cultural insiders and outsiders in the various fields of science and the arts? Why should people be denied certain qualities on the basis of their cultural or geographical or historical origin? Fanon refused to pin human beings down: for him it was 'a question of unleashing the human being' (1952: 26), or, as Sekye-Otu puts it in his excellent *Fanon's Dialectic Experience*: 'From the beginning, the central question for Fanon was always that of releasing possibilities of human existence and history imprisoned by the colonization of experience and the racialization of consciousness' (1996: 17).

Senghor, however, continued to believe in racially determined group characteristics. Answering my question as to whether Africans would have treated Europeans better than the other way round, had they been in a position of colonial power, his answer was positive: he even furnished evidence by referring to historical cases such as the Almoravides who conquered Morocco and parts of Spain, and who had never acted in a racist way against whites. This idea was strongly dismissed for instance by Wole Soyinka when I asked him to comment on Senghor's statement:

> Everything which is happening in Africa today proves to me, confirms what I have always believed in, the Africans have as much capacity for cruelty, banality, sadism, corruption as any other race in the world ... I do not accept any thesis which suggests that Africans do somewhere differ from the human race. (See interviews)

According to Adotevi in his much-discussed *Négritude et négrologues* (1972), the Negritude expressed in the poetry themes constituted the Negritude 'of the first hour ... this pistol shot in the middle of the concert, when Africa, America, and the Caribbean, all the Blacks in the world, found each other back outside white humanity, to assert their own humanity'. Such Panafrican thinking is, from Adotevi's perspective, necessarily provisional in nature. This termination of silence, he says, is the real Negritude, the one that is still not perverted, 'the one that enabled us to make Africa known thanks to the howled themes of our poets' (29). These themes he considers 'the birth certificate of a new African literature' (32). In spite of these positive reflections, Adotevi expresses doubt as to the existence of lasting unity among blacks in various parts of the world. What really unites them apart from the colour of their skin and this 'common foundation of three centuries of slavery or collective subconsciousness'? Even regarding this 'common foundation', Adotevi remains sceptical in view of the variety of historical, geographical and sociological factors that have created different forms of expression in the arts of the peoples of the two continents (46).

The 'howled themes' to which Adotevi refers have indeed travelled to and from the USA, the Caribbean and Africa: they constitute a Panafrican link, a transitory unity due to a common experience of white oppression. Adotevi's conclusion is that no other factor can make us generalize about blacks and their culture.

In this respect, the 'conversion' of American black studies professor Henry Louis Gates is interesting. In the 1960s he studied in England the current ideas about Africa on the basis of the concept *nommo* in which the essence of the whole African culture was supposed to consist, as developed by the German Janheinz Jahn in *Muntu* (1961). It fitted well with Black Arts ideas in the USA at the time. Armed with his *nommo*-knowledge and his Afro hairdo Gates presented himself to Wole Soyinka who was then in exile in Cambridge. Soyinka watched him with some suspicion and asked whether he knew anything about Africa.

> 'Absolutely,' I said, having just memorized the principles of *nommo* in preparation for our meeting. 'Because the fact is,' Soyinka added, 'the only reason I accepted you as a student was that at least you did not talk about that *nommo* nonsense.' '*Nommo?*' I said. 'Never heard of it.' (Gates 1992: 126)

In the USA these *nommo* ideas continue to be advocated by the supporters of Afrocentricity (e.g. Asante and Vandi 1980; Asante 1987). Africa is sometimes imagined in such generalizing terms in these circles that the tremendous diversity of African cultures is completely overlooked. This explains Soyinka's suspicion and initial reservations towards Gates.

The unity of a worldwide black culture has repeatedly dominated discussion and has been critically commented upon because it was sometimes also used to cover up the same kind of internal power struggles as occurred during the Harlem Renaissance debates. This happened, for instance, at the first two congresses of black writers in Paris (1956) and Rome (1959):

While the two congresses asserted an 'African presence' in world affairs and appeared to offer an opportunity for many divergent opinions to be aired, at the same time their quest for unanimity at any cost represented a danger in that they made it possible for a dominant group to assert its power over the others. That group was the politically conservative group at the helm of *Présence Africaine*, which found in Negritude an appropriate ideology and in Léopold Sédar Senghor a fitting *éminence grise*, both consecrated by the Dakar Festival in 1966. (Songolo 1988: 26)

From the very beginning Negritude's strength was also its weakness: it wanted to impress the oppressor. Its critics blamed the followers of the movement for mainly focusing on the white man and 'their ultimate goal, even if couched in sweet, negrified rhetoric, has always been to attain that apogee of "civilization" exemplified by the French society' (Ojo-Ade 1989: 238). The triumph of Negritude was short-lived. In 1969 at the Panafrican festival in Algiers it was discarded as folklore and attacked from all sides by writers and politicians alike (Feuser 1987: 263; Songolo 1988: 26).

As an argument against such thinking, Adotevi, who was among those who criticized Negritude in front of a non-Francophone audience at the Algiers Festival, cites the South African Peter Abrahams and the American Richard Wright in defence of his view (1972). Neither of these two writers experienced the unity of black brotherhood during their stay in West Africa. Wright was shocked in many ways, and concluded after his visit: 'I was black and they were black but it did not help me at all', while Peter Abrahams commented:

The sharp black consciousness of the black American or the South African, victim of Apartheid is foreign to the African of independent Africa. Race and colour were his last preoccupations before he was forced to think of them. And 'Mother Africa' is too vast to inspire him with a total feeling. (qtd in Adotevi 1972: 47)

He could also have referred to Langston Hughes who, to his own surprise, was considered a white man in Africa. Racial consciousness is no longer a central issue among the inhabitants of independent Africa. For Senghor's compatriot, the writer and filmmaker Sembène Ousmane, Negritude is something unreal: 'It does not exist, just like the sex of angels.' As a Marxist, his main reproach is that the movement is 'square to the African revolution' (interview).

At a colloquium in Paris, Caribbean writer Maryse Condé also expressed herself critically concerning the Negritude of Senghor and Césaire because of its racial implications. If the West wanted to be the victim of its own myths on race and colour, as she laconically argued, that was no concern of hers, Negritude being an exclusive and therefore a restrictive concept, she did not go along with: 'I refuse to belong to a certain branch of the human species that has much of this and little of the other.' According to her, liberation can only be realized by refusing any racially determined position and by principally affirming our qualities as human beings who are equal to others (Condé 1973: 154). She clearly agrees with Fanon's views. It may seem then that nothing is left of all the Panafrican views on culture, but from her point of view there is:

> Solidarity is one thing that can be retained from negritude. Black Americans who demonstrated in front of the White House because of South Africa, are very right. It is also our struggle. But it is naive and simplistic to think: I go on a pilgrimage to Africa to mix among my African brothers and sisters. They can do without us. They have their own problems and we have ours (see interview).

Senghor refused Frantz Fanon a job as a psychiatrist in Senegal in 1961 (Feuser 1987: 261). Could one of the reasons have been the psychiatrist's views of Negritude? After Fanon had marked out Negritude as an anxiety syndrome in 1952, he wrote extensively about its dangers in *Les Damnés de la terre* (1961: 147): for him the reactive pursuit of racialization was a cul-de-sac.

As Adotevi (1972) observed, Negritude missed its political and revolutionary vocation. If the old Negritude is a rejection of humiliation, a black person who addresses the Black nowadays must deal with the drama of his people and be conscious of new tasks (151). This is in line with the ways in which Gates and West (1996) address today's black intellectuals' responsibilities towards the 'future of the race' in the USA.

Post-colonial Negritude should include a discussion of neo-colonialism: if not, 'after independence, it degrades into the *black* way of being *white'*. Adotevi based his ideas on Fanon who always refused to belong to one particular branch of the human race and to be pinned down by history, because human beings do have the possibility of breaking through the historical situation and of introducing the era of their own liberty. Fanon also refused to draw up 'the balance-sheet of black values' and stated: 'I am no slave of the Slavery that dehumanized my ancestors' (1952: 207).

South African white liberals and Black Consciousness

In South Africa also, assimilation and protest were the reactions to white racism as institutionalized by apartheid laws. In the literature in particular the protest rang out loudiy. The government's reaction was to enforce an extensive system of censorship, a frantic prosecution of writers and a cultural policy of divide and rule. The dictionary definition of literature as 'the collective literary production of a nation' was for a long time problematic in the case of South Africa due to the systematic division of people according to race, colour and culture. While black and white intellectuals and artists got together frequently during the 1950s, contacts became increasingly difficult and in the end even impossible. Nadine Gordimer remembered:

> In the fifties we mixed quite a lot. There were many love-affairs, close friendships. We were incredibly idealistic and we thought that if we ignored apartheid it would simply disappear. But we forgot that, when a black friend left our house – however intense the relationship might be and however dependent we were on each other inside the house – this friend suddenly had to carry his ID in his pocket, and could be arrested because he was black ... The massacre of Sharpeville set off a series of mass arrests, and for the whites the hour of truth had come: the beginning of the *Black Consciousness Movement*. The blacks severed all political, social, and cultural bonds with the whites, one of the reasons being their disappointment about what the whites had been offering them. The word *liberal* became a dirty word (*De Volkskrant* 13 June 1981).

Even if they did not want to be, the well-meaning whites were pushed back into their own *laager*. In an interesting study on Black Consciousness in South Africa, Themba Sono describes the situation of the whites:

> The Liberals had historically been in a dilemma: opposed to apartheid and seeking to win black approval, they found themselves alienating both. Indeed they did not know what to do; only what *not* to do ... liberals found themselves banished from the black ranks. (Sono 1993: 63).

It was no longer a question of how good was a white voice or view, but rather where the black voice was and the black view on the white problem which the black people had carried for so long. This was a shocking experience for well-meaning whites. It seemed as if the criticisms made by Black Consciousness were directed at them rather than at the apartheid authorities. They felt crippled by it while they were fully prepared to oppose the apartheid system. In 'Black Consciousness and the Liberal Tradition' (1991) Budlender says that there were three kinds of criticism in particular. First, there was the reproach that whites automatically dominated in mixed organizations – which was a political point. Second, there was psychological and cultural criticism: for generations the dominant character of white culture had caused destruction and contempt of black culture by ideological, economic and legislative means. As a result black South Africans had always been at a disadvantage. Moreover, from an economic perspective liberalism is the philosophical base of capitalism: it would only lead to more equal chances of exploitation. Third comes personal criticism: their doubts as to whether whites could be trusted at all. In the 1990s the question raised was to what extent space could be created for 'opting in' rather than 'opting out'.

From Black Power to Black Consciousness

At the beginning of the 1970s black student leaders realized that the time had come for views 'which were not stained by ideas from a group that benefited from the status quo', according to a (1972) stencilled document from the South African Students Organization (SASO). All the same, white South Africans, whether because of self-interest or guilt feelings, were the first to be interested in the new ideas of the young black intelligentsia. What kind of ideas were they and where did they come from?

It has often been said that the South African Black Consciousness Movement owes much to Black Power. How important and how direct this influence was has been painstakingly described by Themba Sono. As a former insider of the movement, Sono wrote a critical analysis about his own experience in 'a work about issues and events I helped raise, formulate and guide. I may therefore be seen ultimately as ending up in the invidious role of judge in my own cause' (1993: 1). He discusses in detail the strong impact of Black Power texts (officially banned and illegally distributed in South Africa) on the leaders of SASO. Founded in 1969, it was the first black South African student organization and Steve Biko was its first president. SASO was a preliminary stage of the Black Consciousness Movement (BCM). Sono's information from within is interesting: he places a number of original political statements by Stokely Carmichael and other black American leaders (illegally available in South Africa in the late 1960s) next to their re-writing in SASO documents from the early 1970s. In between the American and South African versions, the internal discussion about the differences and similarities between BP and BC is reported. He demonstrates, for example, how the Black Power statement: 'Before a group can enter the open society it must first close ranks' was adapted to the South African situation, where – unlike the USA – blacks are the majority. In the USA blacks ran the risk of being swallowed by a culture of integration. From the SASO variant it was made clear who was ultimately in power and who would initiate an open society. The result was the following adaptation of the Black Power statement for South African usage: 'Before creating an open society we must first close our ranks' (Sono 1993: 3).

SASO leaders discussed a tape on which Malcolm X distinguishes between 'negro revolution' and 'Black worldwide revolution'. The former is intended to bring about the desegregation of cafeterias and public conveniences and promotes loving one's enemy. The latter would not be satisfied with these cosmetic changes. According to Sono, before Black Power materials became available it was common among black South African radicals to use the negative term non-white in reference to themselves. Important US sources for BCM were the works of Carmichael and Hamilton, Malcolm X, George Jackson and Eldridge Cleaver's *Soul on Ice* (1966), as well as articles from the magazine *Ebony* (banned in South Africa) and, first and foremost, *Black Viewpoints*, a collection of essays published in New York in 1971. It includes the speech 'Black is an Attitude' by the black American member of Congress, Shirley Chisolm, who argues that blacks have said 'yes' to their being black:

> The skin that was once seen as symbolizing their shame is in reality their badge of honour ... *Black is an attitude!* It is the acceptance of all things past and all things present for what they are or were but it is also the rejection of ever letting many of those things happen to anyone in the future. (in Littleton and Burger 1971: 348)

The term Black Consciousness is taken from Jesse Jackson's contribution to the same book, 'Black Power and Black Churches', in which he states that the rise of Black Consciousness is an indispensable force in the development of a black society: 'Black Consciousness is a psychological foundation for black co-operation' (359).

Thanks to the long and bitter lesson of apartheid and the ideas from the USA, blacks were inclined to close ranks. SASO, which was primarily a student organization, disseminated the new ideas mainly in university circles. Members advocated spreading the Black Consciousness message further afield and in 1971 a number of organizations agreed to start a political Black Consciousness organization (Sono 1993: 81).

The first Black Renaissance convention took place in Hammanskraal during December 1974, about fifty-five years after the beginning of US Black Renaissance. Its participants forcefully advocated the solidarity of all blacks against the white Other, as it had become clear that attempts to initiate a dialogue had failed due to the stubbornness of apartheid.

Steve Biko was at the heart of SASO and the brain behind many Black Consciousness ideas. He could have played a prominent role in a non-violent political development process; instead he was murdered. When in 1971 Black Consciousness was defined some argued that the idea was not new in the history of South African resistance (Bernstein 1978; Gerhart 1978): the concept of African Consciousness had been discussed long before, for instance, at the Pan-Africanist Congress (PAC) in the late 1950s. Others made a clear distinction between African and Black:

> African consciousness is rooted in Africa, while black consciousness finds its locale wherever whites were problematic to blacks. This is why, because of the relative freedom black Americans enjoyed in the US compared with blacks in SA, the doctrine and the movement of the BC emerged first in the US. *So Black Consciousness as we know it today in South Africa is a Black American invention.* Case settled. (Sono 1993: 61)

The movement's first aim was to overcome feelings of black inferiority, and to teach people a sense of self-respect and pride. Biko (1978: 49) identified South African Black Consciousness with similar reactions in other parts of the Third World against white exploitation. His view on Black Consciousness can be found in his collected speeches, *I Write What I Like*:

> Black Consciousness is an attitude of mind and a way of life, the most positive call to emanate from the black world for a long time. Its essence is the realisation by the black man of the need to rally together with his brothers around the cause of their oppression – the blackness of their skin – and to operate as a group to rid themselves of the shackles that bind them to perpetual servitude. It seeks to demonstrate the lie that black is an aberration from the 'normal' which is white. It is based on a self-examination which has ultimately led them to believe that by seeking to run away from themselves and to emulate the white man, blacks are insulting the intelligence of whoever created them black. The philosophy of Black Consciousness therefore expresses group pride and the determination of the black to rise and to attain the envisaged self ... Hence thinking along lines of Black Consciousness makes the black man see himself as a being complete in himself. (1978: 91)

There are striking similarities here with the Black Arts Movement and Negritude. Here too, black and white interconnectedness cannot be denied in what Sekye-Otu called the 'dialectic of experience' (1996). Paradoxically, the two groups, separated by the apartheid system, are at the same time inextricably linked by the history of apartheid.

Michael Chapman (1982: 17) cites Alan Boesak's definition of Black

Consciousness as 'an awareness by black people that their humanity is constituted by their blackness ... It is a determination to be judged no longer by white values, and it signifies a rediscovery of their history and culture'. This is reminiscent of Césaire's earlier definition of 'négritude'. A famous slogan ran: 'Black man, you are on your own' and from this knowledge 'the New Black' was born, the black man who was freed from his old complexes. SASO realized that Black Consciousness should not stand for isolation, nor should it adhere exclusively to an anti-white point of view; it should be a positive ideology. Consequently, according to Gerhart (1978: 71), people 'began to shop for ideas in the black world outside South Africa'. Some ideas were gleaned from Black Power in the USA. However, the ideas of Panafricanism, the points of view of Cheikh Anta Diop on history, Kaunda's African humanism and Nyerere's African socialism were also studied. In *I Write What I Like* Steve Biko refers approvingly to all of them, as well as to the Antillians Fanon and Césaire. For instance, he cites from Césaire's *Cahier* the well-known words: 'No race possesses the monopoly of beauty, intelligence, force, and there is room for all of us at the rendezvous of victory' (Biko 1978: 61). The recognition of a common black experience was more obvious than historical and cultural differences.

On 16 June 1971, Soweto schoolchildren went into the streets to protest against the second-rate 'Bantu educational system' of the South African government. During the outbreak that followed, the police shot more than a thousand people, among them large numbers of children and youngsters on the streets of Soweto, as well as in other townships. On September 5 1977 Biko was killed by the secret police. The people openly protested and stringent anti-black measures were taken by the authorities: most BCM leaders were arrested and many organizations and newspapers, as well as literature and theatre, were banned.

'Into the Heart of Negritude'

The Black Consciousness culture thrived for some time against all odds. Those who were seeking fundamental political changes were increasingly forced to go underground. Against the divide-and-rule policy of the government and its group politics based on language, colour and ethnicity, the blacks (those who were marked 'nie-blankes' by the authorities, hence also the so-called 'kleurlinge' and Indian people) emphasized their solidarity and their collective difference from the whites.

Over the years, apartheid had given rise to the four 'black' themes in South African literature: suffering, revolt, triumph and dialogue. During the 1970s there was a clear thematic shift in both poetry and theatre: instead of emphasizing suffering, injustice and protest against the whites, anger becomes increasingly central. This anger no longer addresses the Other. It is exclusively directed at its own audience in exactly the same way as occurred in the Black Arts Movement in the USA during the 1960s. For instance in Gwala's 'Getting Off the Ride' from *Jol'iinkomo* (1975):

I ask again, what is Black?
Black is when you get off the ride.
Black is point of self realisation
Black is point of new reason
Black is point of: NO NATIONAL DECEPTION! (qtd in Chapman 1996: 336)

As he told me in an interview in 1975, Lewis Nkosi had started writing to prove that he could do what white writers had done before him. During the 1970s this concept was completely abandoned by younger writers. The ghetto generation wrote for its own people. Like the Negritude writers, they also opted mainly for the medium of poetry: in the tense political atmosphere of the townships the sustained effort over a long period needed for novel writing was difficult to achieve. Moreover, militant poetry lends itself well to oral presentation; township readings became very popular. Poetry serves an important purpose, in Oswald Msthali's words (1976: 125): 'The black poets who have sprung from seemingly nowhere are the oases in the bleak desert of black man's life from where he will drink the waters of liberation as he forges his way to the green pastures of complete freedom.' In response to Mtshali's later collection of poems *Fireflames* (which was banned for some time), Mphahlele notes the harsh, apocalyptic tone of recent poetry (*Rand Daily Mail*, 19 December 1980). The black public is only inspired by anger and restricts itself to communication within its own cultural and political circles. White domination has energetically stimulated the attraction of blackness, black culture and Black Consciousness. From the early 1970s SASO leaders had been organizing popular cultural Black Community programmes consisting of poetry performances and theatre productions. These programmes, which were sometimes literally entitled 'Into the Heart of Negritude', included poetry in translation by Francophone African poets such as Senghor, David Diop, Bernard Dadié and other Negritude poets, as well as South African authors such as Mtshali, Serote, Sepamla, Gwala and many others.

In 1972, at a meeting with several SASO leaders in Durban, I was struck by the differences in view concerning Senghor among these radicals, as they called themselves, and my own students in Congo who considered Negritude reactionary and would have preferred to have Senghor's works removed from the curriculum. For SASO members, however, Negritude was an indispensable cultural phase that would only end with freedom and victory, at which point new perspectives would be opened. They aligned the Negritude movement with their struggle for liberation. Still, looking back Sono admits that Negritude played only a marginal role in South Africa, the 'minor role in validating, intellectually, the notion of blackness' (1993: 113). To my question of how people from outside could contribute to the liberation struggle, the answer was quite simple:

> The world is one, but everyone has to work in the place where he lives: we, the people in South Africa, will do what needs to be done here; when you will be back home in the North, your task will be to stimulate structural changes in the place were you live, which will not be without consequences here either, if you people do your job well enough.

In South Africa post-Soweto poetry remained a weapon in the struggle, its aim being 'a revolutionary future' (Chapman and Dangor 1982: 15). The relevant literature was written by blacks for blacks, the writer's political involvement being an unconditional requirement. According to Mothobi Mutloatse (1980: 4) this black literature attracted very few white readers. If they were interested at all, a devastating government policy of censorship denied them the right to be informed about burning issues in their own country — worse for them than for us, Mutloatse commented: whites no longer have the slightest idea of what is going on in the country where they live.

Over the years large numbers of South Africans fled into exile, among them many writers and artists, a tragic loss for the culture. Writers, playwrights and journalists especially had to choose (self-)censorship, imprisonment or exile. Stringent censorship made half of the South African Anglophone writers, of all colours, leave the country by the end of the 1960s. This was a dramatic situation, both for the writers, who in exile had to struggle for a living in a foreign country and for South Africa's literature and culture. Even works by the writers who stayed behind were increasingly banned. In 1979 Richard Rive summarized the consequences for the next generation of writers:

> Black writers in South Africa today haven't got much of a precedent to fall back on, because most of the older writers have been banned, so that the young people have no access to them. There is a big gap in South African literature between 1963 and 1971. The new generation really doesn't know much about us, and they don't know much of the writing that is going on outside. (in Lindfors 1985: 57)

The literature of the South Africans in exile, Stephen Gray concluded (1979: 2) 'no longer exists in any real sense for those who stayed behind, or for those who were born after the first losses'. Not many foreign titles were available in South Africa; in particular books about Africa, Africans, Black Power and black theology were banned. Culturally, South Africa became increasingly isolated, a situation that was enhanced by boycotts from abroad.

In *The African Image* (1974), partly rewritten during exile, the South African writer Ezekiel Mphahlele added a new chapter entitled 'Negritude Revisited'. Like Adotevi, he saw the movement as an impossible artistic programme for an Africa where the historical factors on which it used to be based no longer existed. He considered the 'black is beautiful' message irrelevant to people suffering from hunger and oppression. As far back as the 1960s he had called the Negritude elite dishonest and its policy a form of auto-colonization: 'Negritude remains the intellectual pastime of the governing elite' (in Feuser 1987: 263). At the time he wrote this from the perspective of an exile living in independent Africa, while Black Consciousness was enjoying popularity inside South Africa.

Mphahlele was one of the first exiles to return, in spite of the protests of others about such political incorrectness. In his essay 'Africa in Exile' (1982: 48) he justified his homecoming:

Exile had become a ghetto of the mind. My return was a way of dealing with the concrete reality of blackness in South Africa rather than with the phantoms and echoes that attend exile.

Since the 1980s writers, artists and critics in South Africa have begun to question the emphasis on black–white polarity. They have started to comment on the artistic handling and meaning of 'black reality' and the consequences of obligatory political engagement in art and culture; the restrictive prescriptions for writers and artists as against their freedom of expression; and the relation between literature and propaganda. As argued in Chapter 4, these issues are similar to those addressed in the American context throughout the twentieth century where there never was a unanimous conclusion. The same points were now debated passionately in view of the new South Africa.

Beyond protest

One of the most active participants in this cultural debate has been Njabulo Ndebele, writer and professor of literature. Without actually mentioning Negritude he described the well-known themes as characteristic of the South African poetry of the 1970s and 1980s:

> What we have ... is protest literature that merely changed emphasis: from the moral evil of apartheid, to the existential and moral worth of blackness; from moral indignation, to anger; from relatively self-composed reasonableness, to uncompromising bitterness; from the exterior manifestation of oppression, to the interior psychology of that oppression. That may be why the bulk of the writing was poetry. But while the poetry turns its attention toward the self, it is still very much conscious of the white 'other'. (Ndebele 1988: 210)

Ndebele points out that power relations in South Africa are no longer the same. Partly due to the persistent stream of township poetry, a new collective power has reached workers, students and school children. For literature and the arts, which had been forced for so long to inexorable political commitment, there are tremendous cultural possibilities and new challenges:

> The challenge is to free the entire social imagination of the oppressed from the laws of perception that have characterized Apartheid society. For writers this means freeing the creative process itself from those very laws. It means extending the writer's perception of what can be written about, and the means and methods of writing. (Ndebele 1988: 211)

According to Ndebele, old patterns of thought are giving way to new ideas about the culture of South Africa in which the oppressed, rather than the oppressors, make their own future. The dialectic has changed. It is up to the oppressed to propose new definitions; the former oppressor can react but no longer has the initiative. This is one of the achievements of Black Consciousness. The rhetoric of oppression is replaced by a discourse of exploration signifying 'an open-endedness in the use of language, a search for originality of expression and a sensitivity to dialogue' (216). A post-protest culture has to chart new worlds waiting to be explored in art. Ndebele emphasizes the importance of independent thinking intellectuals and artists who refuse to be controlled by any kind of political power. Even when ANC Arts and Culture representatives speak in the name of the masses, it is not enough to have a culture in which the leaders of the ANC are in power instead of the National Party:

> The oppressed of South Africa will want to re-enter the contest for power in history with both their minds and their hands. They will accept no assurances that the thinking and doing have been done for them. They will want nothing less than the writing of their own texts. (Ndebele 1991: 141)

Albie Sachs's provocative lecture 'Preparing Ourselves for Freedom' was another demand for space and openness in art and culture. This text, originally intended as a contribution to an ANC in-house seminar, provoked heated discussions. Sachs, himself one of the leaders of the ANC (who lost an arm when opening a letter bomb), pleaded for an escape from the solemn commitment to engagement that he and others had imposed on artists and writers. Now space must be created for contradictions and for uncovering hidden tensions. Isn't that what the power of the arts is all about? What have we been fighting for, he wondered, 'if not for the right to give shape to every aspect of humanity?' That is why the ANC should cease to see art as an instrument in the struggle because that is a restriction of art. Then he made a statement that must have caused a shockwave among the closed ranks:

> White is beautiful. In case anyone feels that the bomb has affected my head, I will repeat the affirmation, surely the first time it has been made at an ANC conference: white is beautiful. Allow me to explain. I first heard this formulation from a Mozambican poet and former guerilla, whose grandmother was African and grandfather was Portuguese. Asked to explain Frelimo's view on the slogan: Black is beautiful, he replied – Black is beautiful, Brown is beautiful, White is beautiful. I think that affirmation is beautiful. (Sachs 1990: 26)

His message is the same as Ndebele's: the old structures must disappear and if the whites can shed their arrogance then their contribution can be rich and valuable. In the context of colonial domination, white consciousness means oppression, while Black Consciousness means resistance against oppression. However, in the struggle for freedom, black and white joined hands to fight for the right to be free citizens in a free country and to share the culture of the entire country, for culture in the widest sense of the word stands for our view of ourselves and the surrounding world.

The results of the 1994 elections marked a new phase in South Africa. What have been the achievements of Black Consciousness and what will become of it? Its great achievement, thanks to Steve Biko's inspiring ideas, was to make the majority of South Africans conscious of their own value and dignity:

> No African man and woman today calls a white person *Baas* or *Missus*; nor does a black person quake and shiver at the beckoning call of the white boss. Not only has the black person psychologically empowered himself, that is humanised himself, he has also extended the hand of liberation to the white person; for the latter has been freed from the suffocating burden of being a demigod. (Sono 1993: 86)

From both a psychological and a cultural perspective, this is a positive result. But the success of Black Consciousness was gained to the detriment of attention to class and gender issues in the struggle for liberation. (The gender factor will be discussed in the next two chapters.) The class differences are still poignantly visible in the material distance between black and white, both in South Africa and the USA, but also visible, surely, in the growing class differences and living conditions, not only between black and white, but also between black and black and white and white. The future of Black Consciousness depends on how this problem will be solved. The demise of apartheid has led to a society based on class rather than 'race' relations. Sono concludes that Black Consciousness has to transform itself to human consciousness:

> As a political ideology, then, the BCM formalism has no future. It has already died in the US where it originated. (Afrocentricity in the US may exist as a curricular adjunct but as a political force it is dubious. I should know since I was instrumental in helping launch Afrocentricity in the US).

Since the dismantling of apartheid has 'pulled the rug from under BCM's feet', white racism will be cursed by blacks as before, but this will not be sufficient to mobilize a political force. The movement must stress 'bread and butter' issues rather than ideology if they want the masses to join (130).

Cultural perspectives also altered, along with political change. For a long time art and culture had been influenced, indeed conditioned, by apartheid. According to Njabulo Ndebele (1991: 35), there is nothing so dangerous as the repression of any kind of criticism: 'We must be prepared to subject *everything* to rigorous intellectual scrutiny followed by open and fearless discussion.'

This need for cultural space and freedom, advocated by South African intellectuals such as Ndebele and Sachs, is also felt outside South Africa. Increasingly, voices have been heard over the past decades in the Caribbean, in favour of mutual cultural enrichment by creative syncretism (Glissant 1981; Harris 1983) or *créolité* (Bernabé *et al.* 1989; Condé and Cottenet-Hage 1995).

Maryse Condé summarized diaspora developments:

> People fell victim to the delusion that they had to find their identity in Africa. The Caribbean is a place where people from different origins and different cultures have met. There have been attempts to kind of split us up in an inventory of different origins. This element is from India, this from Africa, this from Europe. That is wrong. It is not very important to know where these elements come from. What is important is that they form a whole, and the Caribbeans have made this whole, a way of life, a culture, an identity. (interview)

6

Black is beautiful or the whiteness of feminism

There is a great stir about colored men getting their rights, but not a word about the colored women; and if colored men get their rights, and not colored women theirs, you see the colored men will be masters over the women, and it will be just as bad as it was before.

Sojourner Truth 1867

She is confronted by a woman question and a race problem, and is as yet an unknown or unacknowledged factor in both.

Anna Julia Cooper 1892

Survival is not an academic skill.

Audre Lorde 1985

Interest in gender evolved from feminism as a political movement. This has resulted in new research questions in the humanities. However, the specific relationship between race and gender, or race, class and gender has long been neglected. Black women and women of Third World countries have changed this situation. This chapter will deal with some reactions and reflections on race and gender as presented and experienced by African-American women. Again, the main issue will be the question of the closing of ranks: whose ranks, in what circumstances and for what purpose? Who were included or excluded and on whose behalf were such decisions made?

Racism and sexism

Women from non-Western parts of the world have often directed fierce criticism at the Western feminist movement which, they say, has marginalized or ignored them completely (Davies 1983; Steady 1993). American black women have been no less severe in their criticism of white feminists in their own country. It is impossible, of course, to give an outline of the many black movements, discussions, streams and suggested solutions. I restrict myself to a discussion of some viewpoints on race and gender and its consequent determination of boundaries between insiders and outsiders, first from the point of view of black women in the USA, then of women in Africa.

The experience in and with one's own group is placed central in the American black women's movement and in research done in the field of black women's studies. Concrete experience is considered an important criterion for credibility:

> Theorizing by Black feminists develops out of Black women's experiences of multiple interrelated oppressions including (but not limited to) racism/ ethnocentrism, sexism/homophobia and classism ... Black feminism's theorizing is rooted in Black communities and nourished by them even as it challenges those very communities to address issues of internal oppressions. (James 1993: 2)

From this perspective, black feminist thinking is produced by African-Americans. Black womens' communities constantly refer this thinking to 'a particular set of historical, material, and epistemological conditions', as Collins (1990: 322) puts it. She adds that black feminist thinking can only develop under these specific conditions. In a footnote she states that while black men, white women and people of another race, class or gender should be encouraged to interpret black feminist thinking, should teach it and analyse it critically; it will be different. The danger could be, however, that this constructed difference is celebrated as an unchanging world of experience. In time it might even become a framework for group characteristics labelling people as inevitably 'natural' (Anthias and Yuval-Davies 1992).

Within one's own group, though, the position of researchers is problematic since it is a mixture of belonging and taking distance.The very theorizing of black feminist thinking necessarily cannot but imply a certain distance towards these women's groups. When justifying their objects and methods of research, American black female researchers often strongly appeal to their shared experience as a woman with other women within their common black culture. An essay written by Elsa Barkley Brown on the history of black women has the revealing subtitle: 'How my mother taught me to be an historian in spite of my academic training' (Collins 1990: 312).

Taking this a step further, we find that the similarities between the black experience and that of the women are being emphasized on the grounds that both involve knowledge gained from shared experience: the best way to understand someone's ideas is to share the experiences which gave rise to those ideas. Empathy makes people connected knowers (Collins 1990: 312). The question is whether male and female researchers should be of the same racial, social or cultural group as the people they study. Here, belief in a common black history seems to make this prerequisite imperative. Further, the feminist view that there are experiences and a history which women share irrespective of race, class, denomination or sexual nature underlines its necessity.

In both cases, an epistomology of divorce is opposed to an epistomology of connection. The first is characterized by 'impersonal knowledge procedures' in its attempt to establish the truth. With the second approach 'truth emerges through care' (Collins 1990: 318). In its extreme form, this exclusive approach implies that there is no question of difference and distance between researchers and members of the group they study. This is expressed by scholars in terms of 'we' and 'us': e.g. 'we' were not interested in the women's movement, or: 'our' institutionalized exploitation (King 1990). In such a context, class differences and the difference in power position between researcher and informer risks not being discussed. In fact during any research a certain distance between subject and object is inevitable for the simple reason that the researcher will process and publish the data retrieved from the exchange of information on the shared experience under his or her name. (This point will be elaborated further in Chapter 8). All the same, a researcher can profit tremendously from close personal experience and inside knowledge and, one hopes, the group being researched will also benefit or profit from the results.

There can also be a disadvantage in being too connected with the object of research. As a scholarly principle the impact of power relations and interests as against or in favour of shared insiders' experience should always be taken into account – not only in the relations between insiders and outsiders, but also between representatives of the same culture, gender and social group. Ultimately, scholarship can only benefit from information and exchange of research results from different perspectives. All kinds of insiders (black, white, men, women) should submit their own group discourse to other groups for comment. This may ultimately result in everyone gaining knowledge. What can be gained from black women's critical perspectives, as from all critical epistemologies, is their continuous challenging and questioning of existing truth and knowledge claims, ideally including their own (see also Chapter 8).

Black and female in the USA

A collective identity can only be understood in the context of its social and political history. The physical as well as cultural resistance of slaves to their masters was the first affirmation of a distinct black cultural identity in the USA (Schulte Nordholt 1960). Slavery meant a complete lack of spare time and therefore an impeded cultural development. Generations of men and women devoted their lives to achieving freedom of expression. Such pioneers as Sojourner Truth, Harriet Jacobs, Frederick Douglass and William Wells Brown wrote about the sexual abuse of slave women by white men. Thus the terrain was created on which later battles were fought.

Some researchers (Lerner 1972; Stimpson 1988; King 1990: 265) trace black feminist thinking to the early nineteenth century with such women as Sojourner Truth and Anna Julia Cooper. Although black women made their own contribution in the struggle for liberation, it took a long time before their share and their names were recognized in historical research. From the 1970s onwards – mainly on the initiative of women – attention has been given to these sisters 'who were doomed to silence by tradition'.

With *Women, Race and Class* (1981), Angela Davis was among the first to link the struggle of the liberation of women with that of black people. She connected the two movements which until then had operated separately and cast new light on both from the perspective of class and class struggle. She underlined the fact that the black woman is the major absentee in the debate which started in 1918 and was taken up again in the 1970s about the culture of slavery. The usual topics for discussion were the black woman's marital situation and her forced or deliberate sex with white men since these were, or so it seemed, especially humiliating for the black man. Davis argues for a more historical study of the extremely heavy task of female slaves: they had to work just as hard as the men on the estates and were additionally the victims of sexual abuse and used as breeding machines of new labour. The resistance of women included poisoning their masters, sabotage, rebellion, and fleeing to the North. Harriet Beecher Stowe's *Uncle Tom's Cabin* creates a false image of the slave Elizah and her decent master and mistress: Eliza does not say a word about the inhumanity of slavery. She is depicted, according to Davis, as a naive mother figure who was widely acclaimed by the cultural propaganda of the whites and in the slave community of those days: 'Eliza is white motherhood incarnate, but in black face' (Davis 1981: 27).

It is ironical, Davis says, that the most important anti-slavery document of the time not only contained racist ideas justifying slavery, but also sexist ideas presupposing that women did not take part in the political arena in which the battle against slavery was fought. This is the real image of the black woman:

she worked under the whip of her master, fought for her family, was beaten and raped, but never gave up:

> It was those women who passed on to their nominally free female descendants a legacy of hard work, perseverance and self-reliance, a legacy of tenacity, resistance and insistence on sexual equality – in short, a legacy spelling out standards for a new womanhood. (Davis 1981: 29)

This is in strong contrast with the white women in the USA who would sometimes describe their marriages in terms of slavery. Such a comparison had a negative effect on the position of blacks: if middle-class white marriages were slavery then slavery was not that bad after all. Thus the relationship between white and black women has often been strained due to a difference in power and from ignorance of each other's situation. American white women often had just as bad a reputation as employers in the time of slavery as European women in colonial Africa.

The movement for equal civil rights was a lost cause: it could have made real progress towards dissolving the inequality between black and white and between men and women, but the two emancipatory movements crippled instead of strengthening each other. bell hooks (1981) argues that, at decisive moments, white women let down their black counterparts and renounced their feminist principles. Instead of promoting women's interests they voted along with their fathers, husbands or brothers at elections. Racism was also an issue in the movement for women's suffrage. White women thought they were more worthy of the right to vote than black men (i.e. men):

> This is a story of a vision betrayed. For the white women who led this movement came to trade upon their privileges as the daughters (sisters, wives, and mothers) of powerful white men in order to gain for themselves some share of the political power those men possessed ... This history of racism in the early women's movement, has been sustained by contemporary white feminists. Within organizations, most twentieth-century black women encounter myriad experiences that deny their reality ... When present at all, women of color are under-represented and have marginal and subordinate roles (Andolsen, in King 1990: 282)

In the struggle for suffrage, black women were in a constant dilemma: whether to support white women who publicly professed racism or to choose for black and consequently agree with a patriarchal social order which does not allow women their own voice.

In the USA black women draw the borderline between insiders and outsiders in various ways. First is the line between black and white in general, and between black women and white women in particular. Second, hesitatingly and cautiously, there is the border between black women and black men; third, only occasionally, between black women in different social strata; fourth, and only by way of exception, between women (white and black) on the one side and men (white and black) on the other. In the next chapter I will look into some African comments on gender relations and some African insiders' reservations concerning American views of and comments on African culture and gender issues.

Borderlines between insiders and outsiders were sometimes denied and at others affirmed or changed, depending on the interests and perspectives of those concerned. As long as racism is experienced as the primary external threat, black women will not be inclined to vote for a white women's movement, nor will they speak out on sexism in their own circles. In such a situation, ranks have to be closed. According to bell hooks, the women told themselves that racism was the worst threat and that sexism was insignificant in comparison; they were too frightened to admit that sexism can be as oppressive as racism (hooks 1989: 21).

Many black women, even those who emphasized their position as women within their own culture, felt safer seeking their identity within their own community. Therefore, it should not be surprising that the matrilineal cultural heritage has been highly valued by consecutive generations of black female writers. A well-known example is Alice Walker who discovered a metaphorical mother in Zora Neale Hurston. She also identified with the silenced female slave poets of the South who were sexually abused and politically oppressed. They passed their visions and dreams to their daughters and granddaughters by way of songs. White women are said to think back through their mothers (in the words of Virginia Woolf), but black women are a different case, Walker argues. Their children do not benefit from a racist society, whereas white children do. She concludes that: 'despite shared motherhood, race separates women; racism, not gender or motherhood, oppress the black woman' (Walker 1983: 361; Sadoff 1990: 205). American 'poor white trash' kids might object here that they have not benefited from society either. Strategically, however, the reasons for emphasizing 'race' instead of class or gender as the main issue in the struggle for political change are deeply rooted in a history of racial oppression.

Gender and the Black Arts Movement

In the collection of essays *Reading Black, Reading Feminist* (1990) Henry Louis Gates indicates the differences between black women and black men. In the introduction he argues that during the time of the Harlem Renaissance and the Black Arts Movement, women never manifested their own culture as bombastically and self-consciously as men. Most of the older black writers denied any black influence 'or they eagerly claim a white paternity – black female authors often claim descent from other black women literary ancestors' (Gates 1990: 3)

Before the 1970s it was rare for black female writers to gain any serious attention from the literary establishment; Gwendolyn Brooks was one of the few exceptions. While an increasing number of female writers, especially poets initially, managed to find publishers and a reading public, the 'real' face of the Black Arts Movement was determined by male writers: 'the legacy of male chauvinism in the black literary world continued to predominate' (Hernton 1987: 40). Women's tasks were restricted to operating the duplicator and collecting documentary material in the library (Stimpson 1988: 31). The women, who had first shown complete solidarity with the consciousness-raising character of the movement, now started to criticize such male chauvinism.

Black female writers carried on the Black Arts Movement in their own way:

Black women's writings since 1970 represent worlds in which the Black Goddess/Black Queen stereotypes of the Black Arts Movement – and the corresponding Black Warrior/Black Prince stereotypes for men – are rejected as cardboard stereotypes just as pernicious as the Sambo-Mammy types of the white plantation tradition. (Gates 1990: 4)

Women reacted more and more critically to the 'Macho philosophy of the Black Power Black Arts Movement [which] resulted in so many demeaning experiences for the women, that many of them began to protest and eventually break away' (Hernton 1987: 42). Following these new developments, a fierce debate on culture and gender was sparked off in the black community. It was a response to Ntozake Shange's Broadway play *For Colored Girls Who Have Considered Suicide When the Rainbow is Enuf* (1977) which was received enthusiastically by critics in the white press. There was also Michele Wallace's *Black Macho and the Myth of the Superwoman* (1978). And there was of course Alice Walker's *The Color Purple* (1976) and the film production of her novel by Steven Spielberg which many felt exacerbated the situation.

Walker's novel shifted boundaries. She greatly shocked the black community — and not only the men — by breaking the most important unwritten rule which had stood from the time of the slave narratives: to write only and exclusively about the white oppression of blacks. Walker describes black men using brutal force against black women. She uses the traditional form of the slave narrative not to affirm the old white–black tradition of violence, but to show that black women are also the slaves of their own husbands. Calvin Hernton (1990: 31) sums up the objections and accusations against Alice Walker and her novel, a long list in which the film and the book seem to be dealt with interchangeably:

1. Negative stereotype images were presented of black men.
2. There were no strong black role models, giving an imbalanced description of the black male.
3. She does not make clear that racism and white hatred and oppression made the black male behave the way he did toward black women.
4. There were negative implications for the family, similar to the outrageous Moynihan Report (see below).
5. Walker should not have aired dirty linen before the eyes of the whites, who will use *The Color Purple* to justify their genocide against the black race.
6. The film should never have been awarded a prize.
7. The novel and film have received too much publicity among the whites: so there must be something wrong with it. Alice Walker's road to fame in white America had been too easy, embraced as she was by white feminists.
8. Steven Spielberg was blamed as being part of the white man's conspiracy against blacks.
9. Too much or too little lesbianism in the film.
10. Blacks like the ones in the film do not exist, they are implausible characters and these were unrealistic false images.

Talkshows, debates and demonstrations in front of cinemas were held over this immense controversy. Here again was the old question of the Harlem Renaissance: How should writers depict black characters? Negative images of men revealed lack of loyalty on the part of black women. It was even said that there was a 'conspiracy' of female writers against black male writers: it was 'alleged that the women were using their pens to 'put down' black men before the eyes of the world.' The strongest accusations were hurled at Toni Morrison and Alice Walker, the latter being accused of being an 'avowed lesbian' (Hernton 1990: xxv). In response to this, it was argued that so far black male literature had been full of discriminatory portraits of black women.

For a long time in the literary history of black America the first black female writers had hardly been discussed. In their struggle for equality black women started to study their own culture armed with new questions. They set out to describe the lives and works of the black women who had taken part in the anti-slavery movement and had been important for black culture.

The New Negro writers had almost all been men. Zora Neale Hurston, had been more or less regarded as an outsider. Only much later did her most important books receive serious attention, thanks mainly to Alice Walker. As the often quoted words of Stokely Carmichael show, manliness still predominated in the Black Arts Movement: 'The only position for women is the prone position' or 'The women's place is seven feet behind the men' (Wallace 1978: 18; Hernton 1987: 41).

In her controversial and much abused *Black Macho and the Myth of the Superwoman* (1978), Michele Wallace presented a rather provocative analysis of the black male–female relationship during and since the Black Arts Movement. She argues that there has never been a discussion concerning black male–female relationships since the Civil Rights' movement (27). She came under severe attack from all sides, from black men and women alike.

In the debate concerning male black sexism, black women were accused of having given in to white feminist propaganda. Such accusations have often been made, as has the other reproach that the women were sowing discord in the black community. The resentment of black men towards black women concerned:

- the growing independence of black female writers;
- their influence on black women;
- their growing visibility in American society;
- the recognition they found in 'mainstream' culture (Hernton 1987: 45).

Wallace admitted that it was hard to blame black men, who were also products of a history of oppression. Nevertheless, she argues, there is a difference in gender power: the black man was in a position to define the black woman. He decided whether and to what extent she was a woman. This has made the black woman vulnerable, doubly vulnerable in fact, as a black and as a woman.

Against this the black sociologist Robert Staples (1973) argued that whether they wanted or not black men were not in a position to be sexist. Therefore black women should be the prop of their husbands. But this was the problem: he was uncertain whether black women played their role very well. This could explain why 'the best' and 'the most brilliant' black men preferred white women as partners (Giddings 1984: 355).

Interracial relations started in the 1960s with the Student Non-violent Coordinating Committee (SNCC). This organisation of black and white students mounted a joint campaign. One result was a sudden flourishing of love relations between black men and white women. The reaction of black women was very unfriendly :

> It all seemed strangely inappropriate, poorly timed. In '67, black was angry, anywhere from vaguely to militantly anti-white; black was sexy and had unlimited potential. What did the black man want with a white woman now? (Wallace 1978: 24)

bell hooks (1981: 112) explains this phenomenon against the background of the American patriarchal vision that women embody sexual badness. Since black is immediately associated with evil, black women are considered even more immoral than their white counterparts: 'Sexual racism has caused black women to bear the brunt of society's need to degrade and devalue women.' The effect is that the white woman rises in the racial hierarchy to the symbol of purity, and in this aspect she can return the man's self-regard.

It is generally assumed that one of the reasons for hatred against black women is the Moynihan Report of 1965 concerning 'The Negro Family'. It argued that there was a link between the social and economic problems of the black community and the reputed matriarchal family structure. Not enough male authority existed in the black family or in the black community. The matriarchal structure laid a crushing burden on the black man. It roughly came down to saying that black men were robbed of their male power by black women. As a matter of fact the same argument was raised by black men in the South African context of apartheid (see chapter 7).

Moynihan advised black men to choose preferably 'male' professions, for instance the army. This suited the administration very well – after all, it was the time of the Vietnam war. It struck women in particular that the author of the report associated manhood with violence (Wallace 1978: 26; Davis 1981: 13; hooks 1981: 103). For blacks who did not follow his advice to join the army, another option was to join the Black Muslim movement, which also prescribed male dominant role patterns and female subservience. Black women who joined the movement felt attracted to the promise that they would be respected, while in those circles all non-Muslim women were by contrast regarded negatively (hooks 1981: 109).

Machos and matriarchs

The myth supposedly spread by the Moynihan Report that black women were castrating matriarchs had far-reaching consequences in the black community.

Frustrations that had accumulated over time were transmuted into feelings of hostility towards women. Black women were totally defenceless; the men agreed with Moynihan:

> The black woman had gotten out of hand. She was too strong, too hard, too evil, too castrating. She got all the jobs, all the everything. The black man had never had a chance. No wonder he wanted a white woman. He needed a rest. The black woman should be more submissive, and above all, keep her big mouth shut. (Wallace 1978: 24)

The matriarchy myth was used to manipulate the black woman and force her exclusively to serve her own race, to restrict her role to the traditional Western image of a woman sitting at home, showing feminine behaviour and devoting herself to housekeeping (King 1990: 278). The black woman adapted or she wrote poems about 'that men's business with white women', like Sonia Sanchez, inspired by the anger of a female student who lost her boyfriend to a white woman. Once again one is reminded of Sophie's remark in Oyono's novel: 'What do they have that I don't have?'

> what a white woman got
> cept her white pussy
> always sucking after blk/ness
> what a white woman got
> cept her straight hair
> covering her fucked up mind
> ... yeah.
> what a white woman got? (in Baker 1990: 331)

The first time Sanchez read it in front of a large audience all the black women got up, stamped their feet and cried out loud 'Yeah!' The uproar continued for five minutes. 'And the white women who were there were shocked because no one had said anything in such a fashion before' (*ibid*).

Black Power did not become the movement of equality but the movement of black manhood, of the black macho, according to Michele Wallace who speaks provokingly about 'deification of the genitals that would later characterize the prose of the Black Movement' (1978: 92). The mythic white belief in black virility (that old projection of the whites since the time of slavery), adopted by black men, confirmed the stereotypical idea that blacks were more emotional than whites or, as Leroi Jones quoted by Wallace put it: 'more "natural" than the white simply because the black has fewer things between him and reality ... therefore "wilder," harder, and almost insatiable in his lovemaking' (98).

It was argued that white culture made the white man impotent and the black men extra macho. Rape was not a crime against women but a political act. Under the influence of leaders such as Leroi Jones and Eldridge Cleaver, machoism and primitivism became manly virtues in the black movement. The black man mistakes the black perspective for the white, complained Michele Wallace, 'unaware that he has accepted a definition of manhood that is destructive to himself and that negates the best efforts of his past' (118). Its 'color line' division reminds somewhat of Senghor's black–white division in *émotion nègre* and *raison hellène*.

As the black woman was blamed for being too strong, the women's movement was a difficult option: she was being expected to become passive, and 'feminine', servile and unemployed, she who had worked outside the home since the time of slavery. Her objections to the women's movement were that she wanted to live in harmony with her husband and that the oppression felt as a black was worse than the oppression experienced as a woman. The whole discussion caused a sense of guilt. Many black women felt disloyal to their own people, as if they were conspiring with the whites in the oppression of the black man (Wallace 1978: 177; hooks 1981: 178).

Gradually women started to rebel more and more conspicuously against sexism. Only a minority opted openly for a joint movement; many preferred a black feminist movement (Joseph and Lewis 1981; King 1990: 278;) separate from the whites.

Michele Wallace concludes that sexual myths about black and white men or black and white women profited no one (1978: 229). The acceptance of black woman without preconceived notions of categories failed. Against this pessimistic view, hooks holds that, although there were many anti-woman noises in the Black Power rhetoric, the whole Black Movement should not be valued negatively; it brought about social and economic improvements. However, there were ambivalences: on the one hand it attacked the whites, on the other the interracial patriarchal ties among men could not be denied. Similar ambivalences have been noticed in Africa (cf. Chapter 7):

> The strongest bonding element between militant black men and white men was their shared sexism – they both believed in the inherent inferiority of women and supported male dominance ... Racism has always been a divisive force separating black men and white men, and sexism has been a force that unites the two groups. (hooks 1981: 99)

Interracial developments

Many black middle-class women continued to stick to the principle of closing ranks: that racial identity was more important than gender or class identity. Many of the central issues of the white middle-class women's movement did not affect them in the same way. In 1978 Michele Wallace argued that black women did not want a feminist consciousness because they were afraid of the disapproval of their own community.

Much has changed over the last two decades. Black women have become more openly interested in feminism, while the white women's movement gradually realized that its own situation and interests were less prototypical of women at large than it had imagined. At the root of this white misconception was the idea that the family was always patriarchal and that an individualistic world view and female separatism were everybody's aim. Black women, with a different family experience, had never felt attracted to this (Sadoff 1990: 281).

The differences between black and white women's political, cultural and racial history have been outlined in detail by the American black women's movement. The importance of black feminist criticism at American university departments of black studies and women's studies has caused a remarkable shift in the relationship between racial and gender solidarity over the past years. The Black Power/Black Arts Movement of the 1960s and 1970s also contributed to black women's growing frustration as to the restrictions imposed upon them by their brothers in the struggle. In different ways these developments stimulated the difficult breakthrough to more outspoken ideas about sexism.

In spite of power relations characteristic of both racism and sexism, black women's responses to the two forms of oppression appear to be diverse. Much depended on what people experienced as a primary threat: racism, sexism or both. These factors are complicated even more by the role of class. This problem will not be discussed in the present context, but the idea that the emancipatory movement of the 1960s and 1970s was mainly in the interest of the black middle class has been generally accepted. The majority of poor blacks did not benefit from the Black Power movement, from liberalization, nor from the new climate of equal rights (e.g. King 1990: 279; Gates and West 1996).

For the majority of women in the world, their liberation from sexual oppression has always been associated with other kinds of oppression such as slavery, imperialism, colonialism, neo-colonialism, poverty, racism and apartheid. Dominant structures restrict the liberty of those who do not belong. What is at stake ultimately is access to the means of production and communication (but doesn't this also hold for men?):

It is increasingly becoming clear that women do not belong to a universal category and that the significance of being female varies with technology, setting, class, context, task, rank, age, profession, kinship, wealth and economics. (Steady 1993: 98)

For a long time the Black Movement of the 1960s was denied its influence on the women's movement. Only in retrospect has it been admitted that the movement for black rights was the first to bring about a growing political awareness in the 1960s: 'Without Black Brotherhood, there would have been no Sisterhood; without Black Power and Black Pride, there would have been no Gay Power and Gay Pride' (Edgar in Bourne 1984: 11).

Critical analyses of the cross-connections between gender, race and colour have resulted in more possibility of intercultural dialogue. According to Frankenberg (1993: 8), 'In the realm of theory, women of color were the first to advance frameworks for understanding the intersection in women's lives of gender, sexuality, race, and class as well as conceptions of multiracial coalition work.' In her book on the construction of 'whiteness', Frankenberg started from the idea that too often there is blindness towards one's own profits. After all, these profits determine who belongs to the dominant race and who does not. She analyses to what extent this system of privileges has had negative effects on women of various classes and cultures.

The gender legacy of slavery

The gap between black and white American middle-class women has narrowed: more white women have started to take jobs and more black women have an academic degree. Statistics show that increasingly more black middle-class women have gained higher educational qualifications in recent years relative to whites and black men, and have improved their standard of living.

Orlando Patterson (1963: 10) suggests with respect to careers in top positions that highly qualified black American women nowadays have an advantage over both white women and black men. On the basis of comparative statistical data he questions the often repeated statement that black women carry a double or triple burden on their shoulders. He wonders if it is still in agreement with the facts, when one compares their position with that of black American men of the middle class and higher: could the double burden thesis now be rejected as a myth?

Black working-class women would certainly not agree with Patterson, but would black middle-class women? Sometimes an optimistic or 'self-conscious' tone can be heard in the works of black academic women: 'Black women who hold the key to the future of America' (Frances Hooks). This is the triumphant quotation with which Paula Giddings 1984: 357) concluded her book on the impact of black women on race and gender in the USA.

Against such optimism, Orlando Patterson (1963) depicts a sombre and harrowing picture of 'the American black man'. His article, framed by the Clarence Hill/Anita Thomas controversy, brings to the fore a huge black gender crisis. He distinguishes between men from the lower classes and the middle class. The mutilating historical experience of slavery made the former group become what the whites had forced on them. The resulting anger and self-hatred then led to serious forms of depression when turned inwards, or, when turned outwards, to destructive violence against black men and sexual aggression towards women.

In Patterson's view blacks of the second group, the middle class, reacted in two ways to the same historical experience: on the one hand they cooled their anger against white oppression through social and political movements for civil rights and racial dignity; on the other, their positive identification took the form of an internalization of the white oppressor's own male ideal in his relationship with white women ... a courtly tradition of genteel male dominance ... [which] was to spell trouble for black women (1963: 23).

Predictably, black women refused to stand on the pedestal offered to them, and to adopt the restricted role of housekeeper, which the white woman had taken for granted for such a long time. Patterson points to the negative effects of the black male identifying with the white paternalist gender ideal. It associated oppression with castration and freedom with manhood and dominance.

Patterson concurs with the mechanism that hooks described: black men 'took over the sexual metaphor of freedom from the very oppressors they claimed to be fighting, forging a bond with them' in sexist (conscious or unconscious) solidarity. The Black Muslim movement assured women that servility was for their own well-being. Male dominance went beyond this rather limited movement and existed among many if not most middle-class men. Sometimes, Patterson argues, 'this was rationalized as part of a nationalistic ideology of 'nigrescence' or Africanness, at other times as a dangerous pseudo-radical form of class unity with the lower-class brothers through a glorification of their pathological, hip-hop sexuality' (23).

Disappointed about the gendered burden of history, Patterson blames slavery, racial oppression and poverty for 'the poisoned relationship' between black men and women of all classes. Since nobody gains from putting all the blame on that history he advises men and women to retrace their traumatic past together to get rid of this poison (26). But how? He does not answer that question. Furthermore, is it true that middle-class men have been overtaken by 'their' women? Is it possible to quantify oppression? And who profits from organizing a racialized and gendered competition in pitifulness?

Patterson's 'Blacklash' provoked a storm of reactions in a later special issue of *Transition* (summer 1995) on the crisis of African-American gender relations. Since it presents so many of the us–them controversies with which we have been dealing, I will briefly go into a few points.

bell hooks reacts with indignation: Patterson has appropriated her observation (that black feminist thought has had little impact on African-American politics) to support his antifeminism, while omitting *pour le besoin de la cause* her argument 'that holds sexist black male leaders responsible for deflecting black feminist critique' (1995: 94). She blames Patterson for putting all black women's thinking under one heading. He had accused her of badly obscuring 'our understanding of gender relations'. hooks, on the contrary, who believes unconditionally in the struggle against 'white supremacist capitalist patriarchy', blames Patterson for not discussing this issue which is so important to her. By not discussing it, she argues, Patterson seems to suggest that patriarchy is not problematic. By asserting that 'black men and women of all classes have a poisoned relationship', hooks complains bitterly, he 'seeks to efface all the work by black feminist thinkers to highlight the ways in which the convergence of racism and sexism creates tensions in black gender relations'. She is concerned about the false assumptions (among both black males and females) that black family life can be saved 'by our collective embrace of patriarchal values and norms' and criticizes Patterson (as do many of the other commentators) for making no practical suggestions for a way out of the crisis he describes. Whereas Patterson blames contemporary African-American feminist thought for badly obscuring 'our understanding of gender relations', hooks blames his unshaded blindness for 'the grave difference between the feminist thought of reformist black women who have simply appropriated both the rhetoric and agenda of their white counterparts, and the critical revolutionary black female thinkers of the left' (97). His not seeing that difference clearly reveals the 'anti-feminist thinking that is at the heart of his essay':

> Truthfully, revolutionary visionary feminist thinking by black females and males is one of the few places we can turn for an account of black gender relations that does not seek to pit black women and men against one another in an endless, meaningless debate about who has suffered more'. (hooks 1995: 98)

Less indignantly Michele Wallace (1995) states that she no longer sees black feminism as the discourse of victimization. There are widely different views and opinions among black women, many of whom often do not want to call themselves feminists: 'in most gatherings of black feminists, one rarely hears the word feminism' (99). Wallace emphasizes that even if some black women have become successful because of their education, at the same time the plight of poor black women has become more alarming. And, if poor black men find themselves, as Patterson argues, in a 'soul-killing dilemma', this is not very different, she adds, for young black girls.

She calls upon Patterson to pay more attention to the present rather than being strangled by the impact of the history of slavery: 'the reality is that when you are poor and black, male or female, it is still very hard to have *any* identity as an individual, psychologically' (100).

A few other comments go against the presumed specificity of blackness, emphasizing the parallels between black and white ghettoized poor people: their bad social circumstances are not very different; there is less and less responsible fatherhood among blacks and whites. As Andrew Hacker puts it: 'Recent increases in transient fathers and homes headed by single mothers cannot be easily attributed to a plantation past' (104).

If Patterson is worried about the role of the dominant mother, others (hooks 1995; Williams 1995) are concerned about absent fathers, so significantly ignored in his essay. Rita Williams wonders, as do several other commentators, why race should continue to be the one and only thing that counts, 'first, last, and always' (133). If it does, she argues, African-Americans adopted this belief from their own oppressors:

> Our identities as racial entities first, rather than human men and women, has skewed our abilities to prioritize. Indeed, there is an almost fascistic insistence in the African American community to put aside one's process of individualization for the supposed good of the race. *This is particularly true for women.* (133, emphasis added)

Thus, she argues, we seem to spend more time 'working on them than on us. And *us* is what we can do something about' (133). She admits that a number of black women have made some economical and educational progress. Nevertheless, there is a constant pressure for black women's aims and identities to be prescribed by men's defining and representing women and their roles: 'as best as we can, we step into those roles and hobble around'. The consequence is fragmented identities related to the services that women are supposed to provide and to roles men expect them to fulfil:

> We become the disembodied pumping genitalia of hip hop, on the one hand, or the Nation of Islam, with Madonna personas in habits, on the

other. Both images inflate or invalidate black female sexuality, but, more importantly, both choices colonize it. (134)

Many women still seem ready to pay the price in order to keep the family intact, but the either/or dilemma creates tremendous tensions, turmoil and frustration. It seems a woman's duty to restore man's vulnerable masculinity. Williams admits that 'black men have had few arenas where they were granted a healthy sense of power' .

The practice Williams describes is not very different for women in non-black communities. In many cultures, strong internalized gender norms prevail and prevent radical change towards more equality in rights and duties. If the first step is awareness, the next is to discuss why gender (and racial) equality looks so threatening to dominant outsiders and what can be done about that threat.

Williams makes another important point. If the basic rights we have according to the Constitution are ours, we should see ourselves as the 'responsible guardians of those rights for each other and citizens outside the African American community', instead of clinging 'to the belief that we are only alienated outsiders – victims in an alien land' (133), as an ongoing short-term policy.

Patterson's conclusions about black gender relations are aptly summarized by Yehudi Webster (1995: 161): 'Slavery was less brutalizing for black females. Black male slaves were twice victimized. Their sons are thrice victimized by white males, other black males, and black women who, on the authority of Michele Wallace, have no respect for black men'.

Webster too pleads against the cul-de-sac of racial classification and black self-identification. He analyses this vicious circle as follows: self-classification as black creates hope. Unfulfilled hope creates anger against one's own group, when people realize that 'a common blackness does not eliminate their educational, regional, generational, normative, and aspirational differences ... Yet, the conviction that America is a racist white society compels a more avid embracing of blackness, even as it fails to provide succor' (162). Thus, he argues, black people seem to have trapped themselves in a self-contradictory racial world view. Once class and gender are introduced, the idea of black poverty loses most of its racial flavour. In other words, Patterson's alleged black female–male crisis is a crisis of racial classification without logical substance. As an alternative solution, Webster proposes no longer to consider sociological classifications as existing realities and advises the 'human beings classified as black men and black women [to] act this out ... by establishing color- and gender-blind relations with other human beings' (164).

Or is it 'still premature to dismiss the political efficacy of strategic essentialism'? (Gibel Azoulay 1996: 135). If we are not satisfied with academic slogans, we have to judge what difference such a strategy makes, and in such a context one might examine white and black American politics in relation to Africa today. Many Africans criticize American policies towards Africa. Carol Moseley-Brown, a Democrat from Illinois and the only black member of the Senate, went to Nigeria in 1996 and visited the military governor, Colonel Dauda Musa Komo, in Port Harcourt; the very colonel who had been responsible for hanging Ken Saro-Wiwa and eight other activists the year before. Senator Moseley-Brown praised him for restoring peace and order in the region and refused to meet with members of Nigeria's democratic opposition. Speaking of closing ranks: the USA buys 40 per cent of all Nigerian oil.

George Ayittey, a Ghanaian who lectures at the University of Washington, is one of the African critics of Clinton's Afro-optimists who refuse to criticize African leaders. Their first priority, as he observes, seems to be to please their black American electorate who might conceive negative statements on African leaderships' crimes and mismanagement as 'racist'. According to Ayittey, the Clinton administration's Africa policy leans mainly on African-American activists who look at Africa along the lines of their own racial black–white paradigm use: 'not only are they latecomers in campaigns for Africa's liberation from black tyrants and criminals, but also are they often standing on the wrong side' (*NRC-Handelsblad*, 21 March 1998: 39).

7

Emerging from the shadows

Changing patterns in gender matters

Never marry a woman with bigger feet than your own.
Sena proverb, Malawi/Mozambique

The hen knows when it is morning, but she looks at the mouth of the cock.
Ashanti proverb, Ghana

Men call you Mother Africa and put you on a pedestal. But they want you to stay there for ever — and unhappy you if you want to step down and live the life of an ordinary human being.

Miriam Tlali

God, when will you create a woman who will be fulfilled in herself, a full human being, not anybody's appendage?

Buchi Emecheta

My heart rejoices each time a woman emerges from the shadows.

Mariama Bâ

Women and blacks

The comparison by Simone de Beauvoir and other Western feminists between 'women and blacks' (Chapter 3) discloses an obvious lack of political insight. It is an outsiders' notion which, at least from a black woman's perspective, is of very little relevance: in this equation she is noticeable by her absence. After all, whenever blacks and women are linked, black women are ignored in two ways — as black people and as women (hooks 1981: 8). Small wonder that a feminism unaware of such mistakes is distrusted by those who feel excluded from it.

Apart from using the analogy between women and black people, Western feminism has also regularly made use of the image of colonial annexation, whereby the Western white male is presented as a colonizer not only of faraway countries but also of the woman 'occupied' and colonized by him. The woman as a victim of colonization is a tried and trusted metaphor, used by Marilyn French (1985) among others. Colonialism has been equated with the relationship between men and women and in line with its well-known power relationships 'the woman' is forced into a subordinate position. She is deprived of her voice and, like those colonized, she is called unreasonable and emotional, thus representing everything that rational men are not or do not want to be. Her situation and that of colonized people are linked in joint martyrdom. Again the colonized woman is ignored.

Western middle-class women have applied this comparison to themselves without taking account of their own contradictory position of being 'both colonized patriarchal objects and colonizing race-privileged subjects' (Donaldson 1992: 6). On the one hand they are privileged beings; on the other they are extensions of their husbands. White men colonized and white women profited and African novels about colonial times reflect these connections. This is similar to how things worked under slavery: it was instituted by white men,yet was advantageous for their women, who achieved a higher status by virtue of slaves and servants.

Literature reveals internalized feelings, one being the desire on the part of those colonized to assimilate with the colonizer: to become as white as possible, the highest achievable goal being to 'conquer' one of 'their' women (Fanon 1952). The frequent descriptions of the beauty of white women in novels about colonial times written by African male authors show the continued effect of ambivalence towards colonial power. White women embody the epitome of beauty because they belong to the domain of the rulers. While African novelists have been conditioned by internalized colonial images of women, both black and white, they show these effects carrying through to 'their own' African sisters, wives and daughters. 'What have they got that I haven't got?' is Sophie's earlier quoted question in Oyono's *Une vie de boy* (1956: 38). It expresses the anger, indignation and despair of those caught in a power structure that mercilessly dictates the norms of femininity and beauty, or for that matter of femininity versus masculinity.

The views of African male authors (Chapter 3) differ from those held by Simone de Beauvoir and her sympathizers. From their point of view there is no self-evident black solidarity with (Western) 'woman' in a common liberation struggle. There is, however, one exception, Léopold Sédar Senghor, whose own essentialist notions of Negritude and its interests led him to agree with Western feminists on this point. At the end of an interview limited to an hour he promised to answer the rest of my questions in writing. One dealt with

Simone de Beauvoir's comment about the equation of women and black people. When asked whether this was a typically Eurocentric view, Senghor disagreed. On the contrary, in his letter he affirmed that both groups were in the process of liberating themselves from the same white paternalism:

> There are certainly similarities, not only between the conditions of the Western woman and the black African, but also between the feminine virtues and the black African virtues. It is absolutely evident that the Western woman's conditions and the Black African's in the world are similar. Euramerica, as we all know, started by ignoring the virtues of Woman. What seems less evident, is the similarity between the Woman's virtues and the virtues of the Black. And yet, there is in both cases the same need to express oneself, to be found in the analogical image and the rhythm. There is, above all, in the Black, as well as in the Woman, the power of emotion and, thus, of identification. Therefore the Euramerican as well as the Western man has got the wrong impression that the Black can be assimilated just as woman can be. Father Dahin, a white missionary in Africa, confessed on his death bed, speaking about Black people: 'We'll never understand them.' What woman has not heard the same statement from a man's mouth? Of course, the capitalists from Euramerica are unable to understand the negroes: they restrict themselves to gazing at their own navel.

His views allow ample scope for comment. The stereotyped contrast between black emotion and white male rationality was eventually rejected as a restrictive myth, as an inheritance of nineteenth-century Western racial theories. Incidentally, this same black emotion has sometimes been trotted out by Black Power supporters (see Chapter 6), but even then this emotional quality was not associated with 'the fate of women': it served only to emphasize the contrast with white men. In this context 'the woman', whether black or white, has never been allowed more than a passive role as an object of beauty, fertility and servitude.

Gender in (pre-)colonial Africa

Theories about Africa and gender emphasize either class or colonization. Class oppression in pre-colonial Africa is often taken to be gender free: women were rarely, if at all, discussed in research into class relations. Conversely, investigations into the position of women in Africa have, as in the USA, often disregarded or neglected class differences. At the same time, the concept of patriarchy has been put forward as a generalized term for the oppression of women, whether or not combined with race. It starts from the premise that forms of male domination of women exist everywhere and uses it as a basis to analyse specific relationships between men and women. A danger with such an approach is not only that historical and other contextual aspects in which gender relationships manifest themselves, such as race and class, are neglected, but also that they 'marginalise active and passive forms of resistance in which women have been implicated throughout the ages' (Anthias and Yuval-Davis 1992: 106ff).

In her description of developments from pre-colonialism to post-colonialism, Cindy Courville (1993: 31) stresses the 'trans-historical' nature of patriarchy as an ideology shaping the construction and reproduction of women's oppression:

> The sex-gender roles and sexual division of labor identified in the family structure reflect the patriarchal ideological determinants of the social formation of the family and the state. Women's productive and reproductive capacity made them a social and economic resource which provided men with political leverage. African women were primarily responsible for the economic, social and political reproduction of the household; the bearing of and caring for children; the production, storage and preparation of food. As well, women had exchange value within the context of marriage, forming alliances between households, clans and nations. (Courville 1993: 33)

Women represented exchange value to warriors, to be used in political alliances and as tribute to elders. Women in pre-colonial times were not entitled to own land, yet they were not powerless victims either (36). Through colonization, capitalism violently intervened in the existing order. One of the consequences was that the value of traditional women's labour was reduced because the home and the workplace were separated under the new system: the state and industrial concerns reserved most urban wage labour for men. From then on, women in rural areas were controlled by men in two ways. Not only traditional but also colonial laws now determined that they had no rights to the ownership of land or control over the produce they cultivated. The unpaid labour of women and children essentially subsidized the colonial wage bill. Their traditional powers of healing and other functions (spirit mediums, midwives, brewers of ritual beer) were undermined by Church and state. Women received little or no education because neither African nor colonial patriarchs regarded it as important. Courville provides a bleak summary of the situation of African women in colonial times:

> Under colonialism many African women were raped into submission,
> were exploited as laborers, and endured subhuman status as slaves as a
> result of colonial European and African patriarchal oppression and
> capitalist exploitation ... The exploitation and oppression experienced
> by African women were shaped by the coexistence of dual political
> systems, dual patriarchal systems and dual modes of production.
> (Courville 1993: 39–40)

Patriarchal culture and its concomitant sexual hierarchy was not only
maintained through colonization but also further enhanced. Courville restricts
herself to outlining the state of affairs in Zimbabwe, where the pre-colonial
position of women was not as ideal as the current state of research would seem
to bear out. Sometimes feminist anthropologists idealized the position of
women in pre-colonial society: men and women were supposed to be equal
before the arrival of Europeans and inequality was only the result of Western
capitalist exploitation. Courville's example of Zimbabwe convincingly shows
how both systems reinforced each other on their common patriarchal ground,
but of course much more research needs to be done. As Davison argues:

> The way that gender intertwines with lineage influences the relation
> between women and the means of production. This relationship also is
> contingent on periodic shifts generated by intercultural contact at many
> levels: precolonial contact between differing social groups in various
> relations of power; the trauma-ridden encounter between colonial and
> indigenous groups; and the postcolonial liberation struggles between
> politicized ethnic groups or nationalities for control over future
> development. (Davison 1997: 6)

Davison's research was carried out in Southern Africa, but Africa is a huge
continent with a large number of cultures. A welcome recent contribution to
the field is Obioma Nnaemeka's *Sisterhood. Feminisms and Power From Africa to
the Diaspora* (1998); it contains contributions on African feminisms, in the plural
because of the variety of views represented in a large volume. Among a
'diversity of views locating power differently in gender analysis' (10) some
contributions argue that African feminism is 'traditional', while others hold the
view that it is new to Africa. Contributions from as many perspectives as
possible are indispensable. The discussion at the Conference in Nsukka, on
which this collection of papers was based, led to the conclusion that
'dialoguing is a necessary strategy for conflict resolution' (423).

Women researchers offer more varied opinions on 'traditional women's
rights' than do African women writers. As Eileen Julien put it in a still

unpublished paper presented at a conference in Stanford on 'Woman of African Descent Retrieving Africa':

> I know of no African woman writer who adheres strictly to the view that life before European intervention was idyllic, whereas for African male writers of the first generation (and for African American cultural nationalists, male or female), that view has prevailed. (Julien 1998: 7)

The present chapter deals with some aspects of gender representation and related insiders/outsiders issues in Africa. Gender matters not only involve the construction of images as such, but also the extent to which the gender of the author affects oral and written literature and how male and female authors respond to each other's work from a sense of gender awareness.

Oral literature

In some local communities custom dictates the age and sex of those allowed to tell particular stories or sing certain songs, but there are also societies where these rules do not exist or are less severe. In some societies women are held to be the most gifted storytellers, whereas in others men are regarded as the experts (Finnegan 1970: 375). Writers such as Chinua Achebe, Birago Diop, Sembène Ousmane and Buchi Emecheta have cited their mothers or grandmothers as their first literary sources: they told the stories later reused by these authors in their own work, or inspired them to write.

In societies where strict rules do not apply, the same stories are variously told by male and female authors. This does not mean that the outcome is similar. Oral narration is by definition infinitely variable, depending both on the occasion and the storytellers' individual contributions. Their authorial intention may be to respect traditional versions as much as possible or to introduce new ideas and take into account social change. Over the last few years, considerable research has been carried out into the gender aspects of oral literature. Often we do not know whether a certain song or story was originally created by a man or a woman. When recorded texts are analysed in detail, one can ask to what extent a myth, story, proverb or song serves or harms certain interests within society. What these interests are and how they are given shape in particular texts are issues increasingly raised by women researchers in recent years – and not only in the context of African literature.

Veronika Görög-Karady and Gérard Meyer (1988) have investigated images of women in West African stories: among the Malinke the right to tell stories appears to be almost exclusively a male preserve. When asked to tell stories the women will only do so after considerable hesitation, even when they are supposed to be experts. Insecurity and embarrassment are at the heart of this reaction. As Molara Ogundipe-Leslie (1987: 35) puts it: '[African] women are shackled by their own negative self-image, by centuries of the interiorization of the ideologies of patriarchy and gender hierarchy. Her own reactions to objective problems are therefore often self-defeating and self-crippling.'

Much more research needs to be done to catalogue which genres are specifically female and why. Among the Bambara in Mali women find it easier to tell stories, yet they are no less likely to adopt the male perspective (Görög-Karady and Meyer 1998: 4): through various literary genres, younger generations are impregnated with the fundamental values they must respect as adults. The consequences of those values differ considerably for girls and boys. During initiation rites, girls learn that their futures will be determined by exogamy and exchange arrangements. Men will remain in an environment familiar to them from childhood for the whole of their lives, surrounded by their own family. Girls will be married off, ending up in another village. They must spend the greater part of their lives among 'strangers', their in-laws. From a very early age girls are instilled with the knowledge that they are 'in transit' at home, in order to prepare them for the trauma of separation: 'from earliest childhood she is an outsider who is being prepared for the central role that she will play at her in-laws [where] disillusionment awaits her', concludes Lauretta Ngcobo (1988: 143), basing herself on the situation in Southern Africa. The girl is doomed to depart and her children will in many cases belong to her husband's clan, while she belongs nowhere. After her marriage she is under the supervision of her husband and his family. However, she remains obliged to follow her brothers' orders, for if she were to divorce she would have to return to her own family. Her identity is rendered uncertain and vulnerable by two completely contradictory loyalties. Such a permanent feeling of alienation in girls only becomes manageable by unconditionally adopting and internalizing the principles of the dominant ideology. Initiation institutionalizes existing relationships between girls and boys.

To sum up, the message is as follows: collective interests always prevail over personal interests; absolute respect is owed to anyone entitled to this on the basis of age or status. Girls are taught that their move to 'the others' is of vital importance to the survival of their own group: 'they are the paths linking the villages'. To be a girl means working hard, being patient and obedient to male relatives. This subservience is compensated for by the importance attached to motherhood. This is therefore one of the main themes in the literature depicting these roles in narrative form: the suffering of the once-maligned wife is eventually transformed into successful motherhood, with children not only prettier than those of the jealous and malicious co-wife, but also incredibly successful (Görög-Karady and Meyer, 1988: 5).

Indeed, not only in West African oral tales but also elsewhere, the character of the mother is the exception: she is treated with great respect, whereas other women, especially wives, are often discussed in critical or even contemptuous tones. Proverbs about women in Africa and throughout the rest of the world also reveal a predominantly favourable evaluation of mothers as well as a negative stereotyping of wives (Schipper 1985, 1991). Such imposed collective norms, inspired by the interests of the ruling group, can be traced in the behaviour of characters in stories. Rules can be broken to suit the demands of the story, but the existing order is triumphantly restored in the end. The tales allow for a certain amount of 'poetic licence' (Vail and White 1991): women transgressing against the norms of society can get away with it for a while.

In stories the rules are indeed temporarily suspended to allow for behaviour which would be socially unacceptable in the real world. A prime example is that of a woman committing adultery, for this poses a threat to the social order. As a rule the woman cannot decide her marital fate, whereas an adulteress would be taking her fate into her own hands. She would be claiming the rights reserved for older men, who would otherwise manage her life for her – in the literal sense of the word – and who regard the woman as an object of exchange. Through adultery she turns herself into the subject. In fact, she reverses the roles and relationships between the sexes and turns her husband, lover and relatives into objects which are dependent upon her behaviour. The fear of this happening is so great that from a young age men are warned that women are unreliable (Lallemand 1985: 61). Therefore, the woman is frequently seen as an outsider incapable of keeping secrets, one who does not belong to the family and who, if not strictly controlled, may wreak havoc. The dangers and consequences of female lawlessness are expanded upon in proverbs and stories. Sanctions follow at the end of the story, the transgressor is punished and order and respect for the rules are restored. What Görög-Karady has established with regard to oral stories from various different societies in West Africa has also been noted for Zimbabwe by Rudo Gaidanzwa (1985), for Southern Africa by Lauretta Ngcobo (1988) and for Kenya by Wanjiku Mukabi Kabira (1991a, 1991b), who has carried out research on gender relationships in Kikuyu oral literature in Kenya.

There is a Kikuyu myth which explains why men are the rulers. The story tells how at the dawn of time women were in charge. They ruled with an iron fist; they were cruel, pitiless and unfair. They made men do everything for them: men tilled the fields, did the cooking, looked after the children, went hunting and protected the home. All the women did was give out orders and mete out punishment if things did not suit them. The men obediently did what they were told. They worked diligently, even though they were treated like slaves. The women were never satisfied and became so demanding that the men decided things could not go on this way. They resorted to a ruse and decided to impregnate all the women at the same time. This would weaken the women and provide the right moment to overthrow their unjust regime. So it happened: the men created a new world order and strengthened their grip upon it. Ever since, the Kikuyu community has known justice and peace (Kabira 1991a: 1).

As always, the existing order is explained or justified through the invention of a creation myth. Subsequently, the community involved will have to believe and internalize this explanation, which begins to lead a life of its own as a self-evident given 'fact'. This myth is referred to by men who do not wish to work the land because they are scared of other men thinking that their women still rule them.

In 'Gender and Politics of Control', Kabira provides yet another example of the way interests are justified through the use of myths. We know that as early as the nineteenth century Kikuyu women were bartering their agricultural produce with the Masai for sheep and goats. This entailed the risk of the women becoming economically powerful. So they were forbidden to own cows, sheep or goats in their own right. According to the myth accounting for this, women did own animals in former times, but they were so cruel that the animals ran away. The story aetiologically explains the existence of wild animals, while at the same time justifying why women who do acquire cattle through barter must immediately relinquish them. On their return, they must submit to a ritual whereby they hand over these animals to their husbands or (if they are widows) to their sons. A Kikuyu proverb underlines the importance of this: 'Women and animals are no friends' (Kabira 1991a: 4). Under the pretext of respect for ancestral tradition, women's economic independence is constantly restricted.

There are also stories warning man that he must continuously protect himself and his property against any malevolent intentions on the part of his wife. If, in a story, a woman goes after another man, she basically turns into a monster, misbehaving in all kinds of ways (Brinkman 1996). The only good woman is a silent woman. This is emphasized through proverbs in countless cultures in Africa (and elsewhere). According to a proverb among the Wolof in Senegal, a wife's family name is 'Yes'; she must always say 'yes' to any command. Among the Kikuyu, her name is Mutumia, 'she who keeps everything to herself': she who has no opinion and never answers back, who is seen but never heard:

Narratives often depict women negatively and the dynamics that create these kinds of stories are rooted in material relationships in the Agikuyu society. The narratives themselves contribute to the social gender construction that explains the control of women in society and justifies the male domination and control of women's productive activities and their benefits (9).

The construction of gender differences hides an ideological power struggle in which one party benefits from the preservation of existing differences,while the other constantly seeks to reduce them. These conflicting interests are expressed in the different ways in which male and female authors tell the same story from oral tradition. Kabira carried out comparative research on the basis of the oral tales she noted down. She came across considerable differences in perspective with regard to well-known stereotypes about men and women. For instance, men are strong, women are weak; men help each other, women fight each other; men are expansive and outward looking, women are domestically minded and inward looking.

However, she also found that in 'female' versions narrative strategies are developed to allow the dominant ideology of the story to be undermined. Instead of fighting each other, female characters such as stepmothers and stepdaughters develop good relations with each other, countering well-known clichés. This solidarity is explained by Kabira 'as a reflection of the self-help women's group movement in the country where solidarity among women is a key issue' (1991b: 6).

In the woman friendly version, the girl rebelling against the norms of society is not punished as severely as in the story told by a male author. In the female version, the girl's rebellious attitude is presented with a great deal of understanding. The character of the cruel stepmother is turned into a cruel stepbrother, so that the stigma of the relationship between stepmothers and stepdaughters disappears. While the woman narrator is critical of the way things used to be, the male narrator would rather complain nostalgically about the loss of old values: 'For him the change has not been for the better' (Kabira 1991b: 11). The opinions of the narrator and his male characters are central to his presentation, whereas the female characters hardly speak at all and remain passive during events. If they speak or act they normally say or do the wrong things. None of this applies, however, to the mother, who is portrayed positively and is often even idealized. Here, the woman is completely dependent on her husband, nature, or the community for her safety or salvation.

In contrast to female versions, the community plays a positive role in male versions, as do male characters. Kabira puts this down to existing power relationships: tradition gives power to the community, which then transfers it to men, who in turn exercise this power over women and children (1991b: 11).

Using tools from narrative theory, Kabira re-examined stories from the oral tradition still told in Kenya up to the present day. The variation between different versions of the same story is not without significance. Male storytellers adhere to the dominant ideology, whereas their female counterparts are out to change those traditions oppressing women. She advocates systematic research into the view of contemporary African women on 'traditions' so often eulogized and romanticized.

In *Anthropologie structurale II*, Lévi-Strauss (1973) describes the almost universally prevailing cultural principle that if a man wants a wife she will have to be relinquished by another man, usually her father or her brother. In this exchange, the woman is not a subject but an object. Men saw themselves as creators of society, treating women as living commodities to be bartered in the interest of enhancing the greater glory of male status (Balandier 1974). According to the South African writer Lauretta Ngcobo: 'the basis of marriage among Africans implies the transfer of a woman's fertility to the husband's family group' (1988: 141). In a number of cultures a woman is only known as some man's daughter or mother. Her identity is dependent on her father, husband or son.

According to Görög-Karady and Meyer, the images of women in stories from the West African oral tradition unquestionably reinforce a male perspective (1988: 3). The same holds for most proverbs concerning women, but there are also female gendered genres. However, I should emphasize that oral literature can never be pinned down on the basis of form, content or perspective. Depending on changes within society, stories are adjusted in various different directions, as Kabira's Kikuyu examples show.

Christine Obbo argues that in her own country, Uganda, the changing roles of women today are often regarded as a betrayal of tradition. Women are expected to function as links between the past and the present, whereas men view themselves as mediators between the present and the future (1981: 143). This message is also propagated in the written texts of many male authors: there are indications of an 'identification of women with 'petrified' cultural traditions and the allocation to male characters or narrators of the role of regaining control over the historical development of their societies' (Stratton 1994: 8).

Written literature

The fact that written literature in Africa mainly emerged from colonial times onwards has undoubtedly influenced the way in which it has portrayed men and women. This is as true for colonial literature written by Europeans and set in Africa as for African literature itself. Originally, it was mostly produced by male authors because of dominant colonial and pre-colonial gender views on education:

> The sex role distinctions common to many African societies supported the notion that western education was a barrier to a woman's role as wife and mother and an impediment to her success in these traditional modes of acquiring status. With few exceptions, girls were kept away from formal and especially higher education. The colonial administrations were therefore willing accomplices because they imported a view of the world in which women were of secondary importance. Clearly then, European colonialism, as well as traditional attitudes of and to women, combined to exclude African women from the educational processes which prepare one for the craft of writing. (Boyce Davies 1986: 2)

Until the 1980s African literature and literary criticism has mainly been the province of male authors. So, the question naturally arises of whether, and to what extent, this has affected the way in which images of men and women are constructed since literature, by its very nature, contributes to this process.

In *Emancipation féminine et roman africain* (1980), Arlette Chemain-Degrange analyses the image of the African woman in French-language African novels. She has examined all novels published up to 1976 (no French-language novels by female authors had appeared at that time) and concludes that male authors often take it for granted that women subject themselves to both men and tradition. Of course, it cannot be denied that women played their own part in pre-colonial society, but that was also true for men and hardly any urban male wishes to return to the 'old days', or as a West African proverb puts it, 'the river never returns to its source'.

Just like the orally transmitted stories, quite a few novels show that women who act independently are eventually punished. There is no suggestion that breaking with the past can have any positive or liberating aspects. 'Modern' women who behave in an emancipated fashion are reproached for losing their 'femininity' and their African identity. Another frequent criticism is that women who seek more freedom are contaminated by Western feminist ideas. This causes feelings of impotent rage, as if the idea that male authority is disadvantageous to women could not occur to them of their own accord (Obbo 1981: 3). Often the term 'feminism' is avoided by African women because of its negative connotations and effects. There are women who associate the term with Western feminism; others avoid using it for strategic reasons:

Although the concept may not enter the daily existence of the average woman, and although much of what she understands as feminism is filtered through a media that is male-dominated and male-oriented, African women recognize the inequities and, especially within the context of struggles for national liberation, are challenging entrenched male dominance. (Boyce-Davies 1986: 10).

Female authors are still in the minority in Africa, but they can no longer be ignored. Until about twenty years ago no one appeared even to notice their existence (Volet 1994). The presence of female authors was in any case minimalized in most studies of African literature until the 1980s or even later – a state of affairs referred to by Florence Stratton (1994) as 'exclusionary practices'. In an engaging analysis, she attempts to connect the writing styles of male and female authors and investigates how both kinds of texts interrelate in African literary traditions.

In most feminist-orientated studies of female authors, the central argument is introduced by a description of the ways in which male researchers and critics have 'kept women writers out of literary criticism', excluding them from general handbooks, anthologies and historical surveys of African literature. How do the women writers themselves feel about this?

The subject was broached at a conference of African writers in Stockholm in 1986. Ama Ata Aidoo gave a lecture entitled 'To Be an African Woman Writer'. She first drew attention to Western critics' neglect of women writers and then admitted with heartfelt regret that there is an equally shocking and growing list of African critics who pretend to the rest of the world that African women writers do not exist or do not merit any serious attention (1988: 162). Only one African man, Oladele Taiwo, has written a study of female authors. (Why must they always be set aside in a separate book or special issue?). In Aidoo's words, he treats women writers 'as if they were his co-wives to whom he dishes out his whimsical favours' (166): the concept of 'gender' as a socio-political category does not appear in his vocabulary.

African women writers have mainly made their way in the world outside Africa through black feminist criticism in the USA, where African-American and African literature have often been regarded as inseparable. Sometimes this unity has been expanded to include some universal school of female writing, supposedly unconnected to any specific culture. In this manner, African women writers have been linked to (and inextricably bound up in) traditions and patterns of thought originating outside Africa, with the danger of their work being submerged in white or black Western feminist issues and interests. In *Beyond the Masks. Race, Gender and Subjectivity* (1995) Amina Mama has emphasized that for a long time black women were writing mainly from the perspective of the African-American woman, excluding from their discussions all kinds of different experiences; 'thus forcing women from other parts of the world to locate their identities within the context of North American hegemony', as she put it in an interview in Capetown in 1997.

A similar situation had occurred earlier to male African writers: the opposition between Western versus non-Western, European versus African models of discourse went on at the expense of other literary relationships and themes, ignoring the different regional, national, social and cultural forms of intertextuality and writing back. Thus, the countless ways in which African writers respond to each other's work has received too little attention outside Africa. One would surely expect a community to discuss its own experiences within its own circle. Because of the exaggerated international attention paid to the dominant Western post-colonial discussion, research into internal African cultural developments has been so neglected that once more the overall suggestion seems to be that nothing happens without Western culture (see also Ogunyemi 1996).

One of the issues overlooked in the discussion of literature and gender is the way in which African women writers have entered into a dialogue with the texts and writing traditions of their male predecessors. Florence Stratton has compared the work of male and female African authors from this perspective. She shows that female authors give a great deal of thematic attention to the experience of the margin, while male authors are more geared towards the ideological implications of power and dominance (1994: 18).

Stratton draws attention to the partial continuation of colonial and patriarchal relationships in the work of African male authors as, for example, in the adoption of the (colonial) image of Africa as a woman which allegorically refers to African culture or nationalism. This allegory shows that the status of their work has changed. Its non-hegemonic status in the discourse relationship between Europe and Africa changes to a hegemonic literary status with regard to female authors. This in turn leads to an African dialogue in which gender plays a new role. An interesting aspect of Stratton's book is her analysis of the Mother Africa trope, which seems ubiquitous but which, strikingly, occurs exclusively in the work of male authors (1994: 39).

In the Negritude movement Senghor linked the dichotomy of Europe versus Africa to the dichotomy of reason versus emotion. This was rejected by his many opponents as contentious because in that way old racist prejudices and colonial stereotypes were affirmed and in fact assimilated. However, according to Stratton, Negritude contains another Manichean allegory: the man–woman allegory, which represents dominance–subjection, mind–body, subject–object (1994: 41). The male African author – she only refers to the Western-educated intellectuals – turns his attention to the woman. He describes her lyrically as a young girl or fertile mother, as the African landscape he discovers and explores. This is done along two different lines: first, there is the strand of idealized, romanticized precolonial culture; second, there is the more politically loaded nationalist line of the recapture of Mother Africa: the new nation. In both cases, Stratton argues, the relationship is based on possession. He is the active subject, the new citizen, while she is the passive object, the nation.

In the positive sense, there is 'the metaphorical potential of her physical ability to reproduce' (Stratton 1994: 41). When the nation is doing badly the metaphor of prostitution may be employed, not to refer to the deplorable fate of women, but to the degradation of men. Stratton concludes that in this male literary tradition women function as bodies upon which texts are written. But apparently women writers have rejected this trope: they have not incorporated this image into their work. She explains this as a refusal to collude in their own sexual exploitation. She also sees it as a rejection of the nationalist view which this trope encapsulates in gender form: nations can be oppressed and raped like women, as history has shown ever since Europe invaded an Africa as 'dark and mysterious as a woman' (54).

The focus of the first generation of African authors on racism and colonialism in Western texts was, from their perspective, a matter of 'first things first'. The issue of gender remained absent in both colonial literature and African texts by male authors. It is all the more striking that male authors have adopted the concept of Africa as a woman from their own opponents; John Donne comes to mind with 'O my America, my new found land', referring to his mistress. Stratton describes this phenomenon as an interracially binding connection of intercontinental male solidarity in a shared ideal of superior active masculinity and female subservience (39). As discussed in Chapter 6, a similar connection was noted by bell hooks among others with respect to interracial male bonding in the USA. And what should be made of the fact that nearly every dictator presents himself as the father of 'the' nation?

The current attention given by male authors to gender aspects indicates that they have read their sisters' work, in which gender issues feature prominently. That they should write back means that they are taking more account of foregoing female perspectives. For its interesting, straightforward analyses of these developments, Stratton's (1994) book is certainly a welcome contribution to the debate, if a somewhat one-sided one. As Ogunyemi (1996) has observed, a large part of her work is indeed concerned with a re-reading of the work of well-known male writers, which she has given 'further exposure at the expense of works by unknown women writers' (3)

Stratton has been severely criticized for her unequivocal preoccupation with gender issues and blamed for having a Western perspective, a point I will return to later in this chapter. She does not discuss the situation in South Africa because of racial implications. Given our subject, that is all the more reason to look into South African gender issues here.

Black Consciousness and gender

The question of gender in the South African social and political context during apartheid was never subjected to any thorough discussion until the 1970s. Here too 'first things first' applied and ranks were closed for decades along racial lines. What role have women played in a movement such as Black Consciousness and how did men and women relate to each other within it? According to Mamphela Ramphele (1991: 215), one of the leading women in the movement, gender was not a political issue. Nevertheless, she confirms that the movement still had a positive effect on women, if only because of the assertive slogan imported from America: 'Black is Beautiful'. This slogan gave women more confidence and helped to free them from the dominant white cultural norm which until then had dictated standards of beauty

> For the first time many black women could fall in love with their dark complexions, kinky hair, bulging hips and particular dress style. They found new pride in themselves as they were. They were no longer 'nonwhites', but blacks with an authentic self, appreciated on their own terms. The skin-lightening creams, hot-oil combs, wigs and other trappings of the earlier period lost their grip on many women. (Ramphele 1991: 217)

This refashioning of self-images applied to men as well as women and influenced the whole of society. Women benefited from this as black people, but their emerging Black consciousness also increased their assertiveness from an intellectual point of view, as well as in their personal relationships and public presence. To Ramphele, being involved in Black Consciousness meant following a path travelled by women everywhere in the world when they no longer conform as individuals to the old role models. She learnt how to react arrogantly and not to be intimidated by men who on the one hand think that single women are naturally 'available' and on the other assume that 'beauty and brains do not combine' (Ramphele 1991: 218). The situation remained ambivalent, involving a sense of camaraderie yet also various instances of sexism. The principle behind the natural assumption that domestic tasks such as cooking and cleaning fell to women was never brought up within the movement. This was due both to men not wanting to do such work and women still being tied to their stereotypical gender roles. These were the same problems confronting women in the American Black Power movement – and everywhere else, for that matter.

Another common mechanism operating in the Black Consciousness movement was that the most outstanding women were treated as 'honorary men' – in the same way that, ironically, apartheid created its 'honorary' whites, such as Japanese businessmen visiting South Africa. This allows traditional role patterns to continue to exist, but also creates the space for a few occasional exceptions. In this particular case, honorary status was awarded to Black Consciousness women who dared to challenge sexism on their own account. For the rest, everything remained the same. People from the periphery who are allowed to join in tend to regard this as an honour and forget existing differences from then on. It was Gayatri Spivak (1987: 106) who summed up this phenomenon as follows: 'The putative center welcomes selective inhabitants of the margin in order better to exclude the margin.'

Mamphela Ramphele's life as described in her strong biography (1995) is an outstanding example of how the transgression of accepted rules and norms as a constant challenge can make women succeed who are determined to realize the dream of equal opportunities.

Black Consciousness missed out on the major developments that feminism went through in the USA during the seventies. This cannot be attributed only to censorship and a lack of relevant documentation: after all, American information from Black Power was available on a clandestine basis. Rather, it was due to the general assumption that South Africa had no need for feminism: 'The feminist movement was dismissed as a 'bra-burning' indulgence of bored, rich, white Americans' (Ramphele 1991: 221).

What happened after the Soweto uprising of 1976? The major emphasis was still on women fighting 'side by side' with their men in the liberation struggle. Yet, according to Ramphele, it was pointed out more openly and more frequently that black women suffered from triple or even quadruple oppression: race, class, gender and national oppression as a result of colonization. Nevertheless, an obvious ambivalence continued to exist, both in the Black Consciousness movement and the South African trade unions, with regard to the unavoidable necessity of treating women as equals and the deep-rooted desire to preserve traditional male and female role patterns (224).

It has become apparent in scores of countries, both outside Africa as well as within, that political independence and the liberation from colonialism do not end sexism: from Algeria to Zimbabwe and Guinea-Bissau the 'back to normal' mechanism in the relationship between men and women soon manifested itself. Examples of this phenomenon outside Africa include women in the IRA and in the liberation movements in El Salvador and Nicaragua (see Schipper 1985). Referring to the clash between the interests of race and gender affecting black women in the USA, Ramphele advocates an integrated approach to racism and sexism in contemporary South Africa. What has often been pointed out in connection with racism and sexism in the USA and Europe also applies to South Africa: people who are themselves oppressed within a racial relationship often take out their frustration on weaker members of their own group, men oppress-ing women and women oppressing children. The sexism in their own environ-ment makes women lose confidence, leading to self-loathing and preventing them from taking any initiatives in the political and cultural field. Apart from the obvious attention being paid to racism in contemporary South Africa, more awareness is growing about sexism and the interconnection between the two issues as they manifest themselves in language, culture, arts and sciences.

Literature in South Africa

The practice of excluding women writers has also been pointed out by female authors in South Africa. In another special issue about women in literature in the journal *Current Writing*, Cecily Locket (1990) notes that the mechanisms of sexism and racism always make certain groups invisible. According to her, the position of white feminist critics with regard to oppression allows them to be shot at from all sides: the power paradigm of race views white people as 'the Self' and black people as 'the Other'. Thus, white women are pigeonholed in the male Self and black men in the female 'Other'. Locket also states that in the South African literary power paradigm, however, the work of black male authors such as Serote, Mtshali and the Soweto poets has been quite widely accepted by the literary establishment; whereas this is not the case with the work of black and white female authors who do not fit in with the established 'paternal tradition'. Locket makes elaborate attempts at politically correct manoeuvring by questioning her own right as a white woman to speak for or about black women, when white women themselves have rejected 'the discourses that oppressors have made about us' (14). She draws attention to the problem that although white women are sometimes in the same position as black women, they are still viewed by the latter as agents of oppression. She then goes on to quote Nkululeko, a representative black woman who argues that black and white women should work in their own respective racial groups to create the conditions for eradicating the oppression of African women (14).

A point hardly enlarged upon in current academic discussions is the fact that these exchanges of theoretical insights between blacks and whites are restricted to a small elite, racism and sexism having completely different social implications for various groups. There is a difference between well-to-do women and those who are less privileged. Women who have to work hard all day in a factory or as a domestic servant, while also doing their own housework, have no time or energy left for telling or writing stories, let alone academic discussion and cultural theorizing. On top of this, they have to deal with jealous husbands to whom they must answer every time they leave the home if they wish to participate in a writing or story telling project. In the discussion of gender, the negative self-image of women is frequently raised as a problematic issue, for example, by Nise Malange:

> Young women from traditional homes have been brought up in conditions where girls must be noticed only through the products of their labour. They would be considered unmodest or rude if they tried to make people aware of their presence in any other way ... When one looks at women in what is traditionally regarded as women's area of activity, there is also a lack of trust in creative ability ... They have come to doubt their own ability to tell stories in exciting ways, and they lack the self-confidence to appear in public. (qtd in Locket 1990: 18)

In the debate taking place in South Africa, the fear has been voiced by white women that, in their turn, they might well become marginalized in the future. One of the questions white women ask is:

> Am I privileged or is it rather my black compatriots in South Africa who have had no access to normal social, educational and other modes of existence? Is it privilege that should be eradicated, or is it the unjust difference 'privilege' marks? If social action is required and demanded to eradicate privilege as difference, how can women embark upon it without solidarity and how can there be solidary within new marginalisations? (De Jong 1992: 162)

Is the white South African women's fear of possible exclusion on the basis of their skin colour (they are after all in the minority) the reason why they seldom criticize black women? The openness of dialogue needs to be stimulated both ways. For too long ideas and opinions prevalent among black women have been unknown outside their own silenced groups. Their information and ideas are all the more interesting in view of the fact that the opinions of black women are diverse rather than uniform.

The black South African writer Zoë Wicomb (1990: 37) sharply reacts to Locket's (1990: 16) uncritical quoting of Ogunyemi's rather essentialist rejection of white feminism on racial grounds. Wicomb indignantly opposes the Nigerian scholar's view. In answers Ogunyemi's plaintive 'What is the point of sexual equality in a ghetto?', Wicomb's very practical response is 'to be able to put your feet up for five minutes and have somebody make you a cup of tea'. She pleads for more attention to be paid to what unites black and white women in their hierarchical relationships with men and then goes on to analyse the patriarchal view of black gender relationships. For the sake of convenience, these have been established purely on the basis of racial solidarity, and she wonders why this patriarchal mentality cannot be combatted together with the fight against apartheid (37). Her argument cuts across Locket's nervous balancing act on the tightrope of political correctness to a vigorous attack on Ogunyemi's glorification of black roots and black solidarity. A positive aspect of such discussions is that apparently black and white women in South Africa are giving each other the benefit of constructive criticism. Apparently, an encouraging new development is under way.

To return to Black Consciousness, this movement has been criticized from various quarters for being an exclusively 'male' concern, on such grounds as its consistent use of the male singular pronoun 'he' and the expression 'the black man'. An example is the definition of Black Consciousness in the manifesto from 1971:

(i)   Black Consciousness is an attitude of mind, a way of life.
(ii)   The basic tenet of Black Consciousness is that the Black *man* must reject all value systems that seek to make *him* a foreigner in the country of *his* birth and reduce *his* basic human dignity.
(iii) The black *man* must build up *his* own value systems, see *himself* as self-defined and not defined by others. (my emphasis)

Black awareness, the black experience and the black perspective in relation to men are highlighted and the female point of view is absent. The role of women – the few 'honorary men' described by Ramphele excepted – is limited to the caring, domestic sphere and motherhood. Black Consciousness is very aware of the black man's suffering, as was the Negritude movement. In *Being Black in the World*, Chabani Manganyi (1973: 10) talks about the dehumanization of the black man. The perspective is quite revealing:

> In the life experience of the African, there is hardly any situation in his life in which his sense of self-esteem is nourished. His wife and children may have been forced by conditions beyond his control to lose the modicum of respect which they had for him as an effective, self-steering agent in his psychosocial environment. If we were to formulate his psychic status in a phenomenological way, we could say that his subjective experience is one of feeling emasculated (qtd in Driver 1990: 235n)

According to Dorothy Driver there is, among men, a widespread feeling that white patriarchal authority has symbolically castrated the African. It therefore falls to the woman to restore his masculinity instead of inflicting further humiliation upon him (236). Manganyi seems to exclude women from the category 'African'.

As in the USA, black women and mothers in South Africa are viewed as indestructibly strong. Just like the American female slaves, black women under apartheid have hardly ever been able to let their lives depend upon what others do for them, in contrast with most white women in South Africa. The strength of women and mothers is also expressed in the works of black South African women writers, such as Ellen Kuzwayo's *Call Me Woman* (1985) or Mamphela Ramphele's *Across Boundaries* (1995). At present South African authors and critics are passionately looking for space beyond the boundaries of the antiquated and ossified categories of black and white, of women and men (Driver 1990; Ndebele 1991).

The trope of Mother Africa also had a role in South Africa's literature; yet here too women writers have rejected it in the awareness that putting women on a pedestal robs them of the freedom to step upon the earth where they rather like (in Miriam Tlali's words) to 'live the life of an ordinary human being'.

Insiders, outsiders and cultural boundaries

Today, however, there is growing attention to the work of African women writers as a special field of study, particularly in the USA, but also in Africa and Europe.

In *Unheard Words* (1985), I made a distinction between *exclusive* and *inclusive* *criticism*. In the exclusive approach, certain (aspects of) literary texts, genres or groups of authors are passed over without justification or explanation or ignored on the basis of a particular set of norms. Exclusion has often been used for the purpose of subjugation. This was common policy in colonial times when Western rulers excluded Africa from what they called civilization. The same practice can be found among African critics with regard to African female writers; Aidoo's complaint referred to previously is a case in point. In my book I gave examples of exclusive critics such as Femi Ojo-Ade (1983: 52) who obviously wanted to impose his norms on African women writers, and blamed them for doing otherwise:

The [women] writers that we have studied dwell too much upon the malady of male chauvinism, a phenomenon that, in its most famous aspect, is no less a western way than the notions of feminism espoused by some female writers. Blackness, Africanness ... is almost foreign to others who have let the questions of male domination blind them to the necessary solidarity between man and woman.

Another much used argument has been that women are in danger of losing their femininity as soon as they demand equal rights. Ojo-Ade put it this way: 'Femininity is the virtue of the traditionalist; feminism the veneer of the progressive striving to become a man' (1983: 53). Buchi Emecheta's comment on her compatriot's view was that it is much too simple to argue that women who stand up for their rights are contaminated by Western feminism (cf. interview).

One of the problems is that many men (whether in Africa or elsewhere) continue to have difficulty in taking a female perspective into account (unless it coincides with their own), because their background has never prepared them to do so. We need to exchange views in order to promote 'intercultural positionality' and reduce 'insiderism' (Gilroy 1993).

I want to conclude this chapter by discussing two African women's comments on Western women's work on African literature. Ama Ata Aidoo has complained regularly that the African woman has been and still is attacked from all sides. On the one hand there are the arrogant European feminists who seem 'to know much more about the oppression of African women writers than the African women writers' themselves, while on the other there are African men who want African women to say that they do 'not want feminism at all in Africa. Because after all, African men also knew better when it came to what the African woman in Africa needed' (1996: 168). From her point of view, what does 'the' African woman want?

In 1991 I dedicated *Source of All Evil. African Proverbs and Sayings on Women*, To Ama Ata Aidoo, Micere Githae Mugo and Miriam Tlali, Daughters, Mothers, Writers'. Ama Ata Aidoo did not appreciate my gesture; nor did she appreciate the book — in contrast with many other people (men and women, Africans and Europeans) she resented it. We exchanged letters and in Harare we talked about it, but she did not change her mind. She thought that I should not have published the book. In her essay 'Literature, Feminism and the African Woman Today' (in Jarrett-Macauley, 1996) she once more came back to the issue and repeated her point of view, quoting from my (personal) letter to her in 1991 and from her reply to me. Since her point is not only addressed to me personally but is a generalized statement blaming 'the European (or Western) woman' (169) for bad behaviour, it might be relevant to discuss it here as an insiders/outsiders issue.

The book became the first volume in a series: after the African proverbs, four other volumes of proverbs on women were published (European, Asian,

Jewish, and Caribbean/Latin American). They all follow the same classification order: *I. Phases of Life*: girl, woman, wife, co-wife, mother, daughter, mother-in-law, widow, grandmother, old woman; *II. Elements of Life* (aspects of women's life dealt with in proverbs): beauty, love, sex, pregnancy, work, arguing and violence, unfaithfulness, witchcraft, power. These categories are well represented in proverbs collected from both oral and written sources.

The title of the African volume refers to a Fon proverb from Benin: 'Woman is the source of all evil; only *our* soul saves *us* from the harm *she* does' (emphasis added). Needless to ask who is speaking in this proverb and whose perspective is presented: the source of all evil is certainly not woman, but the many unflattering sayings on women produced all over the world, including Africa. At my request, the South African publisher added at the end of the blurb (something the publishers of the East African edition found superfluous): 'Of course women are not "the source of all evil", but they are portrayed as such — and have lived with this burden for so long in so many societies.' The dedication to the three women writers, 'daughters, mothers, writers,' meant that it is women themselves who can and do change certain gender perspectives and beliefs thanks to their own writings.

The book contains proverbs from all countries south of the Sahara, originating from some eighty languages. One of Aidoo's reproaches was that I should have started with a collection of European proverbs. But why? Can a scholar be blamed for working in the field of his or her choice, for working on African and not on European material, for publishing collected African proverbs on women?

At the end of the twentieth century Ama Ata Aidoo still speaks as (or in the name of) *the* African woman addressing *the* 'European woman' and, including the rest of the West, *the* 'Western woman' (does she mean the woman with the white skin?) in a generalizing accusatory tone:

> For a number of years now, some of us have been getting more and more convinced that somehow, the European (or Western) woman believes that her position in society is the highest of all women's positions in the world. That conversely, the position of the African woman in society is the lowest. This is in line with the normal European way of looking at Africa and Africans. It is also a dichotomy of conquest. You are the conquerors. We are the vanquished. It stands to reason that you should represent the superior and we the inferior in all things. (in Jarrett-Macauley 1996: 169)

Aidoo invokes, in the words of Gilroy (1993: 33), 'the misplaced idea of a national interest ... as a means to silence dissent and censor political debate'.

She suggests that the collected African proverbs on women reaffirm 'prejudices we have been struggling so hard to change' (170). Alas, these prejudices are persistent in life as in proverbs all over the world. Honestly, our struggle is the same, because the aim of such a comparative research is to make ourselves as men and women more aware of deeply internalized gender patterns. The ideas contained in proverbs do have an enormous impact, transmitted as they have been from one generation to the next. Ama Ata Aidoo's compatriot, Amba Oduyoye (1979), who studied the crucial impact of proverbial imagery in her own culture to 'elicit the realistic situation of women in Asante', underlines that language about women, in particular proverbs, strongly influences sex role socialization:

> Those women who do not fit the composite picture are marginalized by their own social group, other women, as well as by men. Thus one encounters such generalized statements as: women cannot keep a secret, they demand impossible feats from men, they prove to be unfaithful ... Yet the fact remains that it is a composite picture which mediates against the individual woman to be a person. (Oduyoye 1979: 5)

In fact this statement holds not only for Asante but for many, perhaps most, cultures in the world, and Africa is no exception to the rule. As the Nigerian Niyi Osundare (1992) observes in his review of the book, many proverbs are a reinforcement of existing power relations. When we approach proverbs from the speaker's gender perspective 'some of the proverbs are so male-centred that they would sound absurd in the mouths of women' (1072).

Would a woman ever say: 'Women and cutlets, the more you beat them, the better they'll be' (Germany)? or: 'Woman is like a goat, you tether her where the thistles grow (Rwanda). Perhaps sometimes she might, when it suits her. As a Congolese student explained to me: 'Women's solidarity is subservient to clan solidarity. My mother warned my brother the day before he married against his wife to be, with a Lingala proverb: 'To eat with a woman is to eat with a witch.' She meant that a woman from outside will never be 'one of us': she stays 'the enemy'.

During a project that has resulted in an ever-growing intercontinental collection of proverbs, I was trying to answer the question why, again not only in Africa but all over the world, should proverbs and other derogatory statements about women be so widespread. Could it be that fear and uncertainty, sublimated in domination, underlie the imposition of so many dictates and restrictions? Logically, if the situation were ideal and women as humble as many proverbs want them to be, fear and uncertainty would be superfluous and no hostile proverbs would be needed. The (Wolof) ideal of the

'Woman-wife whose name is "Yes"' is more a case of wishful thinking than a matter of fact. In reality, women seem too strong to be handled without all the invented restrictions and rules that the proverbs seek to impose in the name of traditions and the ancestors. Therefore, the ultimate underlying message of the proverb collections is not at all negative for women. Nowhere, as far as I can see (but Ama Ata Aidoo might object that I am a blinded Western outsider) could one in all honesty conclude that African women are vilified by the book.

In South Africa women's groups work with the book. Some of them wrote to the publisher to express their appreciation. In their discussions these women quote and discuss the proverbs, replacing the negative with the positive, the word female with the word male and vice-versa, not as a solution but as an exercise to see and compare the effect of what the proverbs look like from both perspectives. Thus the proverbs provoked a lot of laughter. Indeed, as the Ganda put it: 'An old proverb authorizes a new one.'

I reject the suggestion that I should not have published the African proverbs, either because I am a European, or because dirty linen was washed in public. Ultimately, the same policy applies to this linen as to the women who continue to hide feet that have grown too big, accommodating themselves to the warning of the Sena proverb (Mozambique): 'Never marry a woman with bigger feet than your own.' Discussing the proverb might make clear that it is not so terrible to display those big feet, so that people get used to the idea of women's competence in previously male domains. Proverbs happen to be excellent material for raising gender consciousness, as I have experienced myself while talking about my findings to rural Dutch women's groups. Proverbs reflect the extent to which we have accomodated ourselves unconsciously and unquestioningly to imposed norms. In order to know where we want to go today, we have to know where we have come from, as men and women, as people from different cultures, together; matriarchical protectionism is, in my opinion, no helpful strategy.

In spite of the points made here as well earlier, Ama Ata Aidoo, has apparently extremely not changed her mind and nor have I. Such ongoing discussion is nonetheless enlightening, whether we eventually agree or not.

As a second example I have chosen the article by Nigerian woman scholar Obioma Nnaemeka, 'Feminism, Rebellious Women, and Cultural Boundaries' (1995). Nnaemeka's essay has been praised as 'outstanding', 'superb' and even as 'my bible' in a commentary by Opportune Zongo from Burkina Faso (1996: 183). It is a passionate, outspoken critique of Africanist research on African women and African literatures. With her incisive voice and perspective, Nnaemeka does not shun the debate. She fulminates indignantly against the alarming lack of knowledge (due to laziness and arrogance) among those who write on Africa and African literature. She analyses 'blatant distortions of the works of African women writers by feminist critics' (81); blames Western feminist 'men-bashing and cultural imperialism and intolerance' and speaks 'on behalf of African literature and feminist scholarship' (82).

Sometimes she seems to suggest that there is only one possible 'correct' view of African texts, which I would be inclined to doubt. Still, a number of her observations deserve careful reading and, as usual, outspoken views enliven a critical dialogue, and contribute to further the discussion on insiders and outsiders in the humanities.

Nnaemeka does not reject Western critical theory as such: it has taught her how to handle some tools, but her aim is 'to redeem the creative work of African women writers from some of the distorted misinterpretations' and uncritical 'impositions of culturally-specific Western feminist constructs on texts that speak to different cultural contexts and realities' (81).

Before defining the borderlines between insiders and outsiders as she sees them, she expresses her worries about outsiders who seem to consider the views of (African) insiders as no more than 'informants' views' without appreciating Africans as scholars and producers of knowledge in their own right.

Presenting her own ideas on the respective positions of insiders and outsiders, Nnaemeka refers to an award-winning essay by sixteen-year-old Ikedigbo Nnaemeka, 'Why I Am Proud to Be a Nigerian'. The essay ends with the following statement, approvingly quoted by Obioma Nnaemeka: 'But for me, one thing is certain about being a Nigerian: the hot blood of my ancestors still courses through my veins.' What this 'hot blood' means in terms of knowledge production is elucidated as follows: to be born a Nigerian and to become a Nigerian (by studying it) refers to two types of knowledge: *birthright* (to be) and *empirical right* (to become).

In distinguishing these rights, insiders and outsiders can lay claim to 'different degrees of the *cognitive right* to unlock cultural productions, such as African literary texts' (85). Whereas the insider can lay claim to both the birthright and the empirical right, 'the outsider has only the empirical right available to him or her'. The insider can lose the birthright as well as the empirical right due to 'aberrant behavior' and alienation, while the outsider can also 'lose the *empirical right* and slumber in ignorance' (86). But what fundamental difference can then be made between insiders' and outsiders' rights? 'To have an authentic perspective means, in essence, the ability to maintain an appropriate distance from the object of analysis ... To stand too far (as some outsiders do) or too close (as some insiders do) produces various degrees of distortion' (91).

I would argue that there is not necessarily only one correct distance leading to only one correct view or interpretation. Different perspectives may throw different light on the same material and thus lead to different interpretations. In that sense it may be helpful if some researchers stand close and others far from the object of research, complementing each other's readings. Culture is always an interactive process rather than a body of historical products to be reconstructed from one and the same perspective without distortion. Diversities can be enlightening for all parties in ongoing discussion of research, results of which are always provisional.

We must be careful to respect each other's histories and objectivity is always related to subject positions. That is why I need to mention here my own specific history as a European whose first memory is of German soldiers intruding in to the house and taking away my father. This personal experience made it difficult 'neutrally' to read the 'blood' statement in Nnaemeka's essay. As a scholar and a human being I have always rejected difference made on the basis of blood. History has made clear to me that we cannot talk innocently about blood. For a European with my background, this metaphor is linked with *Blut und Boden* [blood and soil], with Nazi fascism and its terrible consequences which, unfortunately, did not stop there (think of Rwanda, for instance). One might object that I am biased because I was born in Europe. However, I wonder how African-Americans would react if a white American scholar brought the hot blood of his ancestors into the academic arena with statements such as 'the blood has to be there and the blood has to be *hot*' (86, Nnaemeka's emphasis). Perhaps he or she would have risked a law suit for blatant racism. My point is that it is very important *mutually* to explain to each other what hurts and shocks us, without blaming each other and without cutting off the dialogue.

I am sure that Nnaemeka had another reading in mind when she wrote her essay. I suppose she meant the metaphor culturally: people can assimilate insiders' knowledge from the culture they are born in. They can enrich and cultivate that knowledge more easily than those coming from a foreign culture. I completely agree with that. However, the blood metaphor is confusing because this is not a biological process. Does my birth in the Netherlands or my eldest son's birth in Congo guarantee any cultural rights? My birth in the Netherlands does not necessarily make me a better specialist on my culture or its literature, although growing up and living in a culture may be an advantage. One's perspective and research is not automatically more qualified for reasons of birth, class or gender. It depends on the convincing quality of the resulting product. The whole process needs self-criticism, humility, constant efforts, possible failure, and cannot do without a free and open dialogue. Sometimes I am concerned about the fragility of this dialogue.

When I tried to explain this 'blood issue' at a roundtable on insiders and outsiders at the African Literature Association Conference in Michigan (1997), in Nnaemeka's presence, nobody commented on it during the discussion. Only after the session did several colleagues tell me that no white American would have dared to bring such a tricky issue out into the open for fear of reprisals. A Jewish woman came to me with tears in her eyes to thank me for saying 'what no American would have been able to say'. On the other hand, after the session Nnaemeka told me that she had never thought about the connotations of the blood metaphor. She did not show how angry my remarks had made her until much later, when I received a copy of her email letter to another colleague. Apparently it was not possible to communicate openly on this matter, which I deeply regret. If we cannot create a dialogue on such issues, where is our academic openness? Why is it not possible to respect each other's histories and situatedness, and to have a discussion?

Nnaemeka is absolutely right when she observes that much nonsense has been and still is written by Westerners; and not only about Africa. Yet in this they are not very different from people elsewhere: human beings do have their ideological, cultural and gender biases. The positive aspect is that human beings are able to explain to each other in a respectful dialogue where their situatedness comes from.

In her article, Nnaemeka also rightly emphasizes the existing imbalance between scholarly publications from Africa, and those produced in the West. The discussion continues to be dominated by researchers and academics with jobs in the West, who do indeed belong to a privileged group. It is crucial for Africanist scholars carefully to read works and comments by African critical academics, especially those produced in Africa itself. These points will emerge again in the next chapter where the discussion of insiders, outsiders and the academy continues.

8

Knowledge is like an ocean

Insiders, outsiders and the academy

Olofi created the world and all the things in it. He created beautiful things and ugly things. He created Truth and Falsehood. He made Truth big and powerful, but he made Falsehood skinny and weak. And he made them enemies. He gave Falsehood a cutlass, unbeknownst to Truth. One day, the two met and started fighting. Truth, being so big and powerful, felt confident and also very complacent since he didn't know that Falsehood had a cutlass. So Falsehood cunningly cut off Truth's head.This jolted and enraged Truth and he started scrambling around for his head. He stumbled on Falsehood and, knocking him down, Truth felt the head of Falsehood which he took to be his own. His strength being truly awesome, a mere pull from Truth yanked off the head of Falsehood and this Truth placed on his own neck. And from that day what we have is this grotesque and confusing mismatch: the body of Truth; the head of Falsehood.

In order to bring an end to this continuous confusion about truth and falsehood – so we could add to this Afro-Cuban myth quoted by Jeyifo (1990: 33) – people invented science. However, instead of striving for a simplistic dichotomy of true and false one could, as Kwame Anthony Appiah suggested, try to see the diversity of discourse as a source of richness, available to the whole of humankind; a diversity providing us with the multicoloured intellectual landscape we need to understand our place in the universe. Or, in the words of Aimé Césaire, whom Appiah (1992b: 230) quotes: 'Ma conception de l'universel est celle d'un universel riche de tout le particulier, riche de tous les particuliers, approfondissement et coexistence de tous les particuliers' [My conception of the universal is that of a universal that is rich in all of the particular, rich in all particulars, the deepening and the coexistence of all particulars].

This utopian vision is thwarted and hindered by the division of the world into true and false on the basis of the pattern of us and them. 'However long the tree trunk lies in water, it can never become a crocodile', goes the West African Mandinka proverb, with reference to the others, the outsiders who will never really belong, even though they try their utmost. Indeed, the world seems 'naturally' to consist of 'own' and 'foreign'; and 'foreign' never becomes 'own', never a crocodile among the crocodiles. What is true and what is not true, who belongs and who does not, is decided preferably on the basis of established norms.

This also happens in science and scholarship, for example, the nineteenth-century Austrian botanist Mendel. His theory of genetics which later led to laws bearing his name, initially fell outside the existing scientific order. Academic scholars saw nothing in it, probably because they were too much tied to their traditional scientific pedigree. Foucault (1971: 36), who cites the example of Mendel, warned scientists against the danger of becoming a society of insiders that would no longer be sensitive to its own established pre-conditions, rules and mechanisms of inclusion and exclusion. Indeed, scientists are also human beings, and the arguments upon which they base their authority need continuous probing, as do the arguments of those who deconstruct them (cf. Kuhn 1970; White 1978; Korsten 1998).

In the course of history various kinds of people have not only been kept outside the field of the sciences but also outside the boundaries of 'civilized mankind'. Various allegedly scientific reasons have been presented to justify such exclusion, to which the outsider groups have variously reacted. These are as always matters of discourse and counter-discourse, even if the communication is on an unequal footing. Us and them, Self and Other, the drawing of demarcation lines in culture and academia and the reactions of those who were kept outside have long been familiar topics. Scholarship has gradually started to take this history into account.

Much has been written about those Western scholars who held the view that some people could not be fellow human beings because they lacked certain necessary characteristics. It would be straying too far from the subject to raise again the whole series of notorious and sometimes influential Western forefathers who maintained such views, but I cannot resist the temptation to mention briefly a footnote from part three of David Hume's philsophical work, *Essay on Human Understanding* (1748):

I am apt to suspect the negroes and in general all the other species of men (for there are four or five different kinds) to be naturally inferior to the whites. There never was a civilised nation of any other complexion than white ... no arts, no sciences ... Such a uniform and constant

difference could not happen, in so many countries and ages, if nature had
not made our original distinction betwixt these breeds of men. (qtd in
Curtin 1964: 381)

The point here is not to discuss how insiders such as Hume, Kant, Hegel and
others have acted – Wole Soyinka (1986) did this elegantly and eloquently in
his Nobel Prize Address at the Swedish Academy in Stockholm – but to see
how the designated outsiders have reacted; how crocodiles and tree trunks
meet in today's academic discourse. This issue is complicated by the fact that,
in the course of history, a number of Western insiders have critically distanced
themselves from exclusive views such as Hume's, while the so-called outsiders
have often tried to meet them, instead of critically evaluating the dominant
cultural or scientific criteria or fighting them.

   The ability to write was one such criterion. Throughout history people were
scientifically grouped into non-writing and writing peoples. Anthropologists,
as representatives of the writing peoples, committed the cultural 'reality' of the
non-writing peoples to paper in accordance with their discipline, from
perspectives and with vested interests which have changed with the history of
science. Writing was charged with the ambivalence of progress, writes Ton
Lemaire (1984: 106): 'History has been, from the beginning, an accomplice in
hiding the history of the Others'. He quotes Stanley Diamond who remarks
that history has always been written by the victor and that the majority of
people have no say in it.

   This statement holds true not only for history, but also for the whole of
scientific exercise in general: the majority of people have no say in it. This
makes the responsibility of scientists all the greater and the need for precision
more pressing. Written texts start to lead lives of their own. They dominate
oral history and oral literature for writing is, in the words of Walter Ong
(1982: 12), 'a particularly pre-emptive and imperialist activity that tends to
assimilate other things to itself'. In the process of writing, researchers
effectively mould reality according to their own will, but that will is in turn
conditioned by the rules of science. They write within an existing tradition,
even when they write against it. Perspectives are unavoidable, but they are
also reversible and changeable. And they have been changed and reversed, as
discussions in the previous chapters demonstrate.

Intercultural studies

In response to approaches which showed the colonized that they had no
culture and that their history began with the arrival of the Europeans in Africa,

Africans wrote back the success stories of their own cultural history. Cheikh Anta Diop is probably the best example of this. Because of deep-rooted mistrust of old colonial prejudices, researchers from the former colonies were often particularly critical in their approach to Western theory. Owing in part to this, doubt about the self-evidence of one's own truth has strongly increased in the West, which has stimulated in contemporary scholarship a reconsideration of the relation between Self and Other. The traditional exclusive Western boundaries between us and them have opened up.

Intercultural research involves elements from more than one culture. These include, for example, concepts or methods from one culture that are used in the study of another. This immediately poses a problem: where does the other culture start? The delimitation of culture varies with one's perspective. The demarcation line between cultural insiders and outsiders can be very subjective. In each case, it is necessary to specify the cultural criteria that one is following. Intercultural studies oblige researchers to take into account their own legacy of background thinking and taking things for granted, as well as constantly to raise questions about the possible cultural and ideological restraints of their own visions and knowledge. An intensive interdisciplinary discussion is taking place on the danger of authoritarian science in the hierarchical relations between subject and object, between 'scribers' and described. Since this problematic relationship occurs in various disciplines, I will give brief examples from history, anthropology, sociology and literary theory, in that order.

In her study on African historiography, Caroline Neale (1985) discusses African reactions to older visions of Western historians, such as the view of the English historian Hugh Trevor-Roper who, as late as 1963 in a BBC radio lecture, claimed that Africa had no history and that there was nothing to be found on that continent other than 'unrewarding gyrations of barbarous tribes in picturesque but irrelevant corners of the globe'. The Kenyan Ali Mazrui reacted to this in 1970 with the proposal of a new approach that would undo the foregoing vision. There had been enough history of barbarians and savages, he observed; it was now time for something else:

> It now becomes important that the mere accumulation of extra information does not perpetuate the Trevor-Roper myth. Only a process of counter-selection can correct this, and African historians have to concentrate on those aspects which were ignored by the disparaging mythologies. So commitment to the correction of human error in this case might involve purposive discrimination in terms of what is emphasised and what is augmented in the pool of human information. (qtd in Neale, 1985: 9)

Mazrui presented this as the task of African historians – an issue of 'us' (Africans) against 'them' (Westerners). Twenty-three years later the Leiden historian, Henk Wesseling, briefly described in 'History and Africa' the great strides taken by African history in recent decades:

> However, for all that, Africans are not yet freed from their historical problems, for many of the concepts with which they work come from Europe and are very difficult to apply to the African past .... Anyone who reconstructs the African past in terms of the present [political] state structure, actually reconstructs nothing, for that structure is a product of a very recent colonial past. However, to start this history from a universal African culture would also turn one into a victim of a myth, and one that is perhaps even more dangerous than the nationalistic one, for the pan-Africanist ideology is a form of racism, as Appiah shows. That is a brave conclusion, but also one that leaves the African historians with a big problem. Their history has been discovered. But how is it to be written? (in *NRC*, 22 July 1993)

Wesseling does not say who discovered 'their' history, but he is still following the academic 'us versus them' line of thinking; In fact, he puts himself in the position of an outsider in the discussion by once again pretending that it is a problem exclusively of African historians. To anyone who does not wish to be isolated in comfortable cultural relativism, however, this is a theoretical problem that concerns history as a discipline and therefore the profession of historians. New fields and new developments compel researchers to (re)consider problems which arise, and therewith their own positions, their tools, their concepts and the history of their history. In this scientific reconsideration lies the enormous challenge to confer on the applicability of existing concepts and on the question of degree to which certain visions and methods are, or may become, interculturally acceptable, in spite of differences in perspective and background thinking.

Anthropology has been the first of all human sciences in reconsidering the relationship between Self and Other and the scientific consequences of that relationship. Because of the nature and the history of their discipline, anthropologists were forced before their colleagues in other disciplines to reflect on the problem of unequal power relations between researchers and their then non-writing object of research. Many anthropologists have tried to struggle free of the colonial behaviour pattern of their predecessors. One representative of this critical anthropology is Johannes Fabian, who continually questions the assumptions implicit in the contemporary work of anthropologists, including his own. In *Power and Performance* (1990b), Fabian no longer talks in terms of 'us' and 'them', constructing instead a dialogue and thereby establishing a reversible relationship between anthropologists and what used to be called their objects. Fabian sees the work of the anthropologist as a dialogue with the Other in a joint performance. In this way he seeks to avoid the allegation of an unequal and manipulative relationship between subject and object, between researchers and informants, for which a previous generation had been blamed; an uncomfortable but inevitable reproach for which solutions were eagerly sought. Fabian's thesis is that although our academic culture leads us on a separate way our efforts to signify are, in fact, no different from and certainly of no higher an order than those of the people we study from the perspective of that academic culture (xv).

He advocates an encounter on the basis of equality, a true dialogue, a dialogue in which the information relationship is no longer asymmetrical and in which nothing of what really happened is hidden. Nevertheless, during the process the researcher remains a researcher, states Fabian, and therefore we need a further step. On the basis of what he calls his 'discovery', he tries to create a research situation in which there is no longer a question of different roles and everybody involved participates on an equal footing. Thus he explains how the construction of knowledge about a culture can be achieved through a joint effort with the people of that culture. The stage performance that the Congolese actors prepare in response to Fabian's question about the meaning of the expression 'Le pouvoir se mange entier' ['Power has to be swallowed whole'] serves as a model for the kind of research which the author advocates.

The attempt is sympathetic, but if we analyse the final product with some narratological tools from another discipline – literary theory – an inherent contradiction emerges. Narratology can indeed be revealing. *Power and Performance* is an autobiographical book, according to the criteria of autobiography specialist Philipe Lejeune (1975) that an autobiographical pact exists when the identity of author, narrator and main character are one and the same. There is such a pact here: the author, Fabian, is first person narrator and main character in a story about research as performance. As such, he has the first and the last word, although his discussion partners are also able to express themselves directly. They address him so that he in turn becomes the addressee, according to the rules of dialogue. Yet the dialogue takes place in a hierarchically embedded story that, because of the embedding, unavoidably becomes subordinate to the frame text. Moreover, the author/narrator, while telling his story, refers to the ongoing scientific discussion and in so doing does not of course address his Congolese fellow actors and discussion partners in the performance.

In a review of this theoretically interesting book, Mieke Bal (1993: 309) also

points out the insurmountable problem: because of its form, the text cannot but
be subordinate to what she calls an 'extremely self-centered first person'. One
may sympathize with the problem as it is presented by a scholar who is
struggling with the ethical dilemma of how to study cultures other than one's
own — how to study the Other without reducing him or her to a voiceless
object. But Fabian's ardent efforts to create a position of equality cannot
succeed. His performance partners are not in the academic circuit of which he is
a part and for which the results of his research are finally intended. For that
discourse he ostensibly claims all responsibility as the author of the book, for
only his name appears on the cover. The problem has not been solved.
Scientific research narratives lead to a kind of discourse which differs from his
Shaba interlocutors' oral performance traditions.

Besides, the problem also proves insoluble in research within one and the
same culture and even within one and the same subculture, as the sociologist
Geneviève Bollème has shown in her important study, *Le peuple par écrit* (1986).
She describes how in the course of history *le peuple*, 'the people', in Europe
have been studied by European scholars. She too discusses the relationship
between researcher and object of research. Every kind of knowledge reveals a
certain authority. When one speaks about 'popular literature', one usually does
so from a thorough knowledge of the official literature, which of course is not
'popular'.

According to Bollème, interest in 'the people' is always political, or a result
of some specific political policy that occurs from the moment 'the people' are
declared marginal or held at bay. The specialists speak about the people in the
name of the people and they know what is good for the people. The word
'people' is not used by those to whom it refers. Should scholars therefore cease
to study 'the people'? This is not the conclusion drawn by Geneviève Bollème,
but she does warn them no longer to behave as the ones who make the rules
but rather to see themselves as members of a group, a culture, in the midst of
others. An encounter with outsiders inevitably calls into question the
foundation of one's authority and acquired knowledge, so that one's argument
necessarily becomes more modest (74, 77).

In this way the Other cannot simply be reduced to worn out categories and
one's own academic traditions can be viewed more critically. Bollème shows
how over the years 'the people' have been looked at from the outside and
made the object of research and the subject of literature. There has been
continuous fiddling; the image has been repeatedly readjusted and adapted,
exactly as in the image building process with regard to other Others.

Ultimately, the question arises as to whether 'the people' ever recognize
themselves in what is written about them. 'Natives' from among the people
have taken the floor to speak and write on behalf of their own group. The

implication is that the vision from the inside is thus guaranteed. However, in so doing the representatives have, in fact, more or less stepped outside their group. Indeed, writing is an act that also changes the position and the life of the insiders themselves. The discourse of, for and in the name of the Other, whether it concerns 'the people', one's own or another culture, or a piece of the past, is a tricky business. On whose behalf does one speak and for whom is the argument intended? According to Ton Lemaire (1984), the fact that science is 'script-centric' makes impossible all efforts by anthropologists to free themselves from being bound to one specific culture, however well intended: 'as long as anthropology wants to remain a *science*, the anthropologist will remain a professional stranger, who writes about the Other' (112, 120). This also holds true for historians and sociologists. The problem does not lie in writing about the Other, but in the pretension of representing *the* history, the exclusively true history, the only true thought, the true institutions.

Intercultural literary studies

Literary theory has a long and respectable experience of studying Western written texts but, with the exception of some individual researchers, only at a relatively late stage has it begun to look beyond its own Western horizon. The concept of cultural relativism was brought into literary studies towards the end of the 1960s. After Etiemble's strong plea for a real universal literary theory in the 1970s and various interesting Indian and African studies undertaken in the 1980s (Singh 1984; Dev Sen 1985; Amuta 1989), Earl Miner's *Comparative Poetics. An Intercultural Essay on Theories of Literature* (1990) was a solid new attempt to approach the subject of poetics from a global viewpoint on a larger scale. It is not my intention here to discuss this work, or the cultural differences in poetic perceptions with which it deals, but I shall briefly outline the author's perspective and selection of material in relation to what has silently been left out. He obviously addresses colleagues in the West, as can be seen from his use of the pronouns 'us' and 'them'. As for the selection, there are two striking omissions in Miner's book. One is the absence of oral literature, which is not accounted for. Obviously, he is dealing only with what has been written: literature is written literature only. In Miner's study, written literature and poetics follow one and the same line of development, the evolutionist model:

> The subject of poetics deals with what is hitherto implicit in the writings by the poets. We can go back a step further to a time before which there was not even an implicit poetics, since poetry and poets were not distinguished as things autonomous. This holds true for those cultures

today in which 'la pensée sauvage' contains – in undifferentiated, non autonomous status – the elements or kinds of thought we are used to presuming as distinct entities. The clear sign of differentiation is the naming of the poets, of authors of works. (Miner 1990: 13)

This 'pensée sauvage' and the undifferentiated status of literature and poets – they are depicted as non-autonomous so do they then belong to 'the collective soul of the people'? – is reminiscent of the mentalité prélogique and the early childhood of culture in Levy-Bruhl's *Mentalité primitive* (1922), or the seriously criticized perception of the younger Jung that the 'primitive did not think consciously' and 'the primitive mentality cannot invent' (Okpewho 1983: 11).

The persistence of this legacy may well survive the end of the century in some circles of literary theory. I well remember the 1985 ICLA congress at the Sorbonne where participant Indians and Africans found each other in a common rage and futile protest about the fact that, having travelled thousands of miles from home, they were separately programmed, each in their own group once again, to exchange views about their own literature within the sovereignty of their own cultural circles in back rooms on the second floor of the Sorbonne, while below, in the Amphithéâtre Descartes, 'the serious issues' were discussed. The literary theoretical system of rank and status is changing slowly but surely, but mainly as a result of continual protests such as these, which overall have proved far from futile.

The other major absentee in Miner's book is Africa. This has been true of almost all the handbooks of comparative literature that have appeared during the last fifty years and no reason has ever been given. Yet Miner describes the lack of a balanced system of information between scholars from different cultures as alarming:

> People in the departments we have marginalized are more or less forced to keep abreast of what goes on in the study of Western culture. They know what we do, but we do not know what they know otherwise ... The intellectual canons of comparative study also have clear, strong ethical corollaries. Just as the feminist argument rests on the unshakeable rock that justice be done to that half of the race that bears us, so consideration of the other three-quarters or four-fifths of the race must enter into any literary study denominating itself comparative. (Miner 1990: 11)

In literary theory there are several different attitudes concerning literature from cultures other than one's own; the most cautious is one of extreme relativism. I keep away from other cultures because in relation to them I am an outsider. This attitude may have reactionary motives, or be caused by indifference or suffocating modesty. Conversely, the exclusive right to study their own culture may also be claimed by insiders on the grounds that outsiders are incapable of doing so, a regrettable reaction to the equally regrettable colonial misconceptions and denigratory statements. The result, in both cases, is a form of apartheid. In this way, the crocodile-in-its-own-pool mentality continues to flourish, whereas researchers from elsewhere are excommunicated in advance: they can at best achieve the status of tree trunks.

In contrast to such extreme cultural relativism is the evolutionist comparison on the basis of Eurocentric norms from which Miner, despite his good intentions, has not escaped. He could have prevented this by having his text read by the very colleagues whose cultures, as he argues have been marginalized in comparative literature.

Intercultural literary theory deals with oral and written literatures from different cultures. In addition, texts, genres, and movements can be compared, or ideas studied about specific literatures that have connections with more than one culture. The varying relationships and the differing points of view involved in this can be complex, but their existence cannot be denied without injustice to the insights into the literatures in question.

African literary studies

I choose my examples from Africa, a continent where the mapping of cultures and literatures is indeed very complex. Some see the whole area south of the Sahara as a relevant cultural delineation, while others take the line between forest and savannah in a given region as a significant boundary. Africa has also been perceived as a loose conglomerate of separate ethnic units. National culture can be considered as a delineation; language yet another. Language, nationality and culture do not usually coincide and endless linguistic and cultural discussions are centred on cultures that manifest themselves across borders in different countries or even continents, as in the case of *la Francophonie*.

The concept of black culture refers to a common culture of Africans and people of African descent and so, if not exclusively then at least partly, to a biological delineation. However, in the continent of Africa itself national awareness in the separate countries has increased enormously in recent decades, as is apparent from the numerous African publications in the field of national literary history. This nationalism is once again under discussion. As Simon Gikandi (1991: 128) puts it: 'The old narratives of liberation, which assumed that the nation be the fulfillment of human freedom, no longer have legitimacy.' In all cases, the cultural criteria employed have to be established. In these matters, it is of importance to view culture as a construction which never stands apart from the people who (wish to) see it as their reality. Because there were people who viewed culture as exclusively Western, others started to hold a reversed, exclusive point of view: 'black culture' was set against 'white', and African literature, as a large unit, was set against 'European'. That this can be a valid reality to groups of people is demonstrated, for example, in the well-known congresses of black writers such as those held in Paris in 1956 and Rome in 1959, and in the world festivals dedicated to black culture in Dakar in 1966 and Lagos in 1977. In the USA, significantly more commonly than in Africa, numerous universities have departments that concern themselves with Black Studies.

Advocates of Francophone, Anglophone and Lusofone African literature, or of separate national literatures, have yet other realities in mind. These also exist so long as certain groups of people experience them as real or have interests in maintaining them as categories. Every history has to begin with a specification of time and space and this, of course, includes literary history.

Cultural references in and about literary works contain a wealth of information on cultures and societies as provided by authors, readers and researchers. Such references can be expressed as approval or rejection and will vary according to the positions and visions of those concerned. In all cases they generate cultural meanings that will be conditoned by the perspectives and contexts of those authors, readers and researchers.

In African literature that is written in European languages, for example, the conscious insertion of words from an African language can serve as an emphatic means of constructing a certain identity. The importance of being anchored in a specific local or national culture can thus be stressed. Such insertions can also be seen as a reference to Africa as an umbrella unit, as distinct from what does not belong to it. The existence of such varied linguistic and cultural codes within one and the same text has to do with the progressive increase in intercultural relations in the twentieth century, both interregional and intercontinental.

Strangely enough, oral literature seems to be translated into European languages more often than the literature originally written in African languages. This may have to do with the fact that scholars from the West who collect oral 'texts' and transcribe them find funds for translation more easily than African writers who work in their mother tongue and have much less chance of finding a publisher outside Africa. Research into the relationship between oral and written literatures in Africa often limits itself in principle to establishing the traces of the former in the latter, but of course these relationships are considerably more complex.

Oral literature has started to play an ever greater and therefore more instiutionalized role in the African media. It regularly makes use of words and expressions from European languages and refers to actual political situations as well as to contemporary international events. Various derivations from new situations and from other languages and cultures seem to be taken on and embedded without much difficulty in orally transmitted literary forms. Also, new genres such as pop songs are easily adapted and fitted into existing orally transmitted literary forms whenever there is the need. As soon as oral literary texts are transcribed or translated one is immediately confronted with intercultural questions; intercultural literary theory has a formidable task in the field of oral literature. According to Frits Staal (1993), the assumption that someone who is trained in a language would thereby become an authority in the field of what is written in that language is one of the 'wrong-headed and debilitating features of Western academia' (18, 21). That is right, but it does not of course mean that linguists who are thoroughly informed about the literature and culture of the peoples whose languages they have studied do not exist. For literary theory, co-operation with both anthropologists and such linguists is of absolute necessity.

The West and the rest

Today, especially in the USA, there are two views on the task of departments of letters, which are sometimes seen as being diametrically opposed to each other. The first sees its role as one of making heritage accessible; recognized classics are read and explanations are given for their status as classics. The second sees the university as the place where a new debate should be initiated about the role of scholarship and culture in society at large (Culler 1988).

It seems to me that this should not be a question of choice. Both views are equally valid and are not necessarily mutually exclusive. The outcome depends on those empowered to be recognizers of 'the classics' and those entitled to initiate new theoretical issues. How conscious are we of what is left out from perspectives other than our own?

In the USA this debate has been strongly argued and has led to fundamental discussions about the curriculum. The discussion, in its extreme form, has led to two stereotypical models of politically opposed persuasions: the model of the production of knowledge that fights the authority of the existing canon and the model of the reproduction of 'our common' Western culture. Representatives of the second, such as Allan Bloom and E. D. Hirsch, have sounded the alarm about the loss of American Universal Human Values. The debate has polarized into left and right, where the academic left reproaches the new right with populism, and the academic new right accuses the left of having political aspirations instead of concerning itself with eternal cultural values. In an interesting article in *Transition* (1992: 17), W. J. T. Mitchell describes a rhetorical thread in this lamentation of the loss and downfall of American culture: defeatism about a crumbling empire on the one hand and fear of the rise of new centres of cultural power, which are considered a threat, on the other. In the *New York Times* (26 February 1989) Henry Louis Gates called the position of Bloom and Hirsch an antebellum aesthetic position, 'when men were men and men were white, when scholar-critics were white men and when women and people of colour were voiceless, faceless servants and laborers, pouring tea and filling brandy snifters in the boardrooms of old boys' clubs'.

The issue becomes all the more sensitive because belief in the American dream of the cultural 'melting pot' is seriously harmed by the questions raised. From the side of the minorities, strong pressure has been exercised in recent decades to have different cultural identities represented in the curriculum. This has led to such a boom in American publication of works by authors of African, Arab and Asian descent that some 'jalousie de culture' has begun to manifest itself in European literary circles. When, for example, the American rights to Patrick Chamoiseau's Prix Goncourt winning novel, *Texaco*, were bought for US$75,000, the post-colonial success of francophonie was openly greeted with sneers by the 'real French'. The *Nouvel Observateur* sneered at the Americans who, it said, were not at all interested in contemporary 'real' French novels which also won the Goncourt, but who would prefer to 'buy' the Antillian Chamoiseau. It is the irony of history that sometimes intentions end up achieving the opposite of their intended effects. Francophonie had to serve the greater glory of French culture, but now it sometimes attracts more international attention than the 'mother culture' that reared it and therefore claims to be entitled to international appreciation and publicity by right of seniority. In an unpublished paper, the Cameroonian Ambroise Kom (1993) interprets the reaction of the *Nouvel Observateur* as a revealing symptom of an ideological battle in which the 'shut-out of yesterday' establish their own canon and accordingly no longer classify French literature under the heading 'nos grands auteurs', but under 'auteurs étrangers'. This changing African perspective on 'the classics' could well explain the French fear that ultimately in the USA, 'respectable' French authors and intellectuals might be upstaged by Francophone Antillians and Africans such as Maryse Condé, Edouard Glissant and Valentin Mudimbe. 'Whatever the intentions may have been of those who passionately promoted francophonie,' Ambroise Kom knowingly remarks, 'we have to congratulate each other on the contacts and developments we see evolving today' (5).

Chamoiseau is but one of the authors from former colonies who has been awarded important Western literary prizes. In addition there are a remarkable number of other prize-winning 'outsiders' in Western letters. Tahar Ben Jelloun and Amin Maalouf have received the French Prix Goncourt. English Booker Prize winners include Salman Rushdie and Ben Okri. Recent Nobel Prize in Literature winners include Wole Soyinka, Naguib Mahfouz, Octavio Paz, Derek Walcott and Toni Morrison. From an Anglo-American perspective it has often been argued that the most important contemporary creative literature comes from the former colonies, while the most important research in the area of literature is done by the former imperial centres. But on the basis of what criteria would one claim to be able to know, and to measure for that matter, what is going on in the world as a whole? Does importance equal importance in the English-speaking world? Do we have sufficient knowledge to be able to take into account what is happening in the areas of literature and theory in places and languages other than our own? What about China, India or Japan, for example?

It is obvious that universities have often not been able to keep pace with the turbulence of contemporary cultural changes and developments. The publishing world fares no better. The novelist Ahmadou Kourouma told me the story of his famous novel, *Les soleils des Independances* (1970), now translated into many languages, on which he worked for ten years. He thought up his sentences in Mandinka and recreated the flavour of that language in French. The text, which was eventually praised worldwide for its surprising originality and enormous implications for French as a literary language, was initially rejected by all major French publishers (including Editions du Seuil) on two grounds: the novel was too political, and the French was bad. The author shelved the manuscript until someone drew to his attention an advertisement by a Canadian publishing house which was looking for works by African writers. After much persuasion by friends, Kourouma sent in his text. The publisher reacted at once and the book immediately became a big success in Canada: it won Kourouma the Prix de la Francité. In order to open the door to readers in France, Kourouma's publisher sold the rights to Editions du Seuil for a symbolic price of one Canadian dollar. In this way the book also appeared in France a year later. It became a pronounced success and Kourouma was awarded the Prix de l'Academie Française.

The proverb about the tree trunk and the crocodile has, as befits proverbs, a number of meanings, depending on the context in which it is quoted. Thus it may urge researchers to be modest: we are not simply a crocodile among the crocodiles, specialists in the field of a culture which is not ours. Of course, this meaning holds true, but it may also, as we saw earlier, incite people into rigid and sterile thinking in terms of us and them, of insiders and outsiders.

In interdisciplinary theoretical discussions, the rigid dichotomy of insiders and outsiders has gradually given way to intensive comparative studies of various cultural arguments, views and concepts on the basis of interdiscursivity (see next chapter). This may be a start to the hopeful picture sketched by Appiah in his essay 'Inventing an African Practice of Philosophy' (1992: 230). Literary theory can contribute a great deal to this fundamental discussion. That cultures are continuously changing does not make the field of study any less fascinating. The initial French confusion surrounding Kourouma's novel, now highly acclaimed and translated throughout the world, is characteristic of today's worldwide situation. The traditional cultural boundaries between insiders and outsiders have become mutually problematic and the former familiar distinction between tree trunks and crocodiles is questionable instead of self-evident.

Post-colonialities

Now that voices from minorities and from the peripheries have begun to be heard and taken into account in the Western academy, one might rapidly conclude that the distinction between centres and peripheries has become irrelevant. No more Manichean allegories, no more binary oppositions, no more insiders and outsiders in the field of culture and scholarship. Surely we live in the post-colonial era? The question is, once again, who are the *we*? What does post-coloniality mean and for whom does it make sense?

In an interesting article, Arif Dirlik (1994: 332) distinguishes three meanings of post-coloniality:

1. As a literal description of conditions in formerly colonial societies, in which case the term has concrete referents, as in 'post-colonial societies' or 'post-colonial intellectuals';
2. As a description of a global condition after the period of colonialism – this is more vague, comparable to the vagueness of the term Third World for which it is a substitute.
3. As a description of a discourse on Self and Other that followed as the products of the new orientations in world conditions.

The term post-colonialism is striking for the absence of any geographical reference, a reference still present in the term Third World. One has to discover from the discourse itself how post-colonial are the speakers, writers and their perspectives. The undoing of Eurocentrism is no longer an activity from outside the history of the Western world, but is taking place on the liminality of their relation. It is what Homi Bhabha (1994) calls hybridity, an in-between position of practice and negotiation. The critique of Eurocentrism amounts to the unconditional rejection of functioning as Europe's Other. Shifting subject positions replace the earlier binary opposition of Self and Other which was inadequate for the task of including all differences. In this process, the Third World started new connections with like-minded groups in the so-called First World.

To describe the new shifting subject positions is not an easy task, since they have to be acknowledged as changing – historically, socially and culturally. Former categories such as colony–metropolis, Third World–First World, black–white, woman–man as basic oppositions have been replaced by a politics of variable location. Post-terms such as post-modernism and post-colonialism refer to a 'beyond'. What do they mean? Homi Bhaba builds in some reservations:

> If the interest in postmodernism is limited to a celebration of the fragmentation of the 'grand narratives' of postenlightenment rationalism then, for all its excitement, it remains a parochial enterprise. (Bhaba 1994: 4)

What is the 'beyond' of post-coloniality? How post-colonial are Western academics? In *The Empire Writes Back* (1989), Ashcroft *et al* extend post-colonialism to the USA, Canada and Australia, without taking into account their status as First World countries or their colonizing status with regard to their own original populations or minorities.

As for the intellectuals of former colonies, there is an important difference between those living and working in the West and those who remained in their own countries. The intellectuals from Third World countries with jobs in Western universities do have a certain power. They comment critically on cultural imperialist tendencies and the generalizing by Western intellectuals and researchers – a relevant job.

The situation of contemporary intellectuals in the West is marked by contradictory tendencies. On the one hand, there is the human tendency to generalize from one's local to a global situation; on the other there is the emphasis on plurality and diversity. Dirlik (1994) claims that the fact remains that global powers are at work dictating the very conditions for the survival or decline of today's cultural diversity (340).

I am often struck by the optimistic tone of the post-colonial message: this is celebration time, colonialism belongs in the past, and all we have to do is remove the ideological and cultural remains of the colonial heritage from the academic discourse. The Third World seems to be reduced to the discourse of intellectuals operating in the West (whether of Western or Third World origin). The post-colonial language is English; the scientific jargon has been borrowed from post-structural tools and devices with universalistic pretentions. As critics of post-colonial theory have observed, the post-colonial discussion indeed takes place on the tangent plane between insiders and outsiders, but it also means that its geographical location is situated within the Western world, inside its academic institutions (Dirlik 1994: 345).

Scholars in Africa or Asia who are not exiles, migrants or academic tourists may hold reservations about current post-colonial views because they imply that nothing else is happening outside or beyond internationalization and globalization. At the Globalization and Culture Conference at Duke University in 1994, the Indian scholar Geeta Kapur, was highly critical:

> There is much less question of shifting and displacement than Homi Bhabha wants to prescribe us. There should be much more emphasis on dialogues *between* the various spaces. It is not only a question of hybridity ... We refuse to set the languages of nationalism against the language of globalization.

Rajeswari Sunder Rajan agrees that critiques of the West indeed continue to animate intellectuals in India, although she also admits that in the context of independence 'traditional/other knowledges cannot be viewed today in any clear separation from the modern' (1997: 609, 611). She also notes Dirlik's neglect of gender 'as an aspect of the identity of post-colonial intellectuals and of their locations' (604).

Africa and the academy

New data, new insights, new knowledge on Africa have led to new discussions and ideas, particularly in the human sciences. Research in Africa has transformed understandings and the disciplines, as Bate *et al.* have emphasized in their book *Africa and the Disciplines* (1993). This does not mean, however, that the USA, Europe and Africa have profited equally from such new data and insights.

Biodun Jeyifo (1990: 46) notes with concern that in the field of African Studies the shift has been away from the African continent and the African universities. The agenda of Africanists in the West did not seem to have in mind the bridging of the knowledge gap between Africa and the West in the academic field. Its agenda, in Jeyifo's words, 'consists primarily of winning respectability and legitimacy for the discipline of African literary study *in the developed countries*'(44). This shift in location underlines 'the problematic continuous production and reproduction of Africa's marginalization from the centers of economic and discursive power' (46).

As Paulin Hountondji (1990, 1992) states, the scientific and political implications of contemporary post-colonial relations in North and South are dissimilar. In a commentary with the eloquent title: 'Scientific Dependence in Africa Today' (1990) he describes this dependence history from within.

The international division of labour has made scientific invention and development the monopoly of the North, while the contribution of the South is restricted to the importation and the application of what others have found. Most students in African universities, according to Hountondji (1992), share 'the feeling that, whatever their special fields might be, everything that matters for them is located or taking place elsewhere'. Elsewhere, outside Africa that is, methodologies and theories are invented, paradigms for what is considered 'really scientific'. Africans have the choice between staying at home – which means accepting the limited local knowledge situation in which researchers feel trapped – and moving to the West. There are almost no possibilities for exchange between African scholars in Africa among themselves or with colleagues from other Third World countries. No wonder that an enormous brain drain to the West has taken place; the necessary academic infrastructure is mostly lacking in Africa. Hountondji outlines the colonial history of this situation: the theoretical emptiness of colonial science is a side-effect of economic domination and forced integration in the world of the capitalist market, a peripherization of the Third World economy (6, 9).

Totally different conditions pertain, depending on whether a researcher from the North goes to the South or the other way round. The European or American going to Africa is not in search of science but of scientific 'raw materials'. In Africa he is not in search of paradigms, of theoretical and methodological models, he is in search of new information and facts to enrich his own paradigms. The comparison with the proverbial colonial economic greed for African 'material raw materials' may seem obvious.

It is true, as Bates *et al* (1993) have claimed, that much contemporary academic knowledge has resulted from scientific investments from the North in the South. This knowledge contributes to existing disciplines (such as anthropology) or has given rise to new ones. Much of this knowledge went, so to speak, behind Africa's back; but it has been enriching for Europe and the USA. It is knowledge that has systematically been returned from Africa, 'repatriated, capitalized, accumulated in the center of the system', in Hountondji's words (1992: 344-6). In this system, Africa seems no more than a detour to be made on the scientific highway leading to the academic insiders' bulwark of knowledge. In the meantime, what is happening to original local knowledge and skills? In the best case, these continue to exist next to the new knowledge; in the worst, they are wiped from the collective memory. Here the question discussed in Kane's *L'aventure ambiguë* is a crucial one; '... What you learn, does that compensate for what you forget?' (1961: 49).

The African academic situation described above does not give much cause for post-colonial celebration. The term 'post-colonial' has given rise to doubts and scepticism in Africa. Whose post-coloniality are we talking about? 'Ask any African village woman how "posted" her life is', was Ghanaian writer Ama Ata Aidoo's comment on the easy label of post-coloniality. The hierarchical relations are obvious when we look at the ongoing unequal cultural productions in the West and the rest (in Chinweizu's expression).

African literature, for example, is mainly processed in Western academic discourse factories with Western invented tools and mostly meant for students' consumption in the West. The post-colonial centre for African literary studies is situated in Western universities. In the desperately unequal exchange between powerful societies in the Western world and the impoverished societies of the Third World, Africa seems to have little or no say in the international discussion, not even as far as its own cultural products are concerned, except through those Africans who are part of the post-colonial intelligentsia in the West.

Jeyifo and Hountondji, as well as Africans whose voices are not heard in Western academic circles, bring up for discussion the right of self-determination in cultural and scientific matters as far as their own continent is concerned. The problematic fact remains that a discourse from the centre of the economic, technological, cultural and scientific power has at its disposal knowledge and research material from Africa without sharing it with researchers and universities in Africa. In spite of all the Self–Other discussions, power relations continue to determine the casting of roles in all fields; the subjects and objects of knowledge and the perspectives on available materials in all disciplines.

Universalism?

There is much talk today about universalism. For instance, Michel Camdessus, head of the International Monetary Fund (IMF), concluded that with the end of the Cold War the world has become one; within this worldwide unification the IMF was, in his view, a microcosmos. The discussion of universalism versus relativism is fashionable at present. What is new under the sun?

In the past, the academy was often a servant of colonialism. Evolutionism in anthropology helped to justify colonial interests: civilization had to be brought to the natives because they were so far behind on the evolutionary road. However, at a later stage the natives became difficult due to all that imported civilization. The French colonial administrator George Hardy warned the French government in 1929 against the danger 'that we teach them too much'

(78). It was convenient that cultural relativism could justify the restriction of dangerous knowledge and thus justify conservatism. Existing cultures had to be respected and not 'infected' by the West — thus inequalities could be perpetuated. What is the echo of that reasoning in the post-colonial episode of this serial story?

At first sight cultural relativism, with its emphasis on respect for cultural identity, seems very attractive. In practice, it has seldom been more than a theoretical protest against Western domination. Cultural relativism confirms ethnocentrism. Some ethnocentrisms are, however, in Orwell's sense, more equal than others. Eurocentrism differs from a number of other ethnocentrisms as far as its political and economic power is concerned. In the post-colonial discussion on universalism and hybridity, the relation between the local from where the shifting subject positions and fragmentations were studied and determined, has been underexposed. Therefore Arif Dirlik (1994) denounces post-colonialism as a handy foundation of global capitalism.

The idea of a worldwide fragmentation, the crossing of national, ethnic, cultural, gendered and other boundaries is very attractive, a vision or dream of real democratic cosmopolitanism. Outside the world of the academy, however, the practice of fragmentation often leads to a practice of 'murderous ethnic conflict, continued inequalities among societies, classes, and genders, and the absence of oppositional possibilities that, are rendered even more impotent than earlier by the fetishization of difference, fragmentation, and so on' (Dirlik 1994: 347). In the meantime, the transnationalization of economic production has become universal, in the sense that it originated from Europe but is no longer bound to Europe as a geographical or historical centre. The cultural critique of Eurocentrism in fact plays the game of economic universalism, because it throws 'the cover of culture over material relationships, as if the one had little to do with the other' and diverts critical attention from capitalism to the economically innocent criticism of Eurocentrism (347).

Post-colonial intellectuals are keen on noticing the connections between post-colonialism and global capitalism. Is history repeating the colonial past, with intellectuals preferring to ignore their connections with powerful economic interests?

In contemporary global relations then, the inequality in access to data, information and dialogue remains a much neglected issue. First, it has created a divide between academic tree trunks and crocodiles, insiders and outsiders; a divide along the lines of deprivation of or access to contemporary knowledge. As long as this problem is unsolved, academic status will continue to hamper the much-lauded post-colonial diversity of perspectives and dialogues, due to the geographic location where such diversity is celebrated, as well as to its limited scope, globally speaking.

Second and equally hampering is the view that outside the economically dominant Western world nothing of importance happens in cultures and societies elsewhere. Both problems inevitably lead to questionable research. There is a global need for a more balanced exchange and distribution of cultural and scientific knowledge. A strong plea is not enough. The solution is political and the role of academia is to strive for the independence so badly needed for intellectual and scholarly activities anywhere.

If post-coloniality, as Dirlik argues, is the condition of global capitalism, then the task of a global intelligentsia should be not only to share with others what she knows but also to be open to what happens in the world outside post-colonial studies in the academy.

As the Swahili in East Africa say: 'Knowledge is like an ocean: many arms are needed to embrace it.' Or, to put it in terms of the mythical mismatch of Truth and Falsehood with which I began this chapter: those who fervently want to embrace the richly varied body of Truth, not only need the diversity of many arms but also incorruptible bodyguards in many places, keeping watchful eyes on Falsehood's rearing head in all its confusing local and global disguises.

9

Towards a culture of interdiscursivity

In the summer of 1972 I travelled south from Central Africa. Zambia was already independent and Zimbabwe was still a colony. Given a visa application form at the Rhodesian border, I had to fill up the category 'race'. The answer 'human' enraged the responsible colonial officer. He refused to accept the non-existence of the white race and therefore it took a long time before I was allowed to enter the country of Cecil Rhodes and Ian Smith. The next border was South Africa. It was a Sunday and the minister on the car radio explained the validity of apartheid in a sermon about the words spoken by Jesus at the Last Supper 'In my father's house are many mansions': it was not by accident that Jesus used the plural; from the very beginning he had accommodated racial differences and had designated one mansion for the whites, one for 'de bruinmense', one for the blacks and one for the Indians, just like here on earth, starting with South Africa. The validity of apartheid had thus been provided right from the beginning of the Christian era.

Among many publications on Panafricanism, Kwame Anthony Appiah's *In My Father's House. Africa in the Philosophy of Culture* (1992a) is a remarkable book. Appiah points out how Panafricanism was based upon and continued to build itself on very old racist representations in Western history and philosophy of culture. It has rightly received much attention in the international press and media and has provoked a lively critical debate, especially in *Research in African Literatures* (1, 2 1996). Appiah was born in Ghana, took his PhD in Cambridge and is now a professor at Harvard.

The title refers to the aforementioned Bible text about the many mansions, but Appiah's interpretation is diametrically opposed to the preceding one. He rejects labels or restrictions as to race or culture. He wants to create space for intercultural contacts. In his father's house in Ghana there was no room for a 'color line'. Several cultures came together: Appiah's mother belonged to the English aristocracy, his father was the chief of an influential clan and a brother-in-law of the Ashanti king. When his parents married the British press wrote: 'Daughter of Sir Stafford Cripps marries African tribal chief' and: 'Barefooted savages mix with noble blood in London': once more the blood metaphor! In the South African press the question was raised why the Queen had not intervened to prevent the marriage (Ramdas 1993: 104). Yet as a child Appiah hardly experienced the existence of a 'color line'. Everyone, including relatives from other countries in Africa, Asia, Europe and the USA, naturally belonged to the same family in his father's house. His father's house is at the same time a metaphor for Africa as his place of origin.

He came into contact with Panafricanism through his father who was a strong supporter of the movement. In his book he critically explores its origins and does not shy away from questioning the extent to which Panafricanist views can in their turn be considered racist. It takes courage for a professor at an American Department of Black Studies severely to criticize the African-American dream, as he did in this book. It would certainly have been easier to preach Afrocentrism against an inimical Eurocentrism dominating the world.

If cultures of various origins meet more often and more intimately, what will be the consequences? Kwame Anthony Appiah has asked himself that question in relation to the philosophical background and the cultural consequences of Panafricanism. His ideas point in the same direction as those of such South Africans as Ndebele and Sachs and Caribbeans such as Wilson Harris, Edouard Glissant and Maryse Condé . Their central question is how should we, Africans and people of African origin, handle the cultural situation of the present?

Appiah was right in concluding that the illusions of race, which were the basis of the nineteenth-century scientific heritage, affected the ideas of such Panafricanists as Du Bois, Negritude defendants such as Senghor and more recent types of (ahistorical) nativism found among Western educated African academics (Chinweizu and Madubuike 1980) and Afrocentricists in the USA. They are nostalgic for an imagined past or protesting against the undeniable fact that sub-Sahara Africa today is an historical product of the encounter with the West. An African past is invented in response to and in continuation of European racial thinking and a European concept of what the black Other should be. Appiah argues as follows: when the empty rhetoric of the unity of origin is discarded, it is necessary to renew views of Panafricanism and blackness and of the impact of modernization on contemporary culture. This implies that concepts from different cultures have to be brought into contact with each other. The main question then is how to deal with the relations between one's own heritage and the ideas that come from others. How is it possible to deal with ideas from the Panafrican heritage in which race and racial solidarity played such an important role? Why was it so difficult for both whites and blacks to realize that the idea of race could simply be given up or rejected?

Racial solidarity was crucial as a reverse discourse in both continents, but there is a difference between African-Americans and Africans which, in my opinion, the author neglects. Africans in Africa constitute the majority, while blacks in the USA are a minority, afraid of being swallowed by a dominant culture. As a result, race continues to be an issue in their literature and music, while in Africa it is not.

Many middle-class African-Americans, though materially well off, may suffer more often than they benefit from their newly gained integration. The result is again segregation; not so much enforced but out of choice because of the pressure of that integrated society, in which one is seen as a representative of one's 'race'. Examples abound:

Standing on the steps of a fancy hotel in his tuxedo, a black man is seen as a porter, and is asked to carry the suitcases of a new guest. Or a black man is considered a criminal: blacks walking past a row of cars waiting for a traffic light can hear click, click, click as the doors are being locked. When they try to hail a taxi they wave in vain, because the driver will not open his car for fear of robbery. (Huygen, 1994).

The black middle class is larger than ever, yet black nationalism is growing (along with an ongoing process of structural inequality) and is familiar to an increasing audience, thanks to the popularity of rap in the 1990s.

One of Appiah's rhetorical questions is (280) why we cannot take advantage of the interdependences which have come along with history. This is indeed an appealing thought but, as long as the old racist heritage has not been thrown out with the garbage, its realization remains problematic in a white-dominated, Western, multi-cultural society. Over the years, all the arguments against racial theories and racialized views have not been able to exterminate racism, though they have made a difference.

Katya Gibel Azoulay (1996: 135) argued against Appiah's views; she is in favour of the utility of a racial identity as a political tool. Naming, she argues, 'even through the mediating concept of race, is an important part of the process of coming into being' (138). However (as seen in Chapter 6), strategic essentialism has often created false illusions and false hope among the most vulnerable groups in the ghettos. As a result, blackness is nowadays much less a priority for poor black people than for middle-class blacks in the USA (Gates and West 1996). Black essentialist strategies risk preventing people from seeing possible allies among other groups. The South African example of the United Democratic Front as a formidable force against apartheid could serve as a politically successful counter-example against what Fanon referred to as the blind alley solution of essentialism. So far black American political commitment to progressive African causes has not been spectacular.

Paul Gilroy's idea of a black Atlantic including a wide 'web of diaspora identities' pleads against a black American 'project of building an ethnically particular or nationalist cultural canon' (1993: 218). His conclusion is that the history of blacks in the West provides an important lesson which is not restricted to blacks, a lesson for:

> the politics of a new century in which the central axis will no longer be the colour line but the challenge of just, sustainable development and the frontiers which will separate the overdeveloped parts of the world (at home and abroad) from the intractable poverty that already surrounds them. (Gilroy 1993: 223)

This will again be a struggle for badly needed material and cultural space. Intercultural research also learned a lesson from the theories that people and cultures have about themselves; about the formulations which they employ to express themselves in language and about the metaphors linked to sociocultural contexts.

As part of the overall debate on intercultural relations and research today, my main aim in the previous chapters was to look at African and African-American views of themselves and their dealings with outsiders during a climate of cultural racialization.

After Western 'caudatus thinking', the representation of Europeans in oral and written African literatures was discussed, as well as various ideas about Africa and blackness and the settlement of accounts with the problem of whiteness. The answer to the question who belongs to 'us' has to do with group interests. Emphasis on in-group identity often results from fear of outsiders' domination and strengthens the tendency or even the moral obligation to hide detrimental internal controversies from 'them'.

The overriding concern seems to be that outsiders should receive a positive impression, since throughout history they have reacted negatively towards 'us'. Counter-literature has meant engagement; against colonialism and apartheid in Africa and against racism in both Africa and the USA. It has always entailed a discussion on the problematic relation between literature and propaganda, and between commitment and artistic freedom.

There is an important difference, though, between Africans and African-Americans as far as their position as insiders and outsiders is concerned, a difference that cannot be ignored. Americans construct their own Africa from outside; from across the ocean in another continent and another cultural situation. There has been and still is among African-Americans a strong search for roots and a black identity of their own. This obviously often goes hand in hand with a tendency for exoticism and primitivism (which has sometimes also appealed to their white compatriots), for instance, in the Harlem Renaissance. Some black American intellectuals were critical of the romantic exotic representation of Africa – W. E. B. DuBois for example – others needed it as 'their' African reality.

It would be interesting to compare the differences and similarities in America's 'imagining' Africa on both sides of the 'color line' in the twentieth century with African perspectives of their own continent; and to what extent these respective representations have changed over the years as the result of changing agendas. The African images of Harlem Renaissance poetry have been analysed by Elisabeth Mudimbe-Boyi (1992: 182) who concludes that the idyllic Africa of the poets' imagination conforms to that of classical exoticism:

> The sun, the jungle, wild animals, the drumbeat, dance, but also beauty, purity, and innocence. It turns out that the African-American writers, despite their desire to celebrate Africa, integrated into their imaginary the clichés and the stereotypes of their society, popularized furthermore by the movies and the comic strips.

This imagination in itself underlines how far away Africa's realities are and how ambiguous the African-American's situation is, as an insider and as an outsider: he is the Self regarding Africa (and thus the point of departure of the discourse and the gaze) and the Other vis-à-vis the dominant American culture – as the object of the gaze and the discourse (Mudimbe-Boyi 1992: 183).

From their contact with European culture, African Negritude and Black Consciousness representatives were also not averse to romantic Mother Africa metaphors, but there is a noticeable difference. While African-Americans often felt the need for a 'mythologizing representation of that array of peoples and cultures known as Africa' due to their particular history (Julien 1998: 1), African authors continued to write, sing and critically comment on Africa as their own native land.

Contrary to their male colleagues, African women writers have not appropriated the Mother Africa cult (as shown earlier). Instead, their gender perspectives meant a renovating development in African literature.

Diverse conceptions on Self and Other, insiders and outsiders, have left traces in academic questions and answers as well as in literary texts and cultural movements. From the context of their own cultural background, people are not 'naturally' inclined to be interested in what deviates from the reliable safety of their own views; views acquired through their own group in accordance with the norms and interests of that group. Thus, on the basis of 'natural self-evidence' hierarchical distinctions are made along the lines of race and gender.

One conclusion of the previous chapter was that former familiar differences between tree trunks and crocodiles have become problematic: the former clear cultural and scientific borderlines between us and them are blurred and in question. African-American literature and arts do have such a strong impact on American culture that, according to some critics, it will take the lead in the twenty-first century. As the Negritude poets, the Black Consciousness movement, Chinweizu (1980) and Ndebele (1991) have made clear from rather different perspectives, not only in America but also in Africa the debate about dominant norms and cultural borderlines has led to arguments about rules and freedom in matters of literary and cultural creativity.

As for the question of dominant norms, the inequality in access to information and material means is a crucial aspect. It is also part of a much wider intercultural scholarly debate, which includes, among other things, strategies for setting in place minorities' anti-norms; belief or disbelief in absolute universal beauty; scholarship and the role of political and economic interests; the temptations of cultural relativism as an attractive alternative and its problematic side effects.

The academic consequences of the links between post-colonialism and global capitalism urgently need to be seriously addressed. As Malcomson (1993) and Huggan (1993) have noted, it is a cause for alarm that these connections seem to concern so few intellectuals today.

One practical way of approaching culture and culturally conditioned behaviour has drawn upon the concepts *emic* (from inside) and *etic* (from outside) — terms borrowed from the original linguistic distinction between *phonemic* and *phonetic*. Kenneth Pike defined these concepts as follows:

> The etic viewpoint results from studying behavior as from outside of a particular system, and it is an essential initial approach to any alien system. The emic viewpoint results from studying behavior from inside the system ... The etic organization of a world-wide crosscultural scheme may be created by the analyst. The emic structure of a particular system must be discovered ... Two units are different etically when instrumental measurements can show them to be so. Units are different emically only when they elicit different responses from people acting within the system. (Pike 1997: 37)

Pike placed primary emphasis on the emic view, but he did not ultimately answer the question of whether or not intercultural comparative study is possible. Inevitably, a researcher always brings at least some of his or her own concepts and paradigms into the comparison from outside – etically. The emic structures of the cultural system can only be discovered from inside, by asking insiders about their views, concepts, ways of thinking, doing and saying (Rossi and Higgins 1980: 90) – anything in fact related to their identity.

Among others, the sociologist Peter Weinreich (1986) underlined the importance of emic, ego-recognized categorizations of the Self for members of a group. In complex societies, as he points out, one must take into account the relations between the superordinate community and the various subordinate communities that comprise it, while recognizing that influential significant Others can make the social and cultural identities of dominated groups vulnerable.

In the emic approach, individual and group experiences communicated by the participants themselves are studied. In this respect, literature provides an excellent source of material: authors create characters on the basis of cultural and social experience of Self and Other from an emic perspective, reflecting the norms and values as internalized in and between cultural groups.

In intercultural academic theory and practice, a continuous confrontation between discourse and counter-discourse is needed. Emic and etic approaches can complement each other: etic concepts, tools, frameworks and methods are proposed, but emic information and comments are indispensable. It is true that cultural insiders have for too long been used as mere informants by scholars. The fact that so many African scholars have an important impact on the debate in the West has changed this situation, but African scholars also need informants. The unavoidable hierarchical relation between academics and informants cannot be changed: there will always be a difference in position between those who take the initiative, do the research and ask the questions, and those who produce the insiders' information on the researcher's behalf. That difference can never be abolished, not even by representatives of the culture, gender or social class concerned.

The question then is to what extent the different disciplines have been able to resolve the problem of cultural differentness in research and scholarship and what progress has been made in clearing the way for this academic debate.

The ideas of Peter Zima are helpful here. In 'Les méchanismes discursifs de l'idéologie' (1981a) he advocated replacing the individualistic term 'inter-subjectivity' with the critical term 'interdiscursivity'. This concept emphasizes the collective nature of all theoretical discourses. Interdiscursivity and an awareness of historical-cultural relativity are indispensable for all those who are engaged in comparative study, for we tend to be programmed to discount any counter-discourse in advance. The dominance of the system to which scholars professionally belong represents a barrier that should not be underestimated. The assumptions that structure people's background thinking cannot simply be discarded. If academics strive for integrity as scholars, they must always acknowledge and seriously examine the contents of possible counterdiscourses from the outside world.

In describing the power mechanisms of critical discourse, Biodun Jeyifo explains that parallel or competing discourses can be incorporated into the dominant critical one, whereas others are neutralized, marginalized or ignored;

> Where one discourse achieves relative dominance over other discourses, we are beyond the power of individual scholars, critics or theorists to serve as arbiters of opinion, knowledge, or value, no matter how gifted or influential they might be. What gives a particular critical discourse its decisive effectivity under these circumstances is the combination of historical, institutional and ideological factors that make the discourse a 'master' discourse which translates the avowed will-to-truth of all discourse into a consumated, if secret, will to power. In other words, this 'master' discourse becomes the discourse of the 'master,' in its effects and consequences at least, if not in its conscious intentions. (Jeyifo 1990: 34)

Our task as critical readers is to identify the master's (male as well as female) voice; to recognize where 'the will-to-truth masks the will-to-power which pervades all discourse' (34). How can we do this? How can we know whether the master discourse is manipulating us into accepting certain kinds of information simply because it is compatible with our background knowledge? How can we recognize other ways of knowing? In seeking to respond to such questions, we need to focus on the subject — Toni Morrison's 'describers' and 'imaginers', referred to earlier.

Three questions continue to be relevant and need to be posed critically in *all* contexts:

- Who is speaking?
- Who is seeing?
- Who is acting?

These three questions can be amended in a number of ways. They can be asked in the negative form:

- Who is not speaking?
- Who does not have the right to speak in the text?
- Who is not seeing or not allowed to see?

which means

- Whose perspective is not represented?
- Who does not act?
- Who is passive or powerless to act, to take the initiative?
- Who must submit to the acts of others?

The next questions focus on the object of the three basic activities:

- What is the speaker saying?
- What kind of action is he or she taking?
- What does he or she consider worth including in the story?
- What is 'naturally' omitted from it?
- What kinds of opinion are expressed and to what extent are they consistent with other (expressed or silenced) opinions?
- What are the characters doing?
- Are they acting individually or as a group?
- Are they acting in accord with each other or are they opposed to each other's interests? (Bal 1997, Schipper 1985).

Such questions make it possible for us to gain insight into the power effect of the master discourse. They are relevant to theory, literature and the news as reported in the print media or on television. They are also relevant in our attempts to gain insight into the complexity of intercultural relations, as well as those that deal with gender, class or race relations.

In the academic village of our time, we dare not continue to confine ourselves to our own office or garden. In the study of texts, theories and disciplines, intercultural communication in the broadest sense has become inescapable. For this reason, co-operation and dialogue with researchers from different backgrounds is fundamental. Just doing theory while ignorant of languages and cultures is not enough. All who specialize in the study of cultures or sub-cultures need a good dose of modesty, as long as the word 'Occidentalist' does not sound as familiar as 'Africanist' or 'Orientalist'. Nevertheless, one does not have to be a crocodile to swim in the water, just as one does not have to be a woman to engage in women's studies or a member of the culture that one happens to be studying.

Being an outsider is not necessarily negative. In fact, Michael Bakhtin underlies the way in which outsider status can even be a powerful factor in understanding:

A meaning only reveals its depth once it has encountered and come into contact with another, foreign meaning: they engage in a kind of dialogue, which surmounts the closedness and onesidedness of these particular meanings, these cultures. We raise new questions for a foreign culture, ones that it did not raise itself; we seek answers to our own questions in it; and the foreign culture responds to us by revealing to us its new aspects and new semantic depths. (Bakhtin 1986: 7)

The reverse is also true, for interdiscursivity as a dialogical intercultural encounter is by its nature mutually enriching. The Fulfulde express the same idea in somewhat different terms, but they are referring to the same phenomenon when they say: 'One bangle never jingles.'

Earlier in this book I mentioned how enormous is the global imbalance concerning access to data and research, and not only on the subject of imagining insiders and outsiders. This imbalance risks constantly biasing results, especially in the field of the Humanities. This is a reason strongly to plead for the exchange and distribution of cultural and scientific knowledge. Technologically this is possible and it would cost less than even the smallest contemporary war.

Fashionable as they still may be, post-structuralism, post-modernism, post-colonialism, in fact any thinking in terms of post may conceal our orientation towards what lies ahead. Where do we want to go? As academics, fully aware of our relatively privileged position, the challenge is that we do have some choices, in spite of the narrow area of academic influence. We have the choice of being indifferent; or of trying at least not to make things worse for those who are less privileged than we are. In academia this means a commitment to disrupting all racialized discourse and to promoting interdiscursivity in the disciplines.

Chinua Achebe once said that there is at least one thing the North has little of and the South much, and that is hope. The message of 'the end of history' offers no perspective. Those who want to keep up their courage will have to busy themselves with the global future of Selves and Others, since their fate is, for better or for worse, inextricably connected.

INTERVIEWS

artistic resources of other continents. Gradually they discovered the truth that every civilization is but one aspect of human civilization as a whole.

The important thing now is to work together on a *Civilisation de l'Universel* through a dialogue of cultures, as UNESCO has strongly advised, a civilization to which every nation, every continent, and every race contributes its own irreplaceable talents.

(in *NRC-Handelsblad*, 25 October 1974)

Wole Soyinka

I grew up in a colony. We had not yet achieved independence, when I was trying to attain maturity, and so I lived in the midst of these anti-colonial tracts, movements, concerted efforts, etc. And so I became very early aware of what social injustice is. At that time it was reduced to the experience of colonialism, though, even before independence, I was already aware that besides the question of colonialism, we had to answer some internal questions about ourselves. We had to think of the kind of society we wanted.

Not yet in concrete terms such as socialist society, capitalist society, no, no, not at that time. But I knew very well that there was serious inequality, lack of equal opportunity. And there was this disgusting spectacle of the new politicians who just literally took over the mansions of colonialism and just turned all the games inside out and did not think of what all this meant.

There have been a number of writers who, at least for a certain time, spoke quite nostalgically about the purity of the African past, lost paradise, Mother Africa, etc. This idealization made Senghor even state that, if Africa had had the opportunity of colonizing Europe, it would have been a very different colonization, because Africans had never been racist when occupying other territories. Are you more sceptical?

Everything which is happening in Africa today proves to me, confirms what I have always believed in, the Africans have as much capacity for cruelty, banality, sadism, corruption as any other race in the world. In fact, I would rather not belong to any race which is noted for exceptions to this. There must be some penance somewhere for this strange quality, strange definition of ourselves as a race. So, I don't know what would have happened if Africans would have colonized. For me it is idle to guess. But certainly I do not accept any thesis which suggests that Africans do somewhere differ from the human race. There were times when my reaction to the kind of racism I experienced was to wish I had the chance just to give the other side a dose of what racism can be. And I don't know if I would have reacted differently.

As far as racism is concerned, I notice it, but with only a very small fraction of my conscience. In other words, I notice something very familiar to me. And on familiar things you don't comment generally. This problem is essentially a European problem. It is up to people like you to solve it. Not me. And this racism need not affect me ultimately as long as I make sure that the side to which I belong makes itself strong enough to minimize for itself the effect, the impact of this racism, or to make sure that this side is so strong that a European will hesitate before making such racism overt. In other words, I must confess, as recently as a few months ago, I experienced racism in one of its most shattering aspects and I am not about to try and preach to those people. No, my attitude is only: what should I expect any better? And therefore, that compels me to make sure that my environment, my African environment, economic, political, physical, cultural, remains a bastion of my integrity. So that's why I do not get excited to read the news about Africa as it is presented in the European newspapers. I expect nothing different. It is something you notice en passant, and remind people of, and then you go on. And this is the attitude of most Africans today.

What about public opinion? Can we influence it?

Oh yes, for certain things we can influence public opinion, it is related to ideas as well as time, and changes with time. So, I can intend to mobilize public opinion about race, colour, creed, geography, for a concrete event, a concrete situation, like writers in prison and torture. I can intend to contribute to the psychological and social pressure on governments to bring people out of prison.

Now, if you ask me about African writers, whether they should stay in Africa or leave their country – it depends. There are no general rules of course. In general, a writer like all human beings must know when he has become useless in a certain situation. And it's no good his pretending that he has been heroic at a point. It's just useless, not heroic, just useless, and if he can go and be a bricklayer somewhere, or a barman somewhere, and earn a living in the meantime, and of course he maintains contacts from outside, for me that is absolutely valid. Some people have been critical for example about the attitude of some South African writers for leaving, and so on. I think they are talking nonsense. They don't know what they are talking about at all.

Ultimately, it is the individual writer who must decide, who must judge the details of certain chances which he knows and which other people do not ...

and for me there is no real vacuum in leadership, no real vacuum in the struggle. It is only a myth which is pursued either by those who are on the other side who want to demoralize a movement or the ignorants who live on the ideals and activities of others. So, in any case, my experience is that roughly five-sixths of the participants in movements and struggles remain a permanent secret.

You have been in prison yourself. Is that the reason why you have always been so active for writers who are jailed or otherwise muzzled?

Yes, I know what it means and also I believe that I have a debt to pay, because I know how much activity went on while I was in there. And also, I recognize that it's not so much a debt process as, in fact, another dimension of the continuum of the struggle for social justice. The most *literal*, let me put it that way, because there are as many other fighters for social justice. Fighters are the writers, because that's their profession, anywhere. As a professional division of labour, so to speak. So, while a writer is in prison, especially when he is in prison for his concern for social issues, that is quite a few thousands of people really muzzled effectively. I say that because there is a tendency sometimes to ask: why single out writers? First of all, writers do not single out writers in their concern, that's the basic answer to that; and therefore, to be concerned with somebody who has been singled out in his profession in his real work, his own class, his own group, to be concerned for him is to be concerned for groups other than your own.

(in *Vrij Nederland*, 12 August 1978)

Buchi Emecheta

In conferences I heard several African women writers complaining about the one-dimensional African women characters in novels written by male writers. An East African woman critic went so far as to complain that from an African male perspective female characters do not seem to have any other option than the role of being a mother or a whore.

I believe this is true. Yes. And then that mother must slave for her children and maybe die. The kind of woman Nnu Ego is in *The Joys of Motherhood*. They seem to adore women who sacrifice themselves. She should never gain anything for herself. But as long as you're independent, you are supposed to be a prostitute. Why should that be? Most of these men have children. Take for example Cyprian Ekwensi, he has got brilliant daughters. So why, in his books, should he always put down the women? Why? I don't know. And so many others. The only ones who are not so bad are Ngugi, Camara Laye and Sembène Ousmane. Still, women are necessary for building the future.

Could the idea of independent women be threatening?

I think so. That's why they can't cope with me. I had a tough time when I went back to Nigeria, Calabar, after a number of years in England. Had I been a white woman, then it would have been easier. But I was a black woman, writing and publishing while I was raising kids, and I did fairly well. That was too much. Even the women can't forgive me. A lot of them put the blame for not doing much on the back of their children: they could not do this or that because their children needed them. So my case was rather alarming.

The Nigerian critic Ojo-Ade pleaded a reintegration of male and female perspectives in African literature. If men and women in Africa have a conflict with each other in the domain of mutual rights and duties, he argues, this is all due to Western neo-colonialism. Is it true that Western feminism is to be blamed for the fact that African women are more often critically questioning their rights and duties?

No, African woman has always been dependent in the family, though she can say what she likes. But this being so, the position of women has been determined by the man who is her father and then by the man whom she marries. Christianity has reinforced this situation. The argument that a writer who writes about a woman who claims her rights has been influenced by feminists in the West is wrong.

Of course, it is true that Western women do have problems that do not play such a role in our societies in Africa. For example, the mother–daughter conflict is a nuclear family conflict due to the family structure we do not have to the same extent. Loneliness and isolation are much less frequent in Africa than in the West. Still, the issue of equality has become stronger, in Africa too, and women now dare break with their traditional situation, even at great cost of themselves.

To your question about the obliging Mother Africa compliment [it honours you, but you can never step down from that pedestal you've been put on] I react by saying that this is too much for me, I cannot be responsible for all Africa's children. Five is already quite a number! But I want to write for as many people in Africa as possible, and fortunately my books reach more and more readers in Africa today.

How would you define your own identity? What comes first? The writer, the woman, the mother, the African, if you think of yourself?

If you ask me what comes first in my identity, then it is the writer. The writer and the woman come first, and in being a woman, the mother comes first. Mothers are creators – I have extended on that in *The Rape of Shavi*.

When you were in Amsterdam last time, you were talking about racism and sexism. You said that the fact of racism was the main issue for you to deal with in Britain, because your people there were so dominated.

The struggle against racism comes first for both men and women; as long as you are black in a white society you have a common cause. But in Africa it is different. The issues of feminism in the Western world are not at all the same as women's interests in Africa. Take a place like London. However poor you are, you still have social security, you still have medical care. So you are starting from very different angles in Europe and in Africa.

I wrote a book on two girls, one studying and relating with professors, the other not in school, poor. One dies (slimming down) from anorexia nervosa, the other dies of famine. So, what do you want? You speak on different levels. In my opinion, the important thing is education. If you have education, you have a certain level of language. You can pick up a book, you can communicate, resolve problems, go to other countries, deal with immigration, etc.

Adah, in *Second Class Citizen*, sees girls of her own age. She knows that she can be independent: because she has education, she can leave her husband. Without, she probably would still be there. But I had that choice. Most others do not have that choice. What is the use of telling people they're free, if they are forced to marry a man of 70? No choice! If you tell her you're free, you mean free to do what? You get everything through your man, you are not an individual.

In Africa, things are different. You can't afford to have it the same way. African women need to have children. In Europe, you don't have to be a mother to have success, you don't need it, but in Africa you are nowhere as a woman without children. So, feminism is a luxury at the moment for most women in Africa who continue to struggle for the most elementary material things everyday, such as water, firewood, food, and clothing.

(in *NRC-Handelsblad*, 21 May 1983; *Hervormd Nederland*, 16 July 1983)

Sembène Ousmane

We began to write from within a colonial system. The system is now partly covered up by the façade of the black middle classes. My work as a writer is closely connected with the struggle for real independence. In Africa we first thought that, with the independence of 1960, paradise was dawning. We know better now. The whites may have left, but those who are presently in power behave in exactly the same manner. Incidentally, there is one positive side to the situation: we may conclude that, at least in the case of independent Africa, it is not a question of race any more. We are confronted with our own middle class in power, willingly letting itself be carried along to become the equivalent of the white middle class.

These people are willing accomplices of imperialism in Africa. We must have the courage to criticize their practices. They don't like writers and artists, but freedom is never ever given to anybody as a present. We have to create freedom ourselves. Authorities will never give an artist free play to manifest himself as he pleases. In the same way, a nation can never acquire its freedom as a matter of course. It is always a matter of struggle. If freedom of speech has been violated in Africa in the 1970s, I tell you that it will be worse in the 1980s and the 1990s. The prospects are bad. Africa is on its way to what I call African fascism, a combination of Western capitalism and African feudalism. However, we have to make a distinction between freedom of speech in the press and the freedom of the literary writer.

The writer has a special responsibility. If he is silent, it means that the people can't express themselves. In our society the writer has to be the voice of the people. In Africa there is an additional problem, the reading public. Those people who would like to read are often too poor to buy books. Art plays an important role in the lives of the people, especially in Africa, where matters are often alluded to symbolically. The writer takes part in the formation, or rather the reformation of the mentality of the people for whom he writes. The arts must regain their traditional symbolical function.

What do you think of Negritude?

For me Negritude has never existed. It is like the sex of the angels. This is how I see it: one day on the banks of the River Seine a theory was born among a minority who felt crushed under Western civilization, and who had no better occupation than to scratch their belly buttons. In fact, it was a kind of inferiority complex, which manifested itself in this way. Sometimes, perhaps, the Negritude idea can temporarily fulfil a function, as in South Africa. However, only in a post-apartheid South Africa, the South African blacks will be able clearly to understand the core of the problem, and then they will certainly stop running after Negritude.

However, if we take the 'father' of Negritude, Senghor, we see that the same Senghor was negotiating with Vorster, that the same Senghor had contacts with Salazar and his followers. These are, I think, the merits on which the father of Negritude must be judged. As a result, Negritude, as I see it, is one tremendous mystification, that's all. If Senghor's attitude had been different, Negritude could, and I mean *could*, have been a stage in our cultural development.

What we need and what we are looking for in Africa, are new models, examples. We have to create them ourselves. I am sick of European labels. Europe keeps sticking labels on other people. One of the African reactions once was the Negritude movement, but that was exclusively a stage in the lives of Africans living in Europe in the 1930s and 1940s. It did not appeal to the Africans in Africa. In Europe the movement may have served a purpose for some time, but hardly so, if at all, in Africa. May be you can entertain such an idea for a while as a group instinct, yet I can't find anything positive in it. It is a dead end.

My views on the struggle for freedom, carried out by our people, have remained unchanged through the years. Of course my themes have changed with the situation, and so has my technique in some ways. This is true for African literature in general. Anti-colonialism has gone. Nobody will say, this or that is due to the colonials. Not that they can be acquitted, but we appeal more strongly to our own responsibility. Our own politicians, civil servants and religious leaders are scrutinized.

As a result, writers sometimes slip back into Afro-pessimism. You easily get discouraged by the things that go wrong. Take the alarming population explosion, the diseases, drought, the way in which the black middle class enriches itself, how on earth can you get anywhere? The Bible and the Koran already said: Africa is cursed, a race of servants. But I refuse to go along with that. Even if my grandfather was a slave and my father was colonized, I refuse. I will never hold up my hand for begging. It is Europe itself which assumes that we can't do without it.

Europe is responsible for four centuries of slave trade and for one century of colonialism. Colonialism was the right thing for us, according to Europe. Yet how many executives had been installed at the independence of Africa? What have you done for Surinam? How many scientists have you trained there, how many engineers and doctors? You have colonized for a long time without much of a visible result. Are we then supposed to have fixed everything in thirty years of independence?

An important development in our literature is the rise of female novelists. The European media have often given a distorted picture of the African woman. First of all, in our religious art there are more altars for sculptures and masks of goddesses than in Europe. Traditionally, women in Africa have more power than you think. In my own family in the Casamance women were always in charge, while they gave the man the impression that he was the chief.

Our female writers give a very intrinsic picture of contemporary women. With great courage they broach subjects which until recently have been undiscussable. In this way they do away with taboos.

I can see the signs of a new, a more democratic stage, if not yet freedom. If it were up to literature, we would have had an ideal society for a long time, I am sure.

Wole Soyinka once told me that some African leaders called themselves Marxists and subsequently had stopped thinking. In 1975 Sembène, however, assured me that there is no other solution for Africa than Marxism.

That is still my conviction, even if nothing much has come of it in the Eastern bloc. The fact that Mengistu, Bokassa and Idi Amin have made a mess of it tells us just as much about Marxism or capitalism as the fact that Stalin and Hitler were no good at all. We can easily agree on that. However, Europe and I have a basic disagreement on the history of humankind with respect to the deportation of more than one million blacks in bondage for the sake of Western economic development. I like to take a position on that. The West has reacted arrogantly to the collapse of the Eastern bloc; capitalism has entrenched itself in the multinationals. The governments are almost losing grip. Who is in fact responsible for the economic decisions nowadays? It seems to me that it is an urgent question for Europeans, although the West is not the centre that preoccupies me.

Since Africa can no longer rely on anyone, we Africans, with Afro-pessimism left behind, urgently need to organize ourselves. My dream is the wellbeing of Africa and, consequently, the wellbeing of the rest of the world. (in *NRC Handelsblad*, 28 February 1975; *Vrij Nederland*, 20 July 1991)

Maryse Condé

Most of the readers of a novel like *Ségou* read it for reasons other than I intended. They consider it an exciting story, full of adventures and passion. I was interested in placing the decline of Africa in a historical framework, in showing how history encroached upon the lives of people in an African culture, which was harmonious when no outside influence was felt yet. In Antillian literature I have been labelled for a long time as someone who writes novels about Africa. Since *Ségou*, Antillian people have understood that the Africa of the past is also their Africa. In *Ségou* I write about the struggle in which we were all Africans, about the struggle before the slave trade. So *Ségou* is about us. The worst mistake an Antillian can make is to think that his roots are exclusively in Africa and that he has to find his identity there. I thought that for fifteen or twenty years. What we share is that we all come from Africa. But two or three centuries have passed since our departure. In the countries in which we live, the Caribbean or black America, we have built a new culture. This culture is just as fascinating and complex as any culture in the world. Here is where our duty lies, here we must express ourselves, this is what we have to write about, without chauvinism and of course with the recollection of a distant past in Africa.

Do you have any affinity with feminism?

I have never felt attracted towards Western feminism. It contains latent hierarchical thinking, in that the black woman is a kind of zero level of womanhood: she is the most oppressed, has nothing to offer, the opposite of what a woman should be or become. The African sister must be helped by the white woman in her liberation; I detest this paternalism. In their own society African women are often much stronger and much more convinced of their value than white women in an industrialized society.

To come back to this question of identity ...

I solved the problem of my own identity long ago. It has often been said that Antillians are fake Europeans and that a good Antillian is someone who speaks perfect French, Dutch or English. He must know what the colonizer knows, he must fit into the European context. Yet by now, the Antillians understand the refusal of Aimé Césaire, who exclaims in one of his poems: 'Even if the tree trunk is painted white, its bark will cry out nonetheless.'

Unfortunately, maybe as a result, people fell victim to the delusion that they had to find their identity in Africa. The Caribbean is a place where people from different origins and different cultures have met. There have been attempts to kind of split us up in an inventory of origins. This element is from India, this from Africa, this from Europe. That is wrong. It is not very important to know where these elements come from. What is important is that they form a whole and the Caribbeans have made this whole, a way of life, a culture, an identity which is tangible for every visitor, from Trinidad to the Antilles, Jamaica, Cuba, etc. Of course there are internal differences, in language for example, but the charm of the Caribbean is precisely the variety of expression within one cultural society.

And there is another problem. There is a lot of discusssion about *créolité* and *Antillianité*. This discussion has acquired a different meaning over the last few years, with the spread of Caribbean people all over the capitalist countries of the world, from the USA Latin America and Europe. Can these people be denied their *Antillianité*, their *créolité*, because they left the region? That is impossible, even if they start writing in another language. A Haitian girl who comes to the USA or Canada as a little child, and starts to write in English when she is a twenty year old, against *mainstream* American culture is nevertheless a Caribbean, if and as long as she experiences her identity as such. No one can take that away from any individual in New York, Paris or wherever he may be.

I think it is indefensible to reduce *créolité* to fluency in the local Creole language, to the particular island on which someone has to be born and gone to school in order to belong. This point of view does not at all take into account the Antillian reality of today. Fifty years ago the Antillians did not travel, or hardly so, outside their own region. Nowadays, almost 80 per cent of Antillians have lived abroad for at least five years and often more. Their culture mixes with others in all sorts of unpredictable ways and there is no use denying it. The more people are afraid of outside influences, the more they tend to withdraw themselves. Yet the Antillian identity is a spirit which is continually changing, which cannot be defined geographically once and for all. This is the present-day situation.

Is the urge people feel to define and underline their identity a reaction to the racism they are experiencing?

There is certainly a connection between racism and identity. If we believe in our own identity, we don't mind the gaze of other people. As a result the gaze will change. We have to be aware that we are strong and creative, then we can fight better for our rights. It is not a present that the white world should bestow on us out of charity or generosity. We must set the conditions on the basis of our own power, in terms of a society that has a structure. Take South Africa, for instance, where the blacks no longer accepted that they were pushed back into the homelands. The important thing is that black society becomes a strong society, self-conscious, and convinced of the values it represents.

(in *NRC Handelsblad* 8 May1987; November 1994, unpublished)

Bibliography

Achebe, Chinua. *Things Fall Apart*. London: Heinemann, 1958.

Achebe, Chinua, *Morning Yet on Creation Day*. *Essays*. London: Heinemann, 1975.

Achebe, Chinua. 'An Image of Africa,' *Research in African Literatures* 9.1 (1978): 1–15.

Achebe, Chinua. *Hopes and Impediments: Selected Essays 1965–1987*. London: Heinemann, 1988.

Adotevi, S.S.K. *Négritude et négrologues*. Paris: Union Générale d'Editions 1972.

Aidoo, Ama Ata. 'To Be an African Woman Writer – An Overview and a Detail'.
Criticism and Ideology. Second African Writers' Conference. Stockholm 1986. Ed. Kirstin Holst Petersen. Uppsala: Nordiska Afrikainstitutet, 1988: 155–172.

Aidoo, Ama Ata. 'Literature, Feminism, and the African Woman Today'. *Reconstructing Womanhood, Reconstructing Feminism. Writings on Black Women*. Ed. Delia Jarrett-Macauley. London/New York: Routledge, 1996: 156–174.

Ako, Edward O. '*L'Etudiant Noir* and the Myth of the Genesis of the Negritude Movement'. *Research in African Literatures* 15.3 (1984): 341–353.

Alphen, Ernst van. 'The Other Within'. *Alterity, Identity, Image. Selves and Others in Society and Scholarship*. Eds R. Corbey and J. Th. Leerssen. Amsterdam: Rodopi, 1991: 1–16.

Amin, Samir. 'La dimension culturelle du développement. L'Eurocentrisme – critique d'une idéologie'. *Bulletin du Forum du Tiers Monde* 8/9 (1988a): 13–21.

Amin, Samir. *L'Eurocentrisme, critique d'une idéologie*. Paris: Editions du Seuil, 1988b.

Amina Mama. *Beyond the Masks. Race, Gender and Subjectivity*. London: Routledge, 1995.

Amuta, Chidi. *The Theory of African Literature*. London: Zed Books, 1989.

Anderson, Benedict. *Imagined Communities. Reflections on the Origin and Spread of Nationalism*. London/New York: Verso, 1991.

Andrade, Mario de. *La poésie africaine d'expression portugaise*. Paris: Jean-Pierre Oswald, 1969.

Anthias, Floya and Nira Yuval-Davis. *Racialized Boundaries. Race, Nation, Colour and Class, and the Anti-Racist Struggle*. London/New York: Routledge, 1992.

Appiah, Kwame Antony. *In My Father's House. Africa in the Philosophy of Culture*. London: Methuen, 1992a.

Appiah, Kwame Anthony. 'Inventing an African Practice in Philosophy: Epistemological Issues'. *The Surreptitious Speech. Présence Africaine and the Politics of Otherness 1947–1987*. Ed. V.Y. Mudimbe. Chicago/London: University of Chicago Press, 1992b: 227–237.

Appiah, K. Anthony and Amy Gutmann. *Color Conscious: the Political Morality of Race*. Princeton: Princeton University Press, 1996.

Arnold, A. James. *Modernism & Negritude. The Poetry and Poetics of Aimé Césaire*. Cambridge, MA: Harvard University Press, 1981.

Asante, Molefe Kete and Abdulai S. Vandi. *Contemporary Black Thought: Alternative Analyses in Social and Behavioral Science*. Beverly Hills/London: Sage, 1980.

Asante, Molefe Kete. *The Afrocentric Idea*. Philadelphia: Temple University Press, 1987.

Ashcroft, Bill, Gareth Griffith and Helen Tiffin. *The Empire Writes Back. Theory and Practice in Post-Colonial Literatures*. London/New York: Routledge, 1989.

Baker Jr, Houston A. *Modernism and the Harlem Renaissance*. Chicago: University of Chicago Press, 1987.

Baker Jr, Houston A. *Afro-American Poetics. Revisions of Harlem and the Black Aesthetic*. Madison: University of Wisconsin Press, 1988.

Baker Jr, Houston A. 'Our Lady: Sonia Sanchez and the Writing of a Black Renaissance'. *Reading Black, Reading Feminist. A Critical Anthology*. Ed. Henry Louis Gates. New York: Meridian, 1990: 318–347.

Bakhtin, M.M. *Speech Genres and Other Late Essays*. Austin: University of Texas Press, 1986.

Bal, Mieke. 'First Person, Second Person, Same Person: Narrative As Epistemology'. *New Literary History* 24.2 (1993): 293–320.

Bal, Mieke. *Narratology. Introduction to the Theory of Narrative*. Toronto: University of Toronto Press, 1997 (1985).

Balandier, Georges. *Anthropologiques*. Paris: Presses universitaires de France, 1974.

Baldwin, James. *The Fire Next Time*. New York: Del Publishers, 1962.

Bates, Robert H., V.Y. Mudimbe and Jean O'Barr, eds. *Africa and the Disciplines. The Contributions of Research in Africa to the Social Sciences and Humanities*. Chicago: University of Chicago Press, 1993.

Beauvoir, S. de. *Le deuxième sexe I, Les faits et les mythes*. Gallimard: Paris, 1949.

Berger, Peter L. and Thomas Luckmann. *The Social Construction of Reality*. Harmondsworth: Penguin, 1973 (1966).

Bernabé, Jean, Patrick Chamoiseau and Raphaël Confiant. *Eloge de la Créolité*. Paris: Gallimard, 1989.

Bernstein, Hilde. *Steve Biko*. London: IDAF, 1978.

Beti, Mongo (under the pseudonym of Eza Boto). *Ville cruelle. Trois écrivains noirs*. Paris: Présence Africaine, 1954.

Beti, Mongo. *Le pauvre Christ de Bomba*. Paris: Laffont, 1956.

Beti, Mongo. *Mission terminée*. Paris: Correâ/Buchet/Chastel, 1957.

Beti, Mongo. *Le roi miraculé*. Paris: Correâ/Buchet/Chastel, 1958.

Bhabha, Homi. *The Location of Culture*. London/New York: Routledge, 1994.

Biko, Steve. *I Write What I Like. A Selection of his Writings*. Ed. Aelred Stubbs. London: Heinemann, 1978.

Bjornson, Richard. *The African Quest for Freedom and Identity. Cameroonian Writing and the National Experience*. Bloomington/Indianapolis: Indiana University Press, 1991.

Boehmer, Elleke. *Colonial and Postcolonial Literature. Migrant Metaphors*. Oxford/New York: Oxford University Press, 1995.

Bollème, Geneviève. *Le peuple par écrit*. Paris: Seuil, 1986.

Bond-Stuart, Kathy. *Independence is not only for One Sex*. Harare: Zimbabwe Publishing House, 1987.

Borges, Jorge Luis. *Otras inquisiciones*. Buenos Aires: Emece, 1960.

Borges, Jorge Luis. *De cultus van het boek* [The culture of the book]. Amsterdam: Meulenhoff, 1981.

Bourne, Jenny. *Towards an Anti-racist Feminism*. London: Institute of Race Relations, 1984.

Boyce Davies, Carol. 'Feminist Consciousness and African Literary Criticism'. *Ngambika. Studies of Women in African Literature*. Eds Carol Boyce Davies and Anne Adams Graves. Trenton NJ: Africa World Press, 1986: 1–24.

Brantlinger, Patrick. *Rule of Darkness: British Literature and Imperialism, 1830–1914*. Ithaca: Cornell University Press, 1988.

Breman, Jan et al. *Imperial Monkey Business. Racial Supremacy in Social Darwinist Theory and Colonial Practice*. Amsterdam: VU University Press, 1990.

Brewster Smith, M. 'The Metaphorical Basis of Selfhood'. *Culture and Self: Asian and Western Perspectives*. Eds Marsella et al. New York, London: Tavistock, 1985: 56–88.

Brinkman, Inge. *Kikuyu Gender Norms and Narration*. Leiden: CNWS, 1996.

Bruckner, Pascal. *Le sanglot de l'homme blanc*. Paris: Editions du Seuil, 1983.

Budlender, Geoff. 'Black Consciousness and the Liberal Tradition: Then and Now'. *Bounds of Possibility. The Legacy of Steve Biko and Black Consciousness*. Eds. Pityana, Ramphele et al. Cape Town: David Philip/London and New Jersey: Zed Books, 1991: 228–237.

Buikema, Rosemarie and Anneke Smelik, eds. *Vrouwenstudies in de Cultuurwetenschappen*. Muiderberg: Coutinho, 1993.

Burns, Sir Alan. *Le préjugé de race et de couleur et en particulier le problème des relations entre les Blancs et Noirs*. Paris: Payot, 1949.

Calvet, Louis-Jean. *Linguistique et colonialisme. Petit traité de glottophagie*. Paris: Payot, 1974.

Césaire, Aimé. *Cahier d'un retour au pays natal*. Paris: Présence Africaine, 1956 (1939).

Césaire, Aimé. *Les armes miraculeuses*. Paris: Gallimard, 1946.

Césaire, Aimé. *Et les chiens se taisaient*. Paris: Présence Africaine, 1961 (1946).

Césaire, Aimé. 'Liminaire'. *Nouvelle somme de la poésie du monde noir*. (Special edition *Présence Africaine*) 57 (1966): 3.

Césaire, Aimé. 'Truer than Biography: Aimé Césaire Interviewed by René Depestre'. *Savacou* 5 (1971): 71–80.

Chamoiseau, Patrick. *Texaco*. Paris: Gallimard, 1992.

Chapman, Michael, ed. *Soweto Poetry*. Johannesburg: McGraw-Hill, 1982.

Chapman, Michael and Achmat Dangor. *Voices from Within. Black Poetry from Southern Africa*. Cape Town: Ad. Donker, 1990 (1982).

Chapman, Michael. *Southern African Literatures*. London/New York: Longman, 1996.

Chemain-Degrange, Arlette. *Emancipation féminine et roman africain*. Dakar: Nouvelles Editions Africaines, 1980.

Chevrier, Jacques. 'Les littératures africaines dans le champ de la recherche comparatiste'. *Précis de littérature comparée*. Eds Pierre Brunel and Yves Chevrel. Paris: Presses Universitaires de France, 1989: 215–244.

Chinweizu, Jemie Onwuchekwa and Ihechukwu Madubuike. *Toward the Decolonization of African Literature*. Enugu: Fourth Dimension, 1980.

Cissé, E. *Faralako, roman d'un petit village africain*. Rennes: Imprimerie commerciale, 1958.

Clark, John Peper. 'Thèmes de la poésie africaine d'expression anglaise.' *Présence Africaine*, 54.2 (1965): 96–115.

Clifford, James. *The Predicament of Culture. Twentieth-Century Ethnography, Literature and Art*. Cambridge MA/London: Harvard Univerity Press, 1988.

Collins, Patricia Hill. 'The Social Construction of Black Feminist Thought'. *Black Women in America. Social Science Perspectives*. Eds. Micheline R. Malson,

Elisabeth Mudimbe-Boyi, Jean F. O'Barr and Mary Wyer. Chicago/London: University of Chicago Press, 1990: 297–326.

Condé, Maryse. 'Pourquoi la négritude? Négritude ou révolution?'. *Les littératures d'expression française. Négritude africaine, négritude caraïbe.* Paris: Université de Paris Nord, 1973: 150–154.

Condé, Maryse and Madeleine Cottenet-Hage, eds. *Penser la créolité* Paris: Karthala, 1995.

Cook, Mercer and Stephen E. Henderson. *The Militant Black Writer in Africa and the United States.* Madison/Milwaukee/London: University of Wisconsin Press, 1969.

Corbey, Raymond and J.Th. Leerssen. *Alterity, Identity, Image. Selves and Others in Society and Scholarship.* Amsterdam: Rodopi, 1991.

Coulthard, G.R. *Race and Colour in Caribbean Literature.* London/New York/ Toronto: Oxford University Press, 1962.

Coultard, G.R. 'Parallelisms and Divergencies Between "Negritude" and "Indigenismo"'. *Caribbean Studies* 8.1 (1968): 43–68.

Courville, Cindy. 'Reexamining Patriarchy as a Mode of Production: The Case of Zimbabwe'. *Theorizing Black Feminisms. The Visionary Pragmatism of Black Women.* Eds Stanlie M. James and Abena P. A. Busia. London/New York: Routledge, 1993: 31–43.

Culler, Jonathan. *Framing the Sign. Criticism and its Institutions.* Norman/ London: University of Oklahoma Press, 1988.

Curtin, Philip D. *The Image of Africa. British Ideas and Action, 1780–1850.* Madison: University of Wisconsin Press, 1964.

Dadié, Bernard B. *Un nègre à Paris.* Paris: Présence Africaine, 1959a.

Dadié, Bernard B. *Climbié.* Paris: Seghers, 1959b.

Dadié, Bernard B. *Patron de New York.* Paris: Présence Africaine, 1964.

Damas, L. *Black Label.* Paris: Présence Africaine, 1956.

Dash, J. Michael. *Literature and Ideology in Haiti 1915–1961.* London: Macmillan, 1981.

Davies, Miranda, ed. *Third World, Second Sex. Women's Struggles and National Liberation.* London: Zed Press, 1983.

Davis, Angela. *Women, Race, and Class.* London: Women's Press, 1984 (1981).

Davison, Jean. *Gender, Lineage, and Ethnicity in Southern Africa.* Boulder CO: Westview Press, 1997.

Depestre, René, see Césaire 1971.

Depestre, René. *Bonjour et Adieu à la Négritude.* Paris: Robert Laffont, 1980.

Derive, Jean. 'Littérature comparée: problèmes de méthode et positions idéologiques'. *Littérature et Méthodologie.* Ed. Amadou Koné. Abidjan: Céda, 1984: 53–64.

Dev Sen, Nabaneeta. *Counterpoints. Essays in Comparative Literature.* Calcutta: Prajna, 1985.

Diop, Cheikh Anta. *Antériorité des civilisations nègres: mythe ou vérité historique?*. Paris: Présence Africaine, 1967.

Diop, David. *Hammer Blows and Other Writings*. Bloomington: Indiana University Press, 1973.

Dirlik, Arif. 'The Postcolonial Aura: Third World Criticism in the Age of Global Capitalism'. *Critical Inquiry* 20 (1994): 328–356.

Donaldson, Laura E. *Decolonizing Feminisms. Race, Gender, and Empire-building*. London/New York: Routledge, 1993.

Driver, Dorothy. 'M'a-Ngoana O Tsoare Thipa ka Bohaleng – The Child's Mother Grabs the Sharp End of the Knife: Women as Mothers, Women as Writers'. *Rendering Things Visible. Essays on South African Literature*. Ed. Martin Trump. Johannesburg: Ravan Press, 1990: 225–255.

Du Bois, W. E. B. *The Souls of Black Folk*. Chicago: A. C. McClurg, 1903.

Ellison, Ralph. *Invisible Man*. New York: Random House, 1952.

Equiano's Travels. The Interesting Narrative of the Life of Olaudah Equiano or Gustavus Vassa the African, Written by Himself. Ed. Paul Edwards. London: Heinemann, 1977 (1789).

Erikson, Erik H. *Identity and the Life Cycle*. New York: W. W. Norton, 1980 (1959).

Esedebe, P. Olisanwuche. *Pan-Africanism. The Idea of a Movement 1776–1963*. Washington DC: Howard University Press, 1982.

Essed, Philomena. *Diversiteit*. Baarn: Ambo, 1994.

Even-Zohar, Itamar. 'Polysystem Theory'. *Poetics Today* 1.3 (1979): 287–305.

Fabian, Johannes. 'Presence and Representation: The Other and Anthropological Writing'. *Critical Inquiry* 16.4 (1990a): 727–753.

Fabian, Johannes. *Power and Performance. Ethnographic Explorations through Proverbial Wisdom and Theater in Shaba, Zaire*. Madison: University of Wisconsin Press, 1990b.

Fanon, Frantz. *Peau noire, masques blancs*. Paris: Seuil, 1952.

Fanon, Frantz. *The Wretched of the Earth*. Harmondsworth: Penguin, 1961.

Featherstone, Mike, ed. *Global Culture. Nationalism, Globalization and Modernity*. London/New Delhi: Sage, 1990.

Feuser, Wilfried F. 'Afro-American Literature and Negritude'. *Comparative Literature* 28.3 (1976): 289–308.

Feuser, Wilfried. 'The Decolonization of Negritude'. *Research in African Literatures* 18.2 (1987): 259–265.

Finnegan, Ruth. *Oral Literature in Africa*. Oxford: Clarendon Press, 1970.

Finnegan, Ruth, *Oral Poetry. Its Value, Significance and Social Context*. Cambridge: Cambridge University Press, 1977.

Fokkema, D.W. 'Empirische literatuurwetenschap'. *Vormen van literatuurwetenschap*. Ed. R.T. Segers. Groningen: Wolters-Noordhoff, 1985: 249–272.

Foucault, Michel. *L'ordre du discours*. Paris: Gallimard, 1971.

Fox Keller, Evelyn. *Reflections on Gender and Science*. New Haven/London: Yale University Press, 1985.

Fox Keller, Evelyn. *Secrets of Life, Secrets of Death: Essays On Language, Gender and Science*. New York: Routledge, 1992.

Frankenberg, Ruth. *White Women, Race Matters. The Social Construction of Whiteness*. Minneapolis: University of Minnesota Press, 1993.

French, Marilyn. *Beyond Power: On Men, Women, and Morals*. New York: Ballantine Books, 1985.

Gaidanzwa, Rudo B. *Images of Women in Zimbabwean Literature*. Harare: College Press, 1985.

Gates Jr, Henry Louis. *Figures in Black. Words, Signs, and the Racial Self*. New York/Oxford: Oxford University Press, 1987.

Gates Jr, Henry Louis. 'Whose Canon Is It, Anyway?' *New York Times Book Review*, 26 February (1989): 44–45.

Gates Jr, Henry Louis, ed. *Reading Black, Reading Feminist. A Critical Anthology*. New York: Meridian, 1990.

Gates Jr, Henry Louis. *Loose Canons. Notes on the Culture Wars*. New York/ Oxford: Oxford University Press, 1992.

Gates Jr, Henry Louis and Nelly McKay, eds. *The Norton Anthology of African American Literature*. New York/London: W. W. Norton, 1997.

Gates Jr, Henry Louis, and Cornel West. *The Future of the Race*. New York: Alfred J. Knopf, 1996.

Geertz, Clifford, *The Interpretation of Cultures*. New York: Basic Books, 1973.

Geiss, Immanuel. *Panafrikanismus. Zur Geschichte der Dekolonisation*. Frankfurt am Main: Europäische Verlagsanstalt, 1968.

Gérard, Albert. 'Postscript to Nwezeh, "Littérature africaine et littérature comparée"'. *Revue de Littérature Comparée* 1 (1985): 31–42.

Gerhart, Gail M. *Black Power in South Africa*. Berkeley/Los Angeles/London: University of California Press, 1978.

Gibel Azoulay, Katya. 'Outside Our Parents' House: Race, Culture, and Identity'. *Research in African Literatures* 27.1 (1996): 129–142.

Gibson, Donald B. *Modern Black Poets. A Collection of Critical Essays*. Englewood Cliffs NJ: Prentice-Hall, 1973.

Giddings, Paula. *When and Where I Enter. The Impact of Black Women on Race and Sex in America*. Toronto/New York/London: Bantam Books, 1984.

Gikandi, Simon. *Reading Chinua Achebe: Language and Ideology in Fiction*. London: Currey, 1991.

Gilroy, Paul. *The Black Atlantic. Modernity and Double Consciousness*. London/ New York: Verso, 1993.

Giovanni, Nikki. *Racism 101*. New York: W. Morrow, 1994.

Glissant, Edouard. *Le discours antillais*. Paris: Seuil, 1981.

Goffman, Erving. *Stigma. Notes on the Management of Spoiled Identity*. New York: Simon & Schuster, 1986 (1963).

Görög-Karady, Veronika. *Noirs et Blancs. Leur image dans la littérature orale africaine*. Paris: Sélaf, 1976.

Görög-Karady, Veronika with Gérard Meyer. *Images féminines dans les contes africains (aire culturelle manding)*. Paris: Cilf/Edicef, 1988.

Gordimer, Nadine. 'De verbittering stapelt zich op'. (interview with Peter Brusse). *de Volkskrant*, June 13 (1981).

Grant, Joanne, ed. *Zwart Protest*. Tilburg: Nederlands Boekhuis, 1968.

Gray, Stephen. *Southern African Literature: An Introduction*. Cape Town: David Philip, 1979.

Hacker, Andrew. 'We All Drink the same Water.' *Transition* 66. 2 (1995): 101–104.

Hall, Stuart. *Het minimale zelf en andere opstellen*. Amsterdam: SUA, 1991.

Hardy, G. *Nos grands problèmes coloniaux*. Paris: A. Colin, 1929.

Harris, Wilson. *The Womb of Space: The Cross-Cultural Imagination*. Westport CO: Greenwood, 1983.

Hausser, Michel. *Pour une Poétique de la négritude*, vol. 1 Paris: Editions Silex, 1988; vol. 2. Paris: Editions Nouvelles du Sud, 1991.

Henderson 1969, see Cook and Henderson.

Hernton, Calvin C. *The Sexual Mountain and Black Women Writers. Adventures in Sex, Literature, and Real Life*. New York: Doubleday Anchor Books, 1990 (1987).

Herskovits, M. *The Human Factor in Changing Africa*. New York: Alfred Knopf.

Hoffmann, Léon François. *Le nègre romantique. Personnage littéraire et obsession collective*. Paris: Payot, 1973.

Holst Petersen, Kirstin, ed. *Criticism and Ideology. Second African Writers' Conference. Stockholm 1986*. Uppsala: Nordiska Afrikainstitutet, 1988.

hooks, bell. *Ain't I A Woman. Black Women and Feminism*. London: Pluto Press, 1982 (1981).

hooks, bell. *Talking Back. Thinking Feminist, Thinking Black*. Boston MA: South End Press, 1989.

hooks, bell. 'Feminist Transformation'. *Transition* 66. 2 (1995): 93–98.

Hountondji, Paulin. 'Scientific Dependence in Africa Today.' *Research in African Literatures* 21.3 (1990): 5–15.

Hountondji, Paulin. 'Daily Life in Black Africa.' Ed. V.Y. Mudimbe. *The Surreptitious Speech. Présence Africaine and the Politics of Otherness 1947–1987*. Chicago/London: University of Chicago Press, 1992: 344–364.

Huggan, Graham. 'Postcolonialism and its Discontents'. *Transition* 62 (1993): 130–135.

Hughes, Langston. *The Big Sea*. New York: Alfred Knopf, 1940.

Hughes, Langston. 'Black Writers in a Troubled World'. *Colloquium on Negro Art* (organized by the Society of African Culture with the Co-operation of Unesco, under the patronage of the Senegalese Government, 1966). Paris: Présence Africaine, 1968: 505–510.

Hutchinson, George. *The Harlem Renaissance in Black and White*. Cambridge MA/London: Belknap Press of Harvard UP, 1995.

Huygen, Maarten. 'Zwart en Apart in Amerika'. *NRC Handelsblad* 2 July (1994).

Irele, Abiola. 'A Defence of Negritude'. *Transition* 13 (1964): 9–11.

Jackson, Blyden and Louis D. Rubin Jr. *Black Poetry in America. Two Essays in Historical Interpretation*. Charlotte NC: Louisiana State University Press, 1974.

Jahn, Janheinz. *Muntu: An Outline of Neo-African Culture*. Trans. Marjorie Grene. London: Faber and Faber, 1961.

Jahn, J. *A History of Neo-African Literature. Writing in Two Continents*. London: Faber and Faber, 1968.

Jahoda, G. *White Man. A Study of the Attitudes of Africans to Europeans in Ghana before Independence*. London/New York/Accra: Oxford University Press, 1961.

James, Stanlie. 'Introduction'. *Theorizing Black Feminisms. The Visionary Pragmatism of Black Women*. Eds James and Busia. London/New York: Routledge, 1993: 1–9.

James, Stanlie M. and Abena P. A. Busia, eds. *Theorizing Black Feminisms. The Visionary Pragmatism of Black Women*. London/New York: Routledge, 1993.

JanMohamed, Abdul R. *Manichean Aesthetics. The Politics of Literature in Colonial Africa*. Amherst: University of Massachusetts Press, 1983.

Jarrett-Macauley, Delia, ed. *Reconstructing Womanhood, Reconstructing Feminism. Writings on Black Women*. London/New York, Routledge, 1996.

Jeyifo, Biodun. '"Race" and the Pitfalls of Ventriloquial Deconstruction: Gayatri Chakravorti Spivak's Regressive Monoloque on Africa'. Unpublished essay. Ithaca: 1989.

Jeyifo, Biodun. 'The Nature of Things: Arrested Decolonization and Critical Theory'. *Research in African Literatures* 21.1 (1990): 33–46.

Joachim, Sébastien. *Le nègre dans le roman blanc (1945–1977). Lecture sémiotique et idéologique*. Montréal: Presses Universitaires de Montréal, 1980.

Jong, Marianne de. 'Dialogism in Two African Novels'. *Theoria* (1992): 39–54.

Joseph, Gloria I. and Jill Lewis. *Common Differences. Conflicts in Black and White Feminist Perspectives*. New York: Anchor Press Doubleday, 1981.

Julien, Eileen. 'Women of African Descent Retrieving "Africa"'. Unpublished paper presented at Stanford University, May 1998.

Kabira, Wanjiku Mukabi. 'Gender and Politics of Control'. Unpublished paper presented at a Kola Workshop. Nairobi, August 1991a.

Kabira, Wanjiku Mukabi. 'Gender Ideology: The Cultural Context.' Unpublished Paper. University of Nairobi, 1991b.

Kane, Cheikh Hamidou. *L'aventure ambiguë*. Paris: Julliard, 1961.

Kane, Saïdou. 'Where are the Good Children of Zonga and Manicongo?'. *ViceVersa* November (1995): 12.

Kesteloot, L. *Les écrivains noirs de langue française: naissance d'une littérature*. Brussels: Université Libre, 1963.

King, Deborah K. 'Multiple Jeopardy, Multiple Consciousness: The Context of a Black Feminist Ideology'. *Black Women in America. Social Science Perspectives*. Eds Micheline R. Malson, Elisabeth Mudimbe-Boyi, Jean F. O'Barr and Mary Wyer. Chicago/London: University of Chicago Press, 1990: 265–296.

Koffi, Raphaël Atta. *Les dernières paroles de Koimé*. Paris: Debresse: 961.

Kom, Ambroise. 'Francophonie et enseignement des littératures africaines: quels enjeux?'. Unpublished paper presented at the 19th Annual Meeting of the African Literature Association, Guadeloupe: 19–21 April, 1993.

Korsten, Frans-Willem. *The Wisdom Brokers. Narrative's Interaction with Arguments in Cultural Critical Texts*. Amsterdam: ASCA, 1998.

Kourouma, Ahmadou. *Les soleils des indépendances*. Paris: Editions du Seuil, 1970 (Montréal 1968).

Kuhn, Thomas S. *The Structure of Scientific Revolutions*. Chicago: University of Chicago Press, 1970 (1962).

Kuzwayo, Ellen. *Call Me Woman*. London: Women's Press, 1985.

LaCapra, Dominick, ed. *The Bounds of Race: Perspectives on Hegemony and Resistance*. Ithaca/London: Cornell University Press, 1991.

Lakoff, George and Mark Johnson. *Metaphors We Live By*. Chicago: University of Chicago Press, 1980.

Lallemand, Suzanne. *L'apprentissage de la sexualité dans les contes d'Afrique de l'Ouest*. Paris: L'Harmattan, 1985.

Langley, J. Ayodele. *Pan-Africanism and Nationalism in West-Africa, 1900–1945: A Study in Ideology and Social Classes*. London: Oxford University Press, 1973.

Laye, Camara. *Le regard du roi*. Paris: Plon, 1954.

Leacock, Eleanor. 'Women, Development, and Anthropological Facts and Fictions'. *The Politics of Anthropology*. Eds G. Huizer and B. Manheimm. The Hague/Paris: Mouton, 1979.

Leclerc, Gérard. *L'observation de l'homme. Une histoire des enquêtes sociales*. Paris: Editions du Seuil, 1979.

Leclerc, Gérard. *Anthropologie et colonialisme*. Paris: Editions du Seuil, 1972. (*Legitime Défense* 1.1 1932).

Lejeune, Philippe. *Le pacte autobiographique*. Paris: Editions du Seuil, 1975.

Lemaire, Ton. *Over de waarde van culturen. Een inleiding in de kultuurfilosofie tussen europacentrisme en relativisme*. Baarn: Ambo, 1976.

Lemaire, Ton. 'Antropologie en schrift'. *Antropologie & Ideologie*. Ed. Ton Lemaire. Groningen: Konstapel, 1984: 103–126.

Lemaire, Ton. *De Indiaan in ons bewustzijn. De ontmoeting van de Oude met de Nieuwe Wereld*. Baarn: Ambo, 1986.

Lerner, Gerda, ed. *Black Women in White America: A Documentary History*. New York: Pantheon Books, 1972.

Lévi-Strauss, Claude. *Anthropologie structurale II*. Paris: Plon, 1973.

Lévy-Bruhl, L. *La mentalité primitive*. Paris: Presses Universitaires de France, 1960 (1922).

Lindfors, Bernth, ed. *Contemporary South African Literature. A Symposium*. Washington DC: Three Continents Press, 1985.

Littleton, Arthur and Mary W. Burger, eds. *Black Viewpoints*. London/New York/Ontario: Mentor Books, 1971.

Locket, Cecily. 'Feminism(s) and South African Writing in English in South Africa'. *Current Writing* 2 (1990): 1–21.

Lorde, Audre. *Sister Outsider. Essays and Speeches*. Trumansburg NY: Crossing Press, 1985.

Magubane, Bernard Makhosewze. *The Ties that Bind. African-American Consciousness of Africa*. Trenton NJ: Africa World Press, 1987.

Malcolm X. *Malcolm X Speaks. Selected Speeches and Statements*. Ed. George Breitman. New York: Grove Press, 1966 (1965).

Malcolmson, Scott L. 'Time's Valley'. *Transition* 60 (1993): 118–137.

Malson, Micheline R. and Elisabeth Mudimbe-Boyi, eds. *Black Women in America. Social Science Perspectives*. Chicago/London: University of Chicago Press, 1990: 197–222.

Mama, Amina. *Beyond the Masks: Race, Gender and Subjectivity*. London: Routledge, 1995.

Manganyi, Chabani. *Being Black in the World*. Johannesburg: Sprocas/Ravan, 1973.

Marsella, Anthony J., George de Vos and Francis L. K. Hsu, eds. *Culture and Self: Asian and Western Perspectives*. New York/London: Tavistock, 1985.

Martin, Tony. *Race First: The Ideological and Organizational Struggles of Marcus Garvey and the Universal Negro Improvement Association*. Westport CT: Greenwood Press, 1976.

Martin, Tony. *Literary Garveyism. Garvey, Black Arts and the Harlem Renaissance*. Dover MA.: Majority Press, 1983.

Martinus Arion, Frank. *Stemmen uit Afrika*. Rotterdam: Flamboyant/P, 1978 (1957).

Matip, Benjamin. *Afrique, nous t'ignorons*. Paris: Lacoste, 1956.

McKay, Claude. *Home to Harlem*. Boston: Northeastern University Press, 1987 (1928)

Meek, C. K. *A Sudanese Kingdom: An Ethnographical Study of the Jukun-speaking Peoples*. London: Kegan Paul, Trench, Trubner, 1931.

Melone, Thomas. *De la négritude dans la littérature négro-africaine*. Paris: Présence Africaine, 1962.

Memmi, Albert. *Portrait du colonisé précédé du Portrait du colonisateur*. Preface by Jean-Paul Sartre. Paris: Jean-Jacques Pauvert, 1966.

Memmi, A. *L'homme dominé*, Paris: Gallimard, 1968.

Michard-Marchal, Claire, and Claudine Ribery. *Sexisme et science humaines*. Lille: Presses Universitaires de Lille, 1982.

Michaud, Guy et al. *Identités collectives et relations interculturelles*. Paris: Editions Complexe, 1978.

Milbury-Steen, Sarah L. *European and African Stereotypes in Twentieth-Century Fiction*. New York/London: New York University Press, 1981.

Miles, R. *Racism*. London: Routledge, 1989.

Miller, Christopher. *Blank Darkness. Africanist Discourse in French*. Chicago: University of Chicago Press, 1985.

Miner, Earl. *Comparative Poetics. An Intercultural Essay on Theories of Literature*. Princeton: Princeton University Press, 1990.

Mitchell, W. J. T. 'Postcolonial Culture, Postimperial Criticism'. *Transition* 56 (1992): 11–19.

Morrison, Toni. *Playing in the Dark. Whiteness and the Literary Imagination*. Cambridge, MA/London: Harvard University Press, 1992.

Mouralis, Bernard. *Les contre-littératures*. Paris: PUF, 1975.

Mphahlele, Ezekiel. *The African Image*, (revised edition). New York: Praeger, 1974.

Mphahlele, (Ezekiel) Es'kia. 'Africa in Exile'. *Daedalus* 66/69 (1982): 29–48.

Mtshali, Oswald M. 'Black Poetry in South Africa: What it Means'. *Aspects of South African Literature*. Ed. Chris Heywood. London: Heinemann, 1976: 121–130.

Mudimbe, V.Y. ed. *The Surreptitious Speech. Présence Africaine and the Politics of Otherness 1947–1987*. Chicago/London: Chicago University Press, 1992.

Mudimbe, V.Y. *The Idea of Africa*. Bloomington/Indianapolis: Indiana University Press/London: James Currey, 1994.

Mudimbe-Boyi, Elisabeth. 'Harlem Renaissance and Africa: An Ambiguous Adventure'. *The Surreptitious Speech. Présence Africaine and the Politics of Otherness 1947–1987*. Ed. V.Y. Mudimbe. Chicago/London: Chicago University Press, 1992: 174–184.

Mudime-Boyi, Elisabeth. 'Review of *Femmes rebelles: naissance d'un nouveau roman africain au féminin* by Odile Cazenave'. *Research in African Literatures* 39.3 (1988): 207–209.

Mukherjee, Arun. 'Whose Post-Colonialism and whose Post-Modernism?'. *World Literature Written in English* 30 (1990): 1–9.

Mutloatse, M., ed. *Forced Landing. Africa South: Contemporary Writings.* Johannesburg: Ravan Press, 1980.

Naerssen, Ton van. *De gelede ruimte. Inleiding over ongelijke ontwikkeling en imperialisme.* Nijmegen: Anti-imperialisme-werkgroep (AI Cahier 4), 1979.

Ndebele, Njabulo S. 'Beyond "Protest": New Directions in South African Literature'. *Criticism and Ideology. Second African Writers' Conference. Stockholm 1986.* Ed. Kirstin Holst Petersen. Uppsala: Nordiska Afrikainstitutet, 1988.

Ndebele, Njabulo S. *Rediscovery of the Ordinary. Essays on South African Literature and Culture.* Johannesburg: COSAW, 1991.

Neale, Caroline. *Writing 'Independent' History. African Historiography, 1960– 1980.* Westport CO/London: Greenwood Press, 1985.

Nederveen Pieterse, Jan. *Wit over Zwart. Beelden van Afrika en Zwarten in de Westerse populaire cultuur.* Amsterdam: KIT/Den Haag: Novib, 1990.

Ngcobo, Lauretta. 'African Motherhood – Myth and Reality'. *Criticism and Ideology. Second African Writers' Conference. Stockholm 1986.* Ed. Kirsten Holst Petersen. Uppsala: Nordiska Afrikainstitutet, 1988: 141–150.

Ngugi wa Thiong'o. *Decolonising the Mind.* London: James Currey, 1986.

Ngugi wa Thiong'o. *Moving the Centre.* London: James Currey, 1993.

Nnaemeka, Obioma. 'Feminism, Rebellious Women and Cultural Boundaries: Rereading Flora Nwapa and Her Compatriots.' *Research in African Literatures* 26.2 (1995): 80–113.

Nnaemeka, Obioma, ed. *Sisterhood, Feminisms and Power: From Africa to Diaspora.* Trenton NJ/Asmara, Eritrea: Africa World Press, 1998.

Notten, Eleonore van. *Wallace Thurman's Harlem Renaissance.* Amsterdam: Rodopi, 1994.

Ntamunoza, M. M. 'Quelques aspects de la poésie zaïroise moderne'. *West African Journal of Modern Languages* 75/6.2 (1976): 75–86.

Nwezeh, Emmanuel. 'Littérature africaine et littérature comparée'. *Revue de Littérature Comparée* 1 (1985): 31–42.

Obbo, Christine. *African Women. Their Struggle for Economic Independence.* London: Zed Press, 1981.

Obeyesekere Gananath. *The Work of Culture: Symbolic Transformations in Psychoanalysis and Anthropology.* Chicago: Chicage University Press, 1990.

Oduyoye, Amba. 'The Asante Woman: socialisation through proverbs.' *African Notes* 8. 1 (1979): 5–11.

Ogundipe-Leslie, Molara. 'African Women, Culture and Another Development'. *Présence Africaine* 141 (1987): 123–139.

Ogundipe-Leslie, Molara. 'Beyond Hearsay. The Black Woman and Ali Mazrui'. *Research in African Literatures* 24.1 (1993): 105–112.

Ogunyemi, Chinwenye Okonjo. *Africa Wo/Man Palava. The Nigerian Novel by Women.* Chicago/London: University of Chicago Press, 1996.

Ojo-Ade, Femi. 'Female Writers, Male Critics'. *African Literature Today* 13 (1983): 158–179.

Ojo-Ade, Femi. *Black Culture.* Ile-Ife: Obafemi Awolowo University Press, 1989.

Okpewho, Isidore. *Myth in Africa.* Cambridge: Cambridge University Press, 1983.

Okpewho, Isidore. *The Epic in Africa. Towards a Poetics of the Oral Performance.* New York: Columbia University Press, 1979.

Ong, Walter. *Orality and Literacy. The Technologizing of the Word.* London/New York: Methuen, 1982.

Osundare, Niyi. 'Proverb and Prejudice: review of *Source of All Evil: African Proverbs and Sayings on Women* by Mineke Schipper'. *West Africa* June (1992): 1072.

Ousmane, Sembène. *O pays, mon beau peuple.* Paris: Amiot-Dumont, 1958.

Ousmane, Sembène. *Le Mandat* précédé de *Véhi Ciosane.* Paris: Présence Africaine, 1966.

Oyono, Ferdinand. *Une vie de boy.* Paris: Julliard, 1956.

Oyono, Ferdinand. *Le vieux nègre et la médaille.* Paris: Julliard, 1956.

Padmore, George. *Pan-Africanism or Communism? The Coming Struggle for Africa.* New York: Doubleday, 1972 (1956).

Patterson, Orlando. 'Blacklash'. *Transition* 62 (1963): 4–26.

Penel, Jean Dominique. *Homo caudatus. Les hommes à queue d'Afrique Centrale: un avatar de l'imaginaire occidental.* Paris: Société d'Etudes linguistiques et Anthropologiques de France, 1982.

Pike, Kenneth. *Language in Relation to a Unified Theory of the Structure of Behavior.* The Hague: Mouton, 1967.

Pityana, Barney, Mamphele Ramphele et al., eds. *Bounds of Possibility. The Legacy of Steve Biko and Black Consciousness.* Cape Town: David Philip/London/New Jersey: Zed Books, 1991.

Poggioli, R. *The Theory of the Avant-Garde.* Cambridge MA: Harvard University Press, 1968.

Preiswerk, Roy and Dominique Perrot. *Ethnocentrisme et histoire.* Paris: Editions Anthropos, 1975.

Preto-Rodas, A. *Negritude as a Theme in the Poetry of the Portuguese-speaking World.* Gainesville: University of Florida Press, 1970.

Price, Sally. *Primitive Art in Civilized Places.* Chicago: University of Chicago Press, 1991 (1989).

Rajan, Rajeswari Sunder. 'The Third World Academic in Other Places: or the Postcolonial Revisited'. *Critical Inquiry* 23.3 (1997): 596–616.

Ramdas, Anil. *In mijn vaders huis*. Amsterdam: Jan Mets, 1993.

Ramphele, Mamphela. 'The Dynamics of Gender Within Black Consciousness Organisations: A Personal View'. *Bounds of Possibility. The Legacy of Steve Biko and Black Consciousness*. Eds Barney Pityana et al. 1991: 214–227.

Ramphele, Mamphela. *Across Boundaries. The Journey of a South African Woman Leader*. New York: Feminist Press 1996 (1995).

Randall, Dudley, ed. *The Black Poets. A New Anthology*. Toronto/New York/London: Bantam Books, 1988 (1971).

Redding, Saunders. *To Make a Poet Black*. Chapel Hill: University of North Carolina Press, 1939.

Redmond, Eugene B. *Drumvoices. The Mission of Afro-American Poetry. A Critical History*. New York: Anchor Press/Doubleday, 1976.

Rex, John and David Mason, eds. *Theories of Race and Ethnic Relations*. Cambridge: Cambridge University Press, 1986.

Roediger, David. *Towards the Abolition of Whiteness. Essays on Race, Politics, and Working Class History*. London/New York: Verso, 1994.

Roediger, David. *Black on White: Black Writers on What It Means To Be White*. New York: Schocken, 1998.

Rossi, Ino and Edward O'Higgins. 'Theories of Culture and Anthropological Methods.' *People in Culture*. Ed. Ino Rossi. New York: Praeger, 1980: 29–102.

Roumain, Jacques, *La montagne ensorcelée*. Paris: Editeurs Français Réunis, 1972.

Sachs, Albie. 'Preparing Ourselves For Freedom.' *Spring is Rebellious. Arguments about Cultural Freedom by Albie Sachs and Respondents*. Eds. Ingrid de Kok and Karen Press. Cape Town: Buchu Books, 1990: 19–29.

Sadoff, Dianne F. 'Black Matrilineage: The Case of Alice Walker and Zora Neale Hurston.' *Black Women in America. Social Science Perspectives*. Eds. Malson, Micheline and Madimbe-Boyi.

Said, Edward W. *The World, the Text and the Critic*. Cambridge MA: Harvard University Press, 1983.

Said, Edward W. *Orientalism*. New York: Vintage Books, 1979.

Said, Edward. 'Representing the Colonized: Anthropology's Interlocutors'. *Critical Inquiry* 15.2 (1989): 205–225.

Said, Edward. *Culture and Imperialism*. London: Chatto & Windus, 1993.

Sartre, Jean-Paul. 'Orphée Noir'. *Situations III*. Paris: Gallimard, 1949: 22–288.

Sartwell, Crispin. *Act Like You Know: African-American Autobiography & White Identity*. Chicago: University of Chicago Press, 1998.

Schefold, Reimar. 'Marginale culturen'. *Spectrum-Jaarboek*. Utrecht/Antwerpen: Spectrum, 1981: 193–198.

Schipper, Mineke. 'Littérature zaïroise et société décolonisée'. *Kroniek van Afrika* 4 (1972): 187–194.

Schipper, Mineke. *Le Blanc et l'Occident au miroir du roman africain de langue française*. Assen: Van Gorcum/Yaoundé: Editions CLE, 1973.

Schipper, Mineke. *Het Zwarte Paradijs. Afrikaanse scheppings- en oorsprongsmythen*. Maasbree: Corrie Zelen, 1980.

Schipper, Mineke. 'Eurocentrism and Criticism: Reflections on the Study of Literature in Past and Present'. *World Literature Written in English* 24.1 (1984): 16–27.

Schipper, Mineke, ed. *Unheard Words: Women and Literature in Africa, the Arab World, Asia, the Caribbean and Latin America*. London/New York: Allison and Busby, 1985.

Schipper, Mineke. 'Literaire kritiek vanuit intercultureel perspectief'. *Door het oog van de tekst. Essays voor Mieke Bal over visie*. Eds Ernst van Alphen en Irene de Jong. Muiderberg: Coutinho, 1988: 172–182.

Schipper, Mineke. *Beyond the Boundaries. African Literature and Literary Theory*. London: Allison & Busby, 1989.

Schipper, Mineke. *Source of All Evil. African Proverbs and Sayings on Women*. London: Allison and Busby, 1991.

Schipper, Mineke. 'Culture, Identity, and Interdiscursivity'. *Research in African Literatures* 24.4 (1993): 39–48.

Schröder, R. E. V. M., ed. *Eurocentrism and Science, Higher Education and Research in the Netherlands. NUFFIC Bulletin*. 26.3/4 (1982).

Schulte Nordholt, J. W. *Het volk dat in duisternis wandelt*. Arnhem: Van Loghum Slaterus, 1960.

Segal, Ronald. *The Black Diaspora*. London/Boston: Faber and Faber, 1995.

Sekyi-Otu, Ato. *Fanon's Dialectic of Experience*. Cambridge MA/London: Harvard University Press, 1996.

Senghor, L. S. *Poèmes*. Paris Seuil, 1964.

Senghor, L. S. *Liberté I, Négritude et humanisme*. Paris: Seuil, 1964.

Shange, Ntozake. *For Colored Girls Who Have Considered Suicide When the Rainbow Is Enuf*. New York: Bantam, 1977.

Shusterman, Richard. 'The Fine Art of Rap'. *New Literary History* 22.4 (1991): 613–632.

Siebelink, Jan. *De herfst zal schitterend zijn*. Amsterdam: Meulenhoff, 1980.

Sinclair, Andrew. *The Savage. A History of Misunderstanding*. London: Weidenfeld & Nicolson, 1977.

Singh, Gurbhagat. *Western Poetics and Eastern Thought*. Delhi: Ajanta Publications, 1984.

Sollors, Werner. *Beyond Ethnicity*. New York/Oxford: Oxford University Press, 1986.

Songolo, Aliko. 'Early *Présence Africaine*: Muffled Discourse'. *ALA Bulletin* 14.3. (1988): 24–29.

Sono, Themba. *Reflections on the Origins of Black Consciousness in South Africa*. Pretoria: HSRC Publishers, 1993.

Soyinka, Wole. *This Past Must Address Its Present*. Nobel Lecture. Stockholm: Nobel Foundation, 1986.

Spivak, Gayatri Chakravorti. *In Other Worlds. Essays in Cultural Politics*. New York/London: Methuen, 1987.

Staal, Frits. *Concepts of Science in Europe and Asia*. Leiden: International Institute for Asian Studies, 1993.

Staples, Robert. *The Black Woman in Africa: Sex, Marriage, and the Family*. Chicago: Nelson-Hall, 1973.

Steady, Filomina Chioma, ed. *The Black Woman Cross-Culturally*. Cambridge MA: Schenkman, 1981.

Steady, Filomina Chioma. 'Women and Collective Action. Female Models in Transition'. *Theorizing Black Feminisms. The Visionary Pragmatism of Black Women*. Eds. James and Busia. London/New York: Routledge, 1993: 90–101.

Stepan, Nancy Leys and Sander L. Gilman. 'Appropriating the Idioms of Science: The Rejection of Scientific Racism'. *The Bounds of Race: Perspectives on Hegemony and Resistance*. Ed. Dominick LaCapra. Ithaca/London: Cornell University Press, 1991: 72–103.

Stimpson, Catharine R. *Where the Meanings Are*. New York/London: Methuen, 1988.

Stratton, Florence. *Contemporary African Literature and the Politics of Gender*. London: Routledge, 1994.

Tambiah, Stanley Jeyaraja. *Magic, Science, Religion, and the Scope of Rationality*. Cambridge: Cambridge University Press, 1990.

Tevoedjre, A. *L'Afrique révoltée*. Présence Africaine, Paris 1958.

Towa, Marcien. *Léopold Sédar Senghor: négritude ou servitude*. Yaoundé: Editions Clé, 1971.

Towa, Marcien. *Poésie de la négritude. Approche structuraliste*. Sherbrooke: Naaman, 1985.

Vail, Leroi and Landeg White. *Power and the Praise Poem*. Baltimore/London: Johns Hopkins University Press, 1991.

Volet, Jean-Marie. *La parole aux Africaines ou L'idée de pouvoir chez les romancières d'expression française de l'Afrique sub-saharienne*. Amsterdam/Atlanta: Editions Rodopi, 1994.

Voltaire. *The Singularities of Nature*. Nakijen, 1766.

Voltaire. *Candide et autres contes*. Paris: Aux Quais de Paris, 1960 (1759).

Voorhoeve, Jan and Ursy M. Lichtveld. *Creole Drum. An Anthology of Creole*

Literature in Surinam. (with English Translations by Vernie A. February). New Haven and London: Yale University Press, 1975.

Wagner, Jean. *Black Poets of the United States. From Paul Laurence Dunbar to Langston Hughes* (translated from the French by Kenneth Douglas). Urbana/Chicago/London: University of Illinois Press, 1973.

Walker, Alice. *The Color Purple.* New York: Simon & Schuster, 1982.

Walker, Alice. *In Search of Our Mothers' Gardens. Womanist Prose.* London: Women's Press, 1983.

Wallace, Michele. *Black Macho and the Myth of the Superwoman.* New York: Warner Books, 1978.

Wallace, Michele. 'Neither Fish nor Fowl.' *Transition* 66. 2 (1995): 98–101.

Warner, Keith Q., ed. *Critical Perspectives on Léon Gontran Damas.* Washington DC: Three Continents Press, 1988.

Webster, Yehudi. *Transition* 66. 2 (1995).

Weinreich, Peter. 'The Operationalization of Identity Theory in Racial and Ethnic Relations'. *Theories of Race and Ethnic Relations.* Eds John Rex and David Mason. Cambridge: Cambridge University Press, 1986: 299–320.

Weiss, Ruth. *The Women of Zimbabwe.* Harare: Nehanda Publishers, 1986.

Wellek, René. *Concepts of Criticism.* New Haven/London: Yale University Press.

Wesseling, H. L. 'Geschiedenis en Afrika'. *NRC Handelsblad* 22 September (1993).

West, Cornel and Henry Louis Gates Jr. *The Future of the Race.* New York: Alfred J. Knopf, 1996.

Wheatly, Phillis. *Poems.* Philadelphia: A. Bell, 1773.

White, Hayden. *Tropics of Discourse: Essays in Cultural Criticism.* Baltimore/London: Johns Hopkins University Press, 1978.

Wicomb, Zoë. 'To Hear the Variety of Discourses'. *Current Writing* 2 (1990): 35–44.

Williams, Adebayo. 'Towards a Theory of Cultural Production in Africa'. *Research in African Literatures* (1991): 5–20.

Williams, Rita. 'Strangers in the Night.' *Transition* 66. 2 (1995): 130–134.

Wright, Richard. *The Outsider.* New York: Harper & Row, 1953.

Young, Robert. *White Mythologies. Writing History and the West.* London/New York: Routledge, 1990.

Young, Robert. *Miscegenation and Colonial Desire.* London/New York: Routledge, 1995.

Zavalloni, Marisa. 'Ego–Ecology: The Study of the Interaction between Social and Personal Identities'. *Identity: Personal and Socio-Cultural. A Symposium.* Ed. Anita Jakobson-Widding. Stockholm: Almqvist & Wiksell International, 1983.

Zima, Peter V. 'Les mécanismes discursifs de l'idéologie'. *Revue de l'Institut de Sociologie de l'Université Libre de Bruxelles* 4 (1981): 719–740.

Zima, Peter V. *Literatuur en maatschappij*. Amsterdam/Assen: Van Gorcum, 1981.

Zima, Peter V. *Literarische Aesthetik: Methoden und Modelle der Literaturwissenschaft*. Tübingen: Francke, 1991.

Zongo, Opportune. 'Rethinking Literary Criticism: Obioma Nnaemeka'. *Research in African Literatures* 2 (1996): 178–183.

Index

Abrahams, Peter 90
academics 2, 3, 4, 22, 179, 180
  and Africa 166–8
  attitudes 25–9
  and racist theory 19
  see also research
Académie française 87, 163
access 169, 180
Achebe, Chinua 1–2, 66, 127, 180
Adotevi, S. S. K. 88–9, 90, 91, 99
Africa 159–60, 166–8, 172, 194
  independence issues 60, 186, 192
  non-African black people and
    174–5, 195
  Panafricanism and 58
African National Congress
  (ANC) 100, 101
African people
  non-African black people and 60,
    69, 88–90, 173, 174–5
  stereotypes of 1
  whether exceptions 39, 88,
    186–7, 192
  women 3, 54
  see also black people *and under*
    women
African Studies 166

African writers and literature 29,
  146–9, 160–1, 162–3, 168
  study of 25–6, 158
  women writers 74, 84, 134–5,
    142–5, 146, 194
Afrocentricity 89, 102, 172
Aidoo, Ama Ata 134, 142, 143–6,
  168
Albert the Great 15
Algeria 138
alienation 128
alliances 173–4
Amin, Idi 194
Amin, Samir 21–2
Amuta, Chidi 157
ANC (African National
  Congress) 100, 101
Anderson, Benedict 19
anthropology 152, 154–7
Antilles 79
Antillians 195, 196
appearance 137
Appiah, Kwame Anthony 61, 150,
  154, 164, 171–3
Arnold, James 79
arts 36–7, 192
  see also literature

Asante   145
Asante, Molefe Kete   89
Ashcroft, Bill   165
assertiveness   137
assimilation   1, 29, 70, 80, 81, 123
audience   38, 97, 98, 135, 190, 195
Augustine   15
autobiography   155–6
avant-gardism   72
Ayittey, George   121

Bâ, Mariama   122
Baker, Houston   71, 72–3
Bakhtin, Michael   179–80
Bal, Mieke   155–6
Baldwin, James   56, 58, 60
Bambara   128
Baraka, Amiri (Leroi Jones)   72, 113,
   114
Bates, Robert H.   166, 167
BCM (Black Consciousness
   Movement) *see* Black
   Consciousness
beauty issues   137
Beauvoir, Simone de   50, 122, 123–4
Behn, Aphra   59
Ben Jelloum, Tahar   163
Berger, Peter   22
Beti, Mongo   39, 40, 42–3, 45–8,
   49–50
Bhabha, Homi   164, 165, 166
Biko, Steve   77, 93, 94–5, 96, 101
binaries   2, 24, 38, 135, 163–4
   see also Others/Otherness
Bjornson, Richard   45
Black Aesthetics   60
Black Arts Movement   29, 60,
   69–73, 78
   South African Black Consciousness
      movement and   95, 97
   and women   109, 111, 115

see also Harlem Renaissance
Black Consciousness movement
   6–7, 29, 78, 91–102, 175,
   176
   and women   137–8, 141
'Black is beautiful'   70, 85, 99, 101,
   137
Black Muslim movement   112, 117
black people   141–2
   myths of origins   28–9, 30–5, 37,
      54–5
   'white-mindedness'   67
   women compared to   50–1, 106,
      107, 122–4
   see also African people *and* black
      women
Black Power movement   60, 70–1
   Black Consciousness Movement
      and   93–4
   and class issues   115
   women and   115, 138
Black Renaissance   6–7, 57, 94
   see also Harlem Renaissance
black/white symbolism   36, 46, 63
black women   103, 111
   and feminism   103–4, 114, 115,
      119, 122–3, 133–5, 138, 140–1,
      190, 191
   and insider-outsider
      boundaries   108
   as writers   109, 110–11, 134–5
   see also African people
black writers' congresses   89–90
blood, as metaphor   148–9, 172
   see also racism
Bloom, Allan   161, 162
blues   70
Blyden, Edward Wilmot   59
Boehmer, Elleke   30
Boesak, Alan   95–6
Bokassa   194

Bollème, Geneviève 156
Borges, Jorge Luis 22
Boto, Eza *see* Beti, Mongo
boundaries 14, 21–2, 75, 108, 151,
    175–6
  interpretive 2, 11
  see also 'color line', ethnocentrism
    and Otherness
Boyce Davies, Carol 133, 134
Brooks, Gwendolyn 109
Brown, Elsa Barkley 104
Brown, Sterling 57, 69–70
Brown, William Wells 106
Bruckner, Pascal 3
Budlender, Geoff 92

Calvet, Louis-Jean 36
Camdessus, Michel 168
Canada 163
capitalism 169, 170, 176, 194
Caribbean 102, 195, 196
Carmichael, Stokely 93, 94, 111
Caroll, C. 19
caudatus, homo see homo caudatus
censorship 11, 98, 99, 188, 192
centre-periphery relations 20–2,
    24–5
Césaire, Aimé 59, 78, 80–2, 84–6,
    150, 196
  Biko and 96
Chamoiseau, Patrick 79, 162
Chapman, Michael 95–6
Chemain-Degrange, Arlette 133
Chinweizu, Jemie
    Onwuchekwa 168, 172, 176
Chisolm, Shirley 94
Christianity 9, 19, 46, 48, 171
  and position of women 190
  see also missionaries
Churchill, Winston 68
Civil Rights movement (USA) 60

class issues 102, 105, 106, 108,
    115
  in Africa 124
Cleaver, Eldridge 94, 114
Collins, Patricia Hill 104, 105
colonialism/colonization 29, 36,
    79–80, 126, 186, 193–4
  and education 37, 40–5, 79–80,
    168–9
  meanings attached to 3. 135
  as metaphor 123
  research and 167
  see also post-colonialism
'color line' 56, 57, 64, 75, 76, 114
colour symbolism *see* black/white
    symbolism
communication 149
Condé, Maryse 77, 90–1, 102, 162,
    172
  interview with 195–7
conditioning 5, 20
Congo 8–9, 11, 41, 46, 78
congresses of black writers 89–90
Conrad, Joseph 66
Cooper, Anna Julia 103, 106
Coulthard, G. R. 78
Courville, Cindy 125–6
creation myths *see* origin myths
créolité 79, 102, 196
criticism *see* literary criticism
crocodiles and tree trunks 151, 152,
    159, 163–4, 169, 176, 179
Crummell, Alexander 61
Cullen, Countee 57, 68–9, 80
cultural evolutionism 3, 13–14, 25,
    157–8
cultural relativism 3, 158–9, 168,
    169
cultural separatism 67
culture(s) 21–2, 24–5, 148, 153,
    160, 179

Dadié, Bernard   30, 39, 46, 48, 49,
   97
Dakar   73–4
Damas, Léon Gontran   59, 68, 74–5,
   78, 81–2, 85–6
Darwin, Charles   13
Davis, Angela   106–7
Davison, Jean   126
Depestre, René   78, 79, 80
describers   28, 178
Dev Sen, Nabaneeta   157
development   13–14, 20–1
dialogue, possibilities for   1–2
Diamond, Stanley   152
dichotomies *see* binaries
difference   6–7, 172–80
Diop, Birago   127
Diop, Cheikh Anta   96, 153
Diop, David   85, 97
Dirlik, Arif   164, 165, 166, 169, 170
discourses   178–9
diversity   150, 165, 169, 170
Donaldson, Laura E.   123
Donne, John   136
double consciousness   65
double standards   49
Douglass, Frederick   106
Driver, Dorothy   142
Du Bois, W. E. B.   56, 57, 59, 60, 61,
   64–5, 67, 172
   Hughes and   69
   and NAACP   59, 64
   posthumous prize   74
   see also 'color line' and 'Talented
   Tenth'

economics   20–1, 62, 130, 169, 170,
   194
   see also capitalism
Editions du Seuil   163
education   116, 119

colonialism and   37, 40–5, 79–80,
   168–9
gender issues   116, 133, 191
Ekwensi, Cyprian   189
El Salvador   138
Ellis, Trey   58
Ellison, Ralph   67
Emecheta, Buchi   122, 127, 143
   interview with   189–91
emic/etic viewpoints   176–7
emotion, stereotypes
   concerning   114, 124, 134
employment   114, 116
environment, internal operant   23,
   24, 25
equality   2, 6, 7
Esedebe, P. Olisanwuche   59
essentialism   172–4
   see also nommo
ethnocentrism(s)   5–6, 14, 27, 169
   racism and   5–6
   see also Eurocentrism
etic/emic viewpoints   176–7
Etiemble, 157
Eurocentrism   21–2, 164–5, 169
   see also ethnocentrism
Europe   148, 184–5, 193–4
evolutionism   3, 13–14, 25, 157–8
exclusion   60, 134, 142–3, 158
   scientific justifications for   151–2
exogamy   128
exoticism   175

Fabian, Johannes   154–6
family structures and issues   112–13,
   115, 117, 119, 190
Fanon, Frantz   59–60, 87, 88, 91,
   123, 173–4
   Biko and   96
fascism   148, 192
feminism   103–4, 122–3, 143, 195

African/black women and 103–4, 114, 115, 133–5, 140–1, 190, 191
  Black Consciousness movement and 138
  black feminist movement 114, 119
  Black Power movement and 114, 116
Festival Mondial des Arts Nègres (1966) 73–4
Feuser, Wilfried 57, 80, 81
films 109, 110
Finnegan, Ruth 14
Fokkema, D. W. 26
forgiveness 86–7
Foucault, Michel 151
Frank, André Gunder 20
Frankenberg, Ruth 75, 116
French, Marilyn 123
Fulfulde 180

Gaidanzwa, Rudo 129
Ganda 146
Garvey, Marcus 59, 60, 63–5, 66, 67, 75, 82
Garveyism 78
Gates, Henry Louis 28, 58, 68, 75–6, 89, 91, 109, 162
Geertz, Clifford 24
Geiss, Immanuel 59
gender issues 103, 134, 137–42
  Black Consciousness movement and 102
  concerning oral literature 127–32
  myths concerning 129–32
  see also feminism *and* women
Genet, Jean 77
Gérard, Albert 25
Gerhart, Gail M. 96

Germany 145
Ghana 60
Gibel Azoulay, Katya 58, 173
Giddings, Paula 117
Gikandi, Simon 159
Gilroy, Paul 10, 36–7, 57, 144, 174
Giovanni, Nikki 58
Glissant, Edouard 162, 172
Gobineau, Joseph Arthur, Comte de 18–19, 184
Gordimer, Nadine 92
Gorée/Goeree 74
Görög-Karady, Veronika 32, 127–9, 132
Graham, Le 71–2
Gray, Stephen 99
Greece 21, 22
guilt 114
Guinea-Bissau 138
Gwala, M. 97

Hacker, Andrew 119
Haiti 78
Hamilton, Ian 94
Hardy, George 45, 168–9
Harlem Renaissance 61–9, 75, 78, 89, 175
  theory and 29, 57, 60, 62–3, 64, 72–3
  and women 109
  see also Black Arts Movement
Harris, Wilson 172
Hausser, Michel 79
Hayden, Robert 74
Hegel, G. W. F. 152
Henderson, Stephen E. 63, 67, 70
Hernton, Calvin 110
Herskovits, Melville 38, 50
Hirsch, E. D. 161, 162
history 152–4, 156
Hochschild, Jenny 56

homo caudatus   2, 14–18, 19
hooks, bell   107, 108, 112, 114, 118,
    119, 122, 136
Hooks, Frances   117
hope   180
Hountondji, Paulin   166–7, 168
Huggan, Graham   176
Hughes, Langston   57, 62, 66,
    68–70, 74, 80, 82, 90
Hume, David   151–2
Hurston, Zora Neale   62, 108, 111
hybridity   6, 7, 164

identity   4–5, 10–11, 22–4, 197
    black women and   106–7, 108,
        122, 132
    collective   5, 22–6
    dependent   132
    emic/etic viewpoints and   176–7
    oppression and   119–21
    place and   195, 196
    race/racism and   172–5, 197
    and research   25–9, 104–5, 139,
        143–6, 176–9
    and responses to information   25
    see also boundaries
illegitimacy   49
imaginers   28, 178
IMF (International Monetary
    Fund)   168
imprisonment   188
inclusion   23–4
    see also boundaries *and* exclusion
Indigenism   29, 78
information   180
    channels of   1
    identity and responses to   25
insiders/outsiders *see* boundaries
interdiscursivity   163–4, 177–8, 180
internal operant environment   23,
    24, 25

International Monetary Fund   168
IRA (Irish Republican Army)   138

Jackson, George   94
Jackson, Jesse   94
Jacobs, Harriet   106
Jahn, Janheinz   79, 89
James, Stanlie   104
jazz   85
Jerome   15
Jeyifo, Biodun   150, 166, 168, 178
Jones, Leroi (Amiri Bakara)   72, 113,
    114
Jong, Marianne de   140
Julien, Eileen   126–7
Jung, C. G.   158

Kabira, Wanjiku Mukabi   129–32
Kane, Cheikh Hamidou   37, 41–2,
    167
Kane, Saïdou   32, 37
Kant, Immanuel   152
Kapur, Geeta   166
Kaunda, Kenneth   96
Kenya   129
Kesteloot, Lilyan   79, 81
Kikuyu   129–31, 132
King, Deborah K.   105, 106
King, Martin Luther   71, 75
Koffi, Raphael   42
Kom, Ambroise   162
Komo, Dauda Musa   121
Korsten, Frans-Willem   151
Kourouma, Ahmadou   163, 164
Kuhn, Thomas S.   151
Kuzwayo, Ellen   142

Laforest, Edmond   29
Laleau, Léon   84
Lamb, Charles   80
Langley, J. Ayodele   59

language 14, 23–4, 57–8, 82–3, 148–9
  black/white symbolism 36, 46, 63
  blood symbolism 148–9, 172
  sexual symbolism 135, 136, 142
languages 36, 60, 77–9, 159, 160, 163
Laye, Camara 39, 189
Lejeune, Philippe 155
Lemaire, Ton 152, 157
Lerner, Gerda 106
lesbianism 110
Lévi-Strauss, Claude 25, 132
Lévy-Bruhl, L. 158
liberalism 92
Lichtveld, Ursy M. 79
Lingala 145
literacy 28, 152
literary criticism and theory 62–9, 71–3, 134–5, 146–9, 157–64, 168
literature 29–31, 37–55
  colonialism and 30, 80, 132–3
  reality and 22
  responses to 28
  see also Harlem Renaissance, oral literature, poetry *and* writers
Locke, Alain 62
Locket, Cecily 139, 140, 141
Lorde, Audre 103
Luckmann, Thomas 22

Maalouf, Amin 163
machoism 112, 113–14
McKay, Claude 57, 59, 64, 65, 68–9, 80, 82
McKay, Nelly 68, 75
Madubuike, Ihechukwu 172
Magubane, B. M. 59
Mahfouz, Naguib 163

Malange, Nise 140
Malcolmson, Scott L. 176
Mali 128
Malinke 127–8
Mama, Amina 134–5
Mandela, Nelson 74
Mandinka 151, 163
Manganyi, Chabani 141, 142
manicheanism 38, 135
Manicongo and Zonga 31–2, 33, 37
Maran, René 59
marginalization *see* boundaries
marriage 132
Martin, Tony 67
Martinus Arion, Frank 85
Marxism 72, 90, 194
  see also socialism
master discourse 178–9
Matip, Benjamin 39
Mazrui, Ali 153–4
Memmi, Albert 29, 30
men 60, 112, 113–14, 137, 141–2
  as writers 135
  see also sexism
Mencken, H. L. 66
Mendel, Gregor Johann 151
Mengistu Haile Mariam 194
metaphor *see* language
Meyer, Gérard 127–9, 132
Michaels, Walter Benn 1
Michaud, Guy 5
Miles, R. 6
militancy 70
Miner, Earl 157–8, 159
miscegenation 20
missionaries 9, 45–50
Mitchell, W. J. T. 162
money 39
  see also economics
Montaigne, Michel de 13
moralism 48–9, 52–4

Morrison, Toni   28, 66, 68, 110,
        163, 178
Moseley-Brown, Carol   121
'Mother Africa'   135, 136, 142, 175
mothers   142, 189, 190, 191
Moynihan Report   110, 112–13
Mozambique   146
Mphahlele, E.   97, 99
Mtshali, Oswald   97, 139
Mudimbe, Valentin   162
Mudimbe-Boyi, Elisabeth   11, 175
Mugo, Micere Githae   143
Mulisch, Harry   13, 15
music   37, 70, 161
Mutloatse, Mothobi   98
myths   28–9, 30–5, 37, 38–40,
        54–5, 127, 150
    of Africa   175
    concerning gender relations   129–32

NAACP *see* National Association for
        the Advancement of Colored
        People
naming   57–8, 173
National Association for the
        Advancement of Colored
        People (USA)   59, 64, 75
Nazism   148
Ndebele, Njabulo   99–100, 101,
        102, 172, 176
Neal, Larry   70, 71
Neale, Caroline   153
Negritude, theory of, and Negritude
        movement   29, 59, 74, 75,
        77–91, 175, 176, 183–4
    and belief in race   6–7, 61, 87,
        172
    and gender issues   123–4, 135–6
    Ousmane on   193
    poets   68, 86
    South African Black Consciousness

        movement and   95, 96, 97–8, 99
    terms used by   82
'Negro', use of term   57–8
neo-colonialism   91
    see also post-colonialism
Netherlands, the   146, 183
New Black Poetry   71–2
New Negro Movement   57
    see also Harlem Renaissance
Ngcobo, Lauretta   128, 129, 132
Ngugi wa Thiong'o   74, 189
Nicaragua   138
Nigeria   121, 189
Nkosi, Lewis   97
Nkrumah, Kwame   60
Nkululeko   139
Nnaemeka, Obioma   126, 146–9
nommo   89
novels   37–8
    see also literature
Nwezeh, Emmanuel   25
Nyerere, Julius   96

OAU (Organization of African
        Unity)   60–1
Obbo, Christine   132
Obeyesekere, Gananath   37
Oduyoye, Amba   145
Ogundipe-Leslie, Molara   128
Ogunyemi, Chinwenye
        Okonjo   135, 136, 140–1
Ojo-Ade, Femi   82, 90, 142–3
Okri, Ben   163
Ong, Walter   152
openness   149
oppressions, multiple/competing
        115–16, 117–18, 119, 190, 195
oral culture   97
oral literature   30, 35–6, 127–32,
        156, 160–1
    see also myths

Organization of African Unity 60–1
origin myths 28–9, 30–5, 37, 54–5, 150
  concerning gender relations 129–32
Orwell, George 169
Osundare, Niyi 145
Other(s)/Otherness 1–5, 38–40, 64–5, 153, 156–7, 165
  reversed 29
  see also boundaries, exclusion *and* stereotypes
Our Own Things (Wie Eegie Sanie) 79
Ousmane, Sembène 53–4, 87, 90, 127, 189
  interview with 192–4
outsiders/insiders *see* boundaries
Oyono, Ferdinand 43–4, 47, 51–2, 54, 56, 113, 123

PAC (Pan-Africanist Congress) 95
Padmore, George 59
Panafricanism 57, 58–61, 73, 78, 96, 172
  and belief in race 6–7, 61, 171, 172–3
  Negritude and 75
Pan-Africanist Congress 95
'Passion of the race' 83–4
patriarchy 124–6, 141–2
  see also sexism
patronage 62, 64
Patterson, Orlando 116, 117–18, 119, 120
Paz, Octavio 163
Penel, Jean Dominique 15
peripheries 20–2, 24–5
Phillips, Caryl 75
Pike, Kenneth 176
Pliny 2, 15, 16

poetry 68, 83–7, 97, 98, 157–8
poetry readings 97
political correctness/incorrectness 3, 11, 58, 99, 139
polygamy 49
portrayal *see* representation
post-colonialism 135, 164–6, 168, 169, 170, 176, 180
post-modernism 165, 180
power relations 9, 55, 131
  and construction of culture 24
  discourse and 178–9
  in independent African states 192, 194
  myths and 127
  and research 105, 154–5
  theory and 19
power struggles 89–90
Prebisch, Raul 20
Présence Africaine 87
Price-Mars, Jean 59
primitivism 175
privilege 50–1, 116, 123, 139–40, 165
profits 116
progress 152
protest 29
proverbs 1, 122, 129, 130, 143–6, 151, 163, 180
  see also crocodiles and tree trunks
psychology 22–3
public opinion 187
publishing 163

Quakers 59

race, belief in 61, 87, 90–1, 172–3
  see also racism, conceptual basis
racism 6, 26, 77, 187
  American black movements and 61, 62–3, 64

anti-racist 85
aristocracy and 19
conceptual basis and scientific
    justifications for 6, 14–20,
    148, 151–2, 172–4; *see also*
    origin myths
ethnocentrism and 5–6
inverted 154
Negritude movement and 88,
    90–1
responses to 6–7
and sexism 138–9
in women's suffrage
    movement 107
Rajan, Rajeswari Sunder 166
Ramphele, Mamphela 137, 138–9,
    141, 142
rape 38, 53, 114, 126, 136
reality
    as construction 22, 24–5
    literacy and 152
Redding, Saunders 70
regions 20–2
relativism, cultural 3, 158–9, 168,
    169
representation 4, 64, 65–7, 109–10
    see also under white people *and*
    under women
research 3
    access to 180
    and Africa/Europe 167
    identity and 11, 25–9, 104–5,
        139, 143–6, 176–9
    and reality 152
    relationship of researchers to
        researched 154–7
    see also academics
responsibility 1, 13, 86–7
Rhodesia 171
    see also Zimbabwe
Rive, Richard 98

Roediger, David 75
Roumain, Jacques 86–7
Rushdie, Salman 163
Rwanda 145, 148

Sachs, Albie 101, 102, 172
Said, Edward 3, 4, 22
Salazar, Antonio de Oliveira 193
Sanchez, Sonia 113
Saro-Wiwa, Ken 121
Sartre, Jean-Paul 83, 85
Sartwell, Crispin 75
SASO (South African Students'
    Organization) 93–4, 96, 97–8
Schipper, Mineke 8–9, 11, 12,
    143–6, 148–9, 171
scholars *see* academics
schools 37, 40–5, 79–80
science 150, 151, 152, 153, 157,
    167
Sekye-Otu, Ato 88, 95
self-hatred 3, 29, 36, 63, 139
self-image 140, 141–2, 195
    see also identity
Sena 146
Senegal 45, 130
Senghor, Léopold Sédar 68, 74, 78,
    81–3, 85–6, 87–8, 97–8
    and belief in race 61, 82–3, 88,
        114, 172
    and Fanon 91
    and gender issues 123–4, 135
    interview with 82–3, 87, 183–5
    Ousmane on 193
Sepamla, Sipho 97
separatism, cultural 67
Serote, 97, 139
Seuil, Editions du 163
sexism 17, 25
    black men and 109–10, 111, 112,
        118

as bond between black and white
men 114
conceptual basis 6
political change and 138
and racism 138–9
responses to 6–7
sexuality and sexual issues 20, 110,
113–14, 117
sexual taboos 48–9, 52–4
see also love affairs
Shange, Ntozake 109
Shao Yong 14
Siebelink, Jan 20
Singh, Gurbhagat 157
slavery 19, 28, 59, 73, 106–7, 108,
120, 184, 194
marriage and 107
SNCC *see* Student Non-violent
Coordinating Committee
socialism 96, 194
see also Marxism
Songolo, Aliko 90
Sono, Themba 92, 93, 94, 95, 97–8,
101, 102
soul 70, 71, 74
souls 15
South Africa 60, 91–6, 98–9,
100–2, 138–42, 171
gender issues 136–42
literature in 98–9, 139, 142
United Democratic Front 173–4
women's groups 146
see also Black Consciousness
South African Students' Organization
(SASO) 93–4, 96, 97–8
Soyinka, Wole 13, 22, 88, 89, 152
interview with 88, 186–8
on Marxism 194
prizes 22, 74, 152, 163
and 'tigritude' 82–3, 183–4
Soyinka-Ajayi, Folabo 26

Spielberg, Steven 109, 110
spirituals 62–3, 83–4
Spivak, Gayatri Chakravorty 26,
138
sponsors 62, 64
Staal, Frits 161
Staples, Robert 111
stereotypes 1, 2, 38–40, 109
concerning emotion 114, 124,
134
gender-related 131, 135, 136
see also Others/Otherness
Stimpson, Catharine R. 106
storytelling 127
see also oral literature
Stowe, Harriet Beecher 106
Stratton, Florence 134, 135–7
Student Non-violent Coordinating
Committee (USA) 111–12
subcultures 24–5
suffrage movements 107
Surinam 78, 79, 194
symbolism *see* under language
syncretism 102

Tacitus 183
'tail-man' *see homo caudatus*
Taiwo, Oladele 134
'Talented Tenth' 57, 64, 65, 75–6
technological evolutionism 13–14,
20–1, 25
technology 5, 13
Tevoedjre, Albert 40
Thali, Miriam 142
theatre 97
Third World 13, 22, 164, 165
Thurman, Wallace 64, 65
tigers and tigritude 82–3, 183–4
time 39
Tlali, Miriam 143
Toomer, Jean 57, 68–9

Towa, Marcien   79, 184
travel   14–16
tree trunks *see* crocodiles
Trevor-Roper, Hugh   153
truth   150–1, 170
Truth, Sojourner   103, 106
Tutuola, Amos   63

Uganda   132
understanding   124
UNESCO   87, 185
UNIA *see* Universal Negro
    Improvement Association
United Democratic Front (South
    Africa)   173–4
universal civilization   184–5
Universal Negro Improvement
    Association (USA)   63, 64,
    66
universalism   168
USA   11, 60, 61, 161–2
    black culture in   57, 61–76
    black people in   59, 106–21, 142,
       173; and Africa   173, 174–5;
       and South African Black
       Consciousness movement
       93–4, 95; terms for   57–8
    black women in   106–20
    literary criticism in, and African
       writing   134
    policies towards Africa   121
    whiteness in   75

Vandi, Abdulai S.   89
Voltaire   17–18
Voorhoeve, Jan   79
Vorster, John   193

Wagner, Jean   57
Walcott, Derek   163
Walker, Alice   108, 109–10, 111

Wallace, Michele   109, 111, 112,
    113, 114, 115, 118–19
Webster, Yehudi   120
Weinreich, Peter   177
West, the   21–2
Wesseling, Henk   154
West, Cornel   57, 75–6, 91
Wheatly, Phillis   28
White, Hayden   151
'White is beautiful'   101
white people
    myths of origins   28–9, 30–5, 37,
       54–5
    representations of   4, 9, 29–31,
       37–55
    see also under women
white/black symbolism   36, 46, 63
whiteness   116
Wicomb, Zoë   140–1
Wie Eegie Sanie (Our Own
    Things)   79
Williams, Henry Sylvester   59
Williams, Rita   119–20
Wolof   130, 145–6
women   189–91
    African   3, 54
    African oral literature and
       127–32, 133
    'honorary men'   138, 141
    post-colonialism and   168
    proverbs concerning   143–6
    representations of in
       literature   132–3, 135–6, 189
    in traditional African
       cultures   124–7, 190–1, 194,
       195
    white, in colonial societies   50–5,
       123, 140
    see also feminism
Woolf, Virginia   108
Wright, Richard   67, 90

writers 134–5, 187–8, 190, 192, 194
  black writers' congresses 89–90
  black/African women 74, 84,
    109, 110–11, 134–5, 142–5,
    146, 194
  see also literature

X, Malcolm 61, 72, 75, 94

Young, Robert 20

Zaïre *see* Congo
Zavalloni, Marisa 23, 24, 25
Zima, Peter 177–8
Zimbabwe 126, 129, 138
  see also Rhodesia
Zongo, Opportune 146